The
Luftwaffe
Fighter Force

The
Luftwaffe
Fighter Force
THE VIEW FROM THE COCKPIT

Adolf Galland, et al.
Edited by David C. Isby

Skyhorse Publishing

First Skyhorse Publishing Edition 2016

Skyhorse Publishing books may be purchased in bulk at special discounts for sales promotion, corporate gifts, fund-raising, or educational purposes. Special editions can also be created to specifications. For details, contact the Special Sales Department, Skyhorse Publishing, 307 West 36th Street, 11th Floor, New York, NY 10018 or info@skyhorsepublishing.com.

Skyhorse® and Skyhorse Publishing® are registered trademarks of Skyhorse Publishing, Inc.®, a Delaware corporation.

Visit our website at www.skyhorsepublishing.com.

10 9 8 7 6 5 4 3 2 1

Library of Congress Cataloging-in-Publication Data is available on file.

Cover design by Rain Saukas
Cover image from US National Archives

Print ISBN: 978-1-5107-0358-2
Ebook ISBN: 978-1-5107-0367-4

Printed in the United States of America

Contents

List of Illustrations, Maps and Diagrams

24 The Bf 109G-6 introduced 'bumps' to cover the breeches of its 13mm machine guns
25 A 'long-nose' FW 190D-9 runs up for a test flight
26 The Me 410 played an important role against USAAF bombers
27 An Me 163B of JG 400
28 An Me 262 in flight
29 The He 162 Volksjäger was considered by Galland to be a waste of resources
30 The Dornier Do 335

Introduction

This book is a collection of German fighter leaders' views of different elements of their part in the Second World War. The authors all led from the cockpit, often with great success, as is shown by their score of air-to-air victories (indeed, with its multiple authors, this book has the highest victory total of any book on air combat). They were the men who determined – usually through improvisation rather than efficient German staff work – how the Luftwaffe fighter force was to do battle throughout the Second World War. These accounts are written by professionals, for other professionals.

But the accounts here are not those familiar from memoirs of air combat. The reader will not find accounts of contrails in the central blue, the cries of 'horrido!' and 'pauke, pauke' over the radio, or even the dilemma of whether to fall in a doomed cause or abandon the struggle and one's comrades. Rather, they recount the history of the Luftwaffe fighter forces' aircraft, operations, tactics, training, technology, and aircrew.

These documents represent the command 'debrief' of many of the Luftwaffe's fighter leaders, being done weeks or months rather than years after the flying and fighting had stopped. It was good that these debriefs were done while memories were fresh, for the prisoners were without official documents except, in some cases, their flight logbooks. This also explains why there is less emphasis on the successes of the opening years of the war – now faded in memory – and more written about the last years of the Defense of the Reich. It was also the area in which the USAAF was most interested.

The authors compiled most of these documents as prisoners of war, under the authority of the US Army Air Forces, while being held in Germany and England. The Air Prisoner of War Interrogation Unit (APWIU), under Major Max von Rossum-Daum USAAF, started the procedure in occupied Germany, at Heidelberg. The bulk of the work was carried out after the prisoners had been flown to England, at the Combined Services Detailed Interrogation Centre, Camp 7, at Latimer, Buckinghamshire, and another interrogation center at the nearby village of Beaconsfield. The prisoners were, later in 1945, flown back to Germany and the debriefs continued at Kaufberen, Bavaria, for two months before many of the prisoners – some had been released – returned to Latimer, where the process was completed by the end of 1945. After that, some of the prisoners started to work on historical narratives requested by the USAAF.

Overhanging the interrogation process was the shadow of the war crimes trials. Indeed, one of the minor contributors to this volume, Generalfeldmarshall Erhard Milch, the Luftwaffe's Director General of Equipment in 1941–44, was tried and sentenced to 15 years for his involvement with slave labor. The other authors were also under investigation, though they were all eventually cleared. However, the subject matter of these interrogations, which focused on the air war itself rather than involvement with issues that led to prosecution – with the notable exception of some dealing with in-unit discipline – is unlikely to have affected interrogations on other issues.

The accounts cover the full range of German fighter operations. They are, quite literally, the first draft of the history of the Luftwaffe fighter force, and make up in immediacy what they may lack in reflection and opportunities for archival research. They include areas often overlooked in history books, such as the air-ground fighter operations and cooperation with the navy. Each of the subjects was interrogated mainly about topics on which they had direct personal knowledge. The intense internal secrecy of the German war effort made claims to knowledge that did not come from such hands-on experience suspect.

These accounts are earlier and less refined than the better known series of historical studies written by former Luftwaffe officers – some volumes of which have been reprinted by publishers such as Greenhill Press and Garland – collectively referred to as the Karlsruhe studies. The accounts in this volume are similar those incorporated in the Karlsruhe studies. Many of the authors of this volume, including Galland, went on to work on them. However, when they were under interrogation they were unable to make use of Luftwaffe documents and records, the vast majority of them had – by design and fortunes of war alike – been destroyed. There was, and remains, much less original documentation for the history of the Luftwaffe than for the other German services.

These later studies corrected many of the inevitable errors and omissions that were recorded in the initial interrogations. What the Karlsruhe studies did incorporate – and what these debriefs largely omit – are the Luftwaffe authors' political biases, sharpened over the years as the shock of defeat grew less and the time for discussions among them increased. The fact that the authors were, unlike in these interrogations, no longer in uniform and were working for German intermediaries rather than directly for USAAF inter-rogators may also have had an impact. For example, the Karlsruhe studies tended to suggest that Germany lost interest in strategic bombing after the death of General Wever in the 1930s. This suited some of the Luftwaffe authors, for it allowed them to pose as morally superior to the victorious USAAF and RAF: they would never have made war on a civilian population the way they did.

This view also suited the USAF sponsors of the studies, for a different reason. They could show that the Luftwaffe failed because it rejected what the USAF then saw as the true light of airpower – strategic bombing – and was instead left under the control of ground officers and led into the delusions of emphasizing combined arms cooperation with the army, becoming a mere 'tactical' air arm which doomed it to defeat. With the Luftwaffe's documents destroyed, no one could then contradict either view.

We now know – from the more recent works of historians such as Williamson Murray, R. J. Overy and Richard Muller, among others – that the Karlsruhe studies, while remaining valuable sources, present a slanted view of the Luftwaffe's actual operations and thinking. In these documents, it appears unlikely that any of the contributors are much concerned with the use to which their information will be put by the Americans, as so long as it was not for prosecuting them for war crimes. None of these fighter leaders lament the absence of a strategic bombing emphasis. Rather, they complain of too much of an emphasis in this area for too long. Complaints about non-flying generals in the chain of command are also conspicuous by their absence – Galland is respectful of the efforts of contributor 'Beppo' Schmid as a commander of fighter units, even if not as an intelligence officer – though such a thing has been anathema to the USAAF and its successors.

These documents represent the view from the cockpit, rather than from headquarters. The authors were operators rather than strategists. Indeed, while the details of fighter operations and tactics and how the forces that were used to carry them out evolved are explained, there is almost nothing written here about German air strategy. Even Galland's summation of what went wrong for the German fighter force looks at technical and resource allocation issues – the lack of drop tanks in 1940, the lack of Me 262s in 1944 – rather than the more telling lack of a way to win an air war against numerically superior opponents. Similarly, there is little on the realities of domestic politics as they existed in Nazi Germany. For Galland's clashes with Göring over the nature of modern air combat and with Speer over the utility of producing more of the same increasingly non-competitive fighters, one must turn to Galland's own version of the story, written in the 1950s, in his classic book *The First and the Last*.

Galland is the unifying voice in this book. He is the primary 'author' of each of the lengthy chapters except those compiled by his ground attack counterpart, Hitschhold. Galland's force of personality comes through in his accounts, both the interrogations and those he wrote himself. In addition to the postwar debriefs, some of Galland's wartime tactical writings are also included. In them, he can be seen as trying to solve the ultimately insoluble operational problems confronting the German fighter force. The wartime documents show him working with combat experience to determine the best counter to the formations of USAAF heavy bombers, first recommending head-on attacks in 1942, then relegating them to a secondary tactic in 1943, and putting these tactics in the context, a 1944 document on the operational level of the defense of the Reich.

Galland's personality and willingness to help meant that he got on well with the APWIU. In addition to the personnel of the unit – one of his inter-rogators, Captain John M. Whitten, later became a personal friend – he worked with fighter pilots who were brought into the interrogation process. All came away with a respect for Galland. His writings, as with those of the others, focus on operational decisions and organization. He did not have to try to impress his captors or try to change what he did in the war. Galland was by no means the highest-scoring German fighter pilot, but he was the best known and most articulate. These accounts show why.

Heinrich 'Pritzel' Bär, killed in a light plane crash in 1957, is also one of the strong voices in this book. He is the one who says 'this is how we would have done things', what a Luftwaffe fighter leader would have done in hypothetical but typical situations at different points in the war. This is very much 'the view from the cockpit', and shows how the broader operational and tactical ideas developed in the other accounts were actually put into practice – usually by the same men who developed them. The same obvious first-hand leadership knowl-edge applies to the inputs of Walther Dahl – credited with 36 four-engine bombers – on the tactics used against the daylight bombing offensive.

Hubertus Hitschhold, the ground attack expert, also impressed the APWIU with his candor and cooperation. This is apparent in his contribu-tions to this book, and was recognized at the time in that his wife was allowed to rejoin him at Kaufberen. The stress put on air–ground operations, espe-cially on the Eastern Front, in these accounts suggest that the USAAF would soon have to consider how tactical airpower might best be used against the Soviet Army's armored spearheads as the Cold War opened.

The accounts in this book were translated contemporaneously by USAAF personnel. They did, overall, a good job, and the accounts are better than many of the translations done by German personnel that are to be found in many of the US Army's series of reports by German officers. Much of the syntax and capitalization reflects that of the German original. The authors assume that those they are writing from know the abbreviations, equipment and references they use rather freely. A glossary has been provided to help the reader identify them.

There has been no attempt to correct the accounts, even where the authors get things wrong, or insert more recent or superior knowledge via square brackets (except in a few cases). Whenever possible, the original spellings and terminology have been maintained, including even such elementary things as capitalization and the rendering of umlauts into English, which was done without consistency in the original documents. The translation has been edited to bring specific terminology, but not necessarily syntax, into line with standard English-language usage. Scrambled words and meanings have been untangled and paragraphs have been re-ordered. But these changes have been kept to a minimum. These are, after all, the fighter leaders' stories, and some of them – like Bär – never got to tell them again.

The editor would like to thank Dr. Robert Johnson of the US Air Force Historical Research Agency, Maxwell AFB, for his help in making the original documents available.

David C. Isby
Washington, 1998

Biographies

Generalleutnant Adolf Galland

Born 19 March 1912. He began glider flying in 1929 and soon became well known for his endurance flights. He entered the German Air Line Pilots School in 1932, where he came in contact with certain 'discharged' Reichswehr officers who were also training on heavy aircraft. After completion of his course, he entered secret military air training, which he completed in May 1934. He then was sent to Italy with other German pilots for training which proved to be very poor. In February of 1934, he started the course for Luftwaffe officers which was disguised as 'Sports Training'. He was posted to J.G. 2 in February 1935. Galland volunteered for the Legion Kondor in the fall of 1935, where he served as a fighter pilot, being in command of the Stabs-Kompanie. From the time of his return from Spain until after the end of the Polish campaign, he was concerned with setting up the ground attack arm. He went back to fighters after the Polish Campaign. He took part in the Battle of France and the Battle of Britain, becoming C.O. of J.G. 26. He was installed as General der Jagdflieger in December of 1941 and was awarded the Ritterkreuz in January 1942. He was relieved by Goring about 1 January 1945, and posted as C.O. of J.V. 44, a Me.262 unit, remaining there until wounded soon before the surrender.

Generalmajor Hubertus Hitschhold

Born 1912. He began training as an airline pilot in 1930, and entered the army in 1931. In 1935, he joined the GAF and taught at fighter schools the entire year. In 1936, he became a Stuka pilot, and was a Staffel C.O. at the start of the Polish campaign. He took part in the Battle of Poland, France, Britain, Greece and Crete, always with Stukas. He became a Geschwader C.O. in 1942, and was equipped with Me.109's and F.W.190's. In 1943, he was Fliegerfuhrer in Sardinia and then went with Luftflotte 2 in Italy. In November 1943, he took over the job of General der Schlachtflieger when Kupfer was killed and held the job until the end of the war, being officially given the job and promoted to Generalmajor on 1 January 1945. He was awarded the Oak Leaf to the Ritterkreuz and has 410 war flights.

Oberstleutnant Heinrich Bär

Born 1911. He was a commercial airline pilot for the Bavarian Air Line, prior to joining the GAF in 1935 as an N.C.O. During the Battle of Britain, he was promoted to officer rank. He was promoted to Hauptmann. He was then transferred to Africa with J.G. 77 where he became a Gruppe C.O. He returned to Germany after the invasion of Italy and was posted to J.G. 1, which he took over after the fall of Oesau. His next command was J.G. 3. In January 1945, he took over an experimental unit at Lechfeld, where he flew Me.262s. In April 1945, he joined J.V. 44 which he led after Galland was wounded. He is credited with 240 victories and was awarded the Swords to the Knights Cross. He flew about 1200 sorties.

Oberst Gordon Gollob

Born in 1912. Joined the GAF about 1936, and was a Gruppe C.O. in Crimea and the Battle of Britain. He later rose to the position of C.O. of J.G. 77. In early 1944, Galland put him in charge of technical development of the Me.163 and 262. He was relieved in the fall of 1944. Goring installed him as General der Jagdflieger after relieving Galland about 1 January 1945. He was awarded Diamonds to the Knights Cross.

Oberst Edgar Petersen

A pilot since about 1925. He joined a special Relslame Staffel to work with the army, and trained further in DVS. As a Hansa pilot, he entered the army in 1934. During the war, he was C.O. of K.G. 40, and then C.O. of the experimental station at Rechlin.

Oberst Robert Kowalewski

Born 1914. He trained as a civilian airline pilot until 1932, when he entered the German Navy as an officer candidate. He transferred to the Luftwaffe in 1935, and was put in the naval branch and took part in the Spanish Civil War on the cruiser Nürnberg. At the outbreak of World War II, he was a pilot in K.G. 40 and took part in operations against England. He was in the headquarters of Fliegerkorps X. In 1941 he was the C.O. of a Gruppe in II/K.G. 26, the torpedo unit in the Mediterranean. From late 1941 to 1943 he was Gruppe C.O. in K.G. 40, bombing shipping in the Atlantic. From February to July 1944, he was C.O. of Z.G. 76, the TE fighter unit in the Defense of the Reich. In the latter part of 1944 he was the first night fighter C.O. and later in November took over K.G. 76 which had Me.262s and Ar.234s operating as bombers over the Western Front. He was in this position until the end of the war.

Major Hans Schmoller-Haldy

Born 1911. He was an insurance employee until he entered the army in 1934. He transferred to the Luftwaffe in 1935, and to a fighter Gruppe in 1936. He served as an adjutant in 1937 and 1938. He flew in the Spanish war in 1939 and took part in the Battle of France and Britain. He was twice wounded in Russia, and was grounded in 1942. Since then he served on Galland's staff as tactics and training expert at various times. He was credited with 12 victories, and was awarded the EK I and II.

Major Hans Jacob

Joined the Luftwaffe in 1936. He took part in the occupation of Sudetenland, and was with Stuka units in Poland, France, during the Battle of Britain, Malta and Africa. He was C.O. of a Gruppe in 1943, and later acted as a liaison officer from the General der Schlachtflieger to the Chief of Staff of the Luftwaffe. In April 1944, he joined the General Staff as an operations and training expert.

Leutnant Klaus Neumann

Born 1924. Pilot in J.G. 51, later transferred to J.G. 3 Sturmgruppe (IV/JG3). He is credited with 14 heavy bombers shot down. In late 1944, he was transferred to II/JG7, and in April 1945 to J.V. 44, where he scored four victories with the Me.262. He was awarded the Ritterkreuz in May 1945. Credited with 37 victories.

Other Contributors

Generalfeldmarschall Erhard Milch. Director General of Equipment for the Luftwaffe from November 1941 to May 1944.

Generalleutnant Joseph 'Beppo' Schmid. Intelligence chief of the Luftwaffe from January 1938 to November 1942. Considered by Galland 'a complete wash-out as an intelligence officer'. Given command of I Jagdkorps September 1943 to November 1944, despite being a non-aviator. Commanded Luftwaffe Command West for remainder of war.

Oberstleutnant Walther Dahl. Fighter ace with 128 or 129 victories, including 36 heavy bombers. Flew throughout most of the war with JG 3, including commanding a Gruppe, then took over JG 300. Developed anti-bomber tactics used by FW 190-equipped Sturmgruppen. In 1945 switched to Me 262s, flying with EJG 2 and Galland's JV 44.

Glossary

AA	Anti-aircraft
A/B Schule	Flight training school
Abschittsführer	Section leader
a/c	Aircraft
AUS	Army of the United States
Benito	Fighter direction based on tracking by ground radars, first introduced in 1941. Unlike the Egon system, it did not require the fighters to transmit a signal. Used by night fighters as well.
Bf	Bayerische Flugzeugwerke, later Messerschmitt
C-stoff	Liquid catalyst used by rocket motors
CO	Commanding officer
Commentary	The Reichsjägerwelle, a running commentary on the tactical situation in defense of the Reich. Rather than vectoring specific formations, it allowed formations to navigate towards the enemy and be warned of major threats.
Deckungs-schwarm	Cover flight
EJG	Reserve/replacement fighter Geschwader
Egon	A navigation system, similar to the British 'Oboe' system
Elfe	Radar blind-firing device for cannon. Not used operationally.
Epsilon	Code-name for Y-Gerät (q.v.) ground and air stations
Erganzung	Reserve/replacement unit
Erstling	Codename for FuG 25a IFF transponder
Erpobung	Test or evaluation
Fliegerführer	Air officer commanding a specific operation, usually also a commander of one of the units involved
Fliegerdivision	Air division. 'Jagd' prefix indicates one mainly of fighter units.

Fliegerkorps

Air corps. Operational formation composed of an unspecified number of units, but usually multiple Geschwader, several hundred aircraft strong. Could be under a Luftflotte command or, as in the case of von Richtoften's VIII Fliegerkorps, independent.

FüG 16ZY

Standard German VHF fighter radio system. Used for R/T, W/T. It provided 'Y-Control'. In addition to standard air-air and air-ground frequencies, would also receive the Reichsjägerwelle.

FüG 125

Lorenz VHF signal beacon receiver, code-named 'Hermine'

Führungsstab

Operations staff of the OKL

F.W.

Focke-Wulf

GAF

German Air Force

General der Jagdflieger

Inspector of Fighters (not a rank). Responsible for readiness, training and tactics rather than an operational command. Galland's post November 1941– January, 1945.

General Staff Officer

A member of the German General Staff, a small body whose members received extensive training and provided almost all Army general officers. Tended to look down at fighter pilots, according to Galland.

Generalfeld-marschall

Equivalent to US General of the Army or RAF Marshal of the Royal Air Force

Generalleutnant

Equivalent to US Major General or RAF Air Vice-Marshal

Generalmajor

Equivalent to US Brigadier General or RAF Air Commodore

Generaloberst

Equivalent to US General or RAF Air Chief Marshal

Gefechtsverband

Combat formation. The standard tactical formation could range from a few fighters to multiple Gruppe formations of about 100. Formations grew larger to meet large daylight bomber raids.

Gefr.

Gefreiter, equivalent to RAF Aircraftsman First Class or USAAF Private First Class

Geschwader

Wing, usually composed of three or more Gruppen

Geschwader Z.b.V

Wing-sized force of miscellaneous units

GM 1

Nitrous oxide

von Greim	Generalfeldmarschall Robert, Ritter von Greim. Operational commander of Fliegerkorps V and Luftflotte 6, in which position he was senior Luftwaffe commander in the East. Replaced Göring in April 1945.
Gruppe	Unit, in the fighter force, of 40–80 aircraft. Three or more made up a Geschwader. Designated by a roman numeral and the designation of its parent Geschwader (e.g. III/JG 26) or by arabic numerals if independent.
Gruppenkom-mandeur	CO of a Gruppe
Hauptmann	Equivalent to US Captain or RAF Flight Lieutenant
Hermine	Code-name for FüG 125 VHF beacon receiver (q.v.)
Hptm	Hauptmann (captain)
HQ	Headquarters
i.G	im Generalsstab. On the General Staff.
Jabo	Jagdbomber, a fighter-bomber or an air-to-air fighter with a secondary air-ground role.
Jafü	Jagdführer. Area fighter leader.
Jagddivision	Fighter division
Jagdfliegerführer	Fighter leader
Jagdkorps	Fighter corps
Jagdwaffe	Luftwaffe fighter force
Jagdstab	Staff of the General der Jagdflieger
JG	Jagdgeschwader, fighter wing
JK	Jagdkorps
JLO	Jägerleitoffizer. Fighter Control officer.
JV	Jagdverband, fighter unit
Kammhuber	General der Flieger Joseph Kammhuber. Built up night fighter force, but was relieved after Hamburg raids in 1943. Afterwards commanded in Denmark and Norway and, in 1945, was put in charge of jet- and rocket-powered aircraft programs.
Kdre	Kommodore (commanding officer)
Kette	Three-plane tactical formation, usually flown in a 'v'
Kommando	Independent detachment, often named for its commander or base
Kommodore	Commanding officer of a Geschwader
Kommandeur	Commanding officer of a Gruppe
Kompanie	Company or squadron

Lehr	Instructional
Lufbery	A defensive maneuver in which aircraft form a circle, each covering the tail of the one in front. Used especially by Bf 110s and Ju 87s.
Luftflotte	A formation of Fliegerkorps or multiple Geschwader of different types. Roughly equivalent to a USAAF numbered air force.
Martini	Generalmajor Wolfgang Martini. Chief of Luftwaffe Signal Troops (including radar) from September 1941 to the end of the war.
Mölders	Oberst Werner Mölders. Ace with 115 victories and a keen tactician. Served as General der Jagdflieger. Killed in crash in November 1941. Friend of Galland.
MW50	Methanol-water injection
Luftgau	Air zone. Used as administrative and support command echelon pre-war.
Nachrichten	Signals (including radar)
Nafu	Signals unit
Natter	Experimental vertical-launch rocket-powered fighter. Never used operationally.
NSFK (HJ)	National Socialist Flieger Korps (Hitler Youth)
Oberleutnant	Equivalent to US First Lieutenant or RAF Flying Officer
Oberst	Equivalent to US Colonel or RAF Group Captain
Oesau	Oberst Walter 'Gulle' Oesau, tactician, trainer and fighter ace with 117 victories. Commanded JG 1 and JG 2. Shot down and killed in 1944.
Ofw.	Oberfeldwebel, equivalent to RAF Flight Sergeant or USAAF Staff Sergeant
Ogr.	Obergefreiter, equivalent to RAF Leading Aircraftsman or USAAF Corporal
OKL	Oberkommando der Luftwaffe, Air Force High Command
Panzerschreck	Anti-tank rocket
Peltz	Generalmajor Dietrich Peltz. Bomber commander in the West 1940–44 and commander of Fliegerkorps IX. Given command of Jagdkorps II in December 1944 over Galland's strong objections.
RAF	Royal Air Force

Reichsjägerwelle	'Reichs fighter waveband'. *See* Commentary.
Rotte	Two-plane tactical formation, usually flown by a leader and wingman
RP	Rocket projectile
R/T	Radio (voice) telephone
Schwarm	Four-plane tactical formation, usually flown in a 'finger-four' formation.
Schlachtflieger	Assault units. Ground attack units which engage in air-to-air combat only in self-defense.
SE	Single-engine
'Spoof service'	Allied designation for German camouflage and diversionary efforts. Included both construction of dummy targets on the ground and use of misleading and jamming transmissions.
Stab	Staff of a unit
Stab-	Prefix of a unit or formation size, indicating the staff of a unit or a sub-unit of aircraft flown by that staff
Staffel	Unit of about 9–16 aircraft. Three or more usually made up a Gruppe.
Staka	Staffelkapitän. Commanding officer of a Staffel.
Stuka	A dive-bomber, but especially the Ju 87
Sturmgruppe	Fighter group dedicated to the anti-bomber mission and comprising up-armed fighters, usually with external armament.
Sturmjäger	Anti-bomber, single-engine fighter units, usually up-armed and armored FW 190s.
TE	Twin-engine
T/O	Table of organization
TOE	Table of organization and equipment. A unit's war establishment, indicating the personnel, equipment and subordinate units it is supposed to have under it.
Uffz.	Unteroffizier, equivalent to USAAF Sergeant or RAF Corporal.
USAAF	US Army Air Forces. Became US Air Force (USAF) in 1947.
Verteidigungs-zone	Air defense zone.
Waffengeneral	A position such as General der Jagdflieger (and its counterparts for the bomber and ground attack forces)

concerned with a specific force rather than a particular operational unit. Could be held by a colonel.

Water-methanol injection   *See* MW50.

WT   Wireless telegraphy (morse).

'Y'   Standard method of fighter guidance by VHF radio, using direction-finding from the ground on signals transmitted by an aircraft. The aircraft would receive signals transmitted from the ground. Capable of providing both range and bearing.

Y-Gerät   Equipment for using 'Y' guidance on German aircraft

'Y' service   Allied designation of monitoring of enemy radio transmissions

z.b.V.   For special duties (zur besonderen Verwendungen)

Zerstörer   Twin-engine day fighter

ZG   Zerstörergeschwader, twin engine day fighter wing

Ia.   Operations officer/section on a German staff, equivalent to USAAF A-3 or S-3

Ic.   Intelligence officer/section on a German staff, equivalent to USAAF A-2 or S-2

Part 1
The Fighter Force

The chapters in this section, written primarily by Galland, are his account of how he saw the Luftwaffe fighter force organization change from his pre-war service to the last battles. In this way, as well as setting out the different organizational terms and levels used in the other chapters, they also function as an overview of the entire conflict. They also include a focus on the twin-engine fighter force throughout the conflict and how it overcame its defeat in the Battle of Britain to become a key part of the Luftwaffe's defensive efforts. However, because these interrogations are being carried out for the benefit of the USAAF rather than the RAF, night fighter operations are not emphasized.

CHAPTER 1

History and Developments of GAF Fighter Commands

Interrogation of Generalleutnant Adolf Galland and Generalfeldmarschall Milch
At Kaufbeuren, Germany, 1–4 September 1945

Before the War

When fighter units were set up in 1935–36 they came under the Luftgau for purposes of administration, supply, and operations. The emphasis on defense in organization at the time was due, in Galland's opinion, to the fear in Germany that other lands might take military action to interfere with her rearmament program. Since no operations took place in this period, it is impossible to judge the rectitude of the idea of having the fighter units controlled by geographical commands, the Luftgau.

The Spanish Civil War, Poland and France

Germany's fighter superiority, proved in the Spanish War and corroborated by intelligence reports, led to a much more aggressive type of organization shortly before the Sudetenland incident. All the fighter units were taken from the Luftgau and put under the Fliegerkorps (and the one Nahkampfkorps VIII under Richthofen). Those Fliegerkorps controlled all kinds of flying units. One Gruppe of J.G. 1 stayed under the control of a Luftgau on the Frisian Coast, but all the other Luftgau had no more to do with the fighter units operationally, except for control of the home bases of the various units where a small detail of men from each Gruppe stayed behind to keep contact with home matters and do housekeeping.

The organization of the Fliegerkorps was very flexible. Each was headed by a General, usually a veteran of World War I who had a younger General Staff Officer as his Chief of Staff. Fighter Geschwader under a Korps might take their operational orders directly from the Korps Staff Operations Section, which also gave out orders to all the bomber, recce, ground attack, and dive-bomber units under the Korps. In some Korps a Fliegerfuhrer (operational command) might be set up to control all the fighters, or all the bombers, and so on. This officer was often merely the senior Geschwader Kommodore of the Geschwader in the Korps, and therefore had no elaborate staff. His function was merely to implement the general battle missions passed down to him by Korps.

In some cases the Korps had under it a number of Fliegerdivisionen each with bombers, fighters and other types under it. Each division had a large staff and simply relieved the Korps of the burden of detailed work. In all these organizational set-ups, supply and repair units were controlled by the Luftgau, which merely expanded their boundaries to take in any new territories which Germany overran.

This type of organization with Fliegerkorps, Fliegerdivisionen, and Fliegerfuhrer controlling at different levels of command all different types of units, without separating the control of fighters from bombers and so on, was continued in the West until the end of the French campaign in Summer 1940 and in Russia until 1944. The great evolutionary changes in fighter command organization took place in the West and in Germany itself from Fall of 1940 up to the end of the War. Russian front organization remained fairly static because the role of the Luftwaffe there as a ground support arm did not change much through the war.

The West – The Battle of Britain and 1941

After the campaign in France, the Luftwaffe forces in France arrayed against England were under Luftflotte 2 and Luftflotte 3. Luftflotte 2 had under it Fliegerkorps II, and Luftflotte 3 had Fliegerkorps VIII and IX. There were no Division headquarters at the time in France.

The great fighter activity of the Battle of Britain soon necessitated the setting-up of specialized Fighter Commands under the two Luftflotten. In August 1940 Jagdfliegerfuhrer 2 was set up under Fliegerkorps II and Jagdfliegerfuhrer 3 was set up under Fliegerkorps VIII. (Note that each Jagdfliegerfuhrer was numbered after the Luftflotte which it came under, though this was not a general rule.) (Jagdfliegerfuhrer means *fighter leader* and is usually abbreviated *Jafu*; this abbreviation will be used throughout this report.)

The main reason for setting up the Jafu at this time was that fighter operations were becoming so important and complicated that special operational staff work was required. Each Fliegerkorps found it more simple to give orders to its Jafu. During the Battle of Britain there was no Jafu control of fighter units after take-off, because the GAF had at that time no radar that could observe fighter action over England. Instead, the Jafu busied themselves planning the missions, consulting frequently with the Geschwader COs, and developing the signals network which later became the skeleton of the reporting and radar systems in France and the low countries. They reported directly to the Korps and had considerable operational freedom. Usually they were informed of the time when German bombers were to be over the target and were told to provide fighter escort.

In 1941 the fighter force in the West went on the defensive. When the Russian campaign began in June all the Geschwader (except J.G. 2 and J.G. 26) went to the Russian Front. Luftflotte 2 (with its Fliegerkorps II) left France and went to the Eastern front. Fliegerkorps VIII with its fighters left the domain of Luftflotte 3 and also went to the East. Luftflotte 3 now took over command authority over those parts of France and the low countries which had belonged to Luftflotte 2.

That left in the West Fliegerkorps IX which had mostly bombers and no fighters under it. The bombers of Fliegerkorps IX were at this time engaged mainly in night operations where they needed no fighters. Jafu 2 and 3 remained, Jafu 2 now coming under the domain of Luftflotte 3. Since the old Fliegerkorps II and VIII to which they had been subordinated were now in the East and since the one remaining Fliegerkorps in the West, IX, was flying night operations, the two Jafus had no headquarters over them except Luftflotte 3 itself. Jafu 2 controlled J.G. 26, and Jafu 3 controlled J.G. 2. The Jafu continued their signals development work.

In mid-1941 another step in development was taken. The Jafu headquarters began to control the fighters, rather than the headquarters of the individual Geschwader. Ground control intercept radar and a radio Listening Service were now functioning, and fighter control in the air by the Jafu was a reality.

Each Jafu sent a representative to the Geschwader Hq. to work with the Geschwader Kommodore in directing operations. By Autumn 1941, however, it was seen that this practice prevented the Kommodore from leading his unit in combat; so it was discontinued. Control of fighters was exercised directly from the Jafu headquarters.

The Organizing of the Jagddivisionen and Jagdkorps

Up until the latter months in 1941 the largest unit of command for fighters was the Jafu. English night bombing operations over Northwestern Germany had developed to such a point that German night fighter forces had to be considerably enlarged. Fliegerkorps XII under Kammhuber controlled almost all of the night fighters, which were located in Holland, Belgium, and N.W. Germany. Fliegerkorps XII developed, for its night fighting, a fine signals and radar network, which became the finest in Europe. In the Fall of 1942, when the first American daylight raids penetrated into Germany and the Low Countries, Fliegerkorps XII organized a Jafu Holland-Ruhrgebiet as well as continuing the night fighter control work.

The setting-up of other Jagddivisionen continued into 1943 until almost all German fighter units in France, the Low Countries, Germany and Austria came under one of them. J.D. 2 was set up in the Bremen vicinity and J.D. 3 at Berlin. Later the numbering was changed and J.D. 1 and J.D. 3 exchanged numbers. Jafu 2 in France became J.D. 4 and Jafu 3 became J.D. 5. The number 6 was left vacant for a J.D. which was to be set up in Southern France, but never was. J.D. 7 was set up in the Munich vicinity and J.D. 8 was later set up with its headquarters in Vienna.

The fighter units on the Russian front stayed under the control of the simple Fliegerdivisionen and Fliegerkorps until 1944. German fighters in Norway, Italy, Africa, the Balkans and other outlying areas were controlled by newly created Jafu headquarters.

The Jagddivisionen based in the western part of Germany and in France were under another type of unit, the Jagdkorps (fighter corps), corresponding to the Fliegerkorps. Jagdkorps II was initiated to control the Jagddivisionen under Luftflotte 3 and Jagdkorps I was formed from Kammhuber's old Fliegerkorps XII, in Germany. It was planned as well to set up a Jagdkorps III for southern Germany but the strength of the fighters there was always too small to warrant it. These Jagdkorps exercised the necessary coordinating functions in the employment of the now much expanded fighter force. The Jagddivisionen were principally interested in the operational functions which involved directing the Geschwader in the air. Matters of policy and supervision had to be left to the higher unit, the Jagdkorps.

By this time the four Luftflotten which had formerly divided Germany between them had now moved into occupied countries to keep up with the fronts, leaving the administration of the Defense of the Reich to the newly created Luftwaffenbefehlshaber Mitte (GAF Commander for the Middle Area), which was renamed Luftflotte Reich. Jagdkorps I therefore came under Luftflotte Reich, while Jagdkorps II came under Luftflotte III now situated in France and the Low Countries.

Each Jagddivision was a definitely bounded geographical area, although boundaries were changed from time to time. All units based in the area of the Jagddivision were responsible to it for operational purposes. This included day fighter, Zerstorer and night fighters. The Division could actually control its Geschwader when they passed beyond its borders during a mission, but on occasions where either the fighters themselves or the enemy forces were outside the range of the Division's radar and R/T, control of the units would, on the Jagdkorps order, be passed over to another Division which was still in touch with the whole situation. This change-over was never accomplished without great difficulty and confusion and was one of the main weaknesses of the Division system. The difficulty arose from the simple physical complexity of the task of establishing communications with all of the units and overloading the staffs of those Divisions which usually had the burden of suddenly assuming operations thrown onto them.

The Jagddivision Headquarters

Each division was under a General officer, usually a World War I veteran, who unfortunately understood little of modern fighter combat. His Chief of Staff was a General Staff officer. The serious shortage of General Staff officers who knew anything about fighters seriously impaired the efficiency of the divisions all through the War. Another handicap was that Goring had a way of replacing the division commanders at the slightest pretext, so they rarely gained experience in their vastly complicated task. Every time in 1943 that an Allied bomber formation accomplished a mission unscathed, the division commanders feared for their positions. In 1944 some younger fighter pilots like Lutzow were put in as commanders and enjoyed considerable success.

The rest of the staff had to be a dual one, with duplicate positions for night and day fighting. Since the headquarters of the unit had to operate on a 24 hour basis, all positions from the highest to the lowest had to be in duplicate. It was really necessary for the Jagddivision commander on duty to be on the job all the time and this was impossible. The absence of any Deputy Commander impaired operations. There were simply too few experienced fighter pilots to provide good deputies. Neither the CO, his Chief of Staff, nor any of their immediate subordinates ever flew on operations, which did not present them with the necessary insights for proper operational control.

The headquarters of the various Divisionen varied considerably, those in Germany itself being the most elaborate. The building was heavily reinforced against bombs and was usually well camouflaged. The Hqs. of J.D. 1 at Doberitz and J.D. 2 at Staade were good examples. The headquarters was the

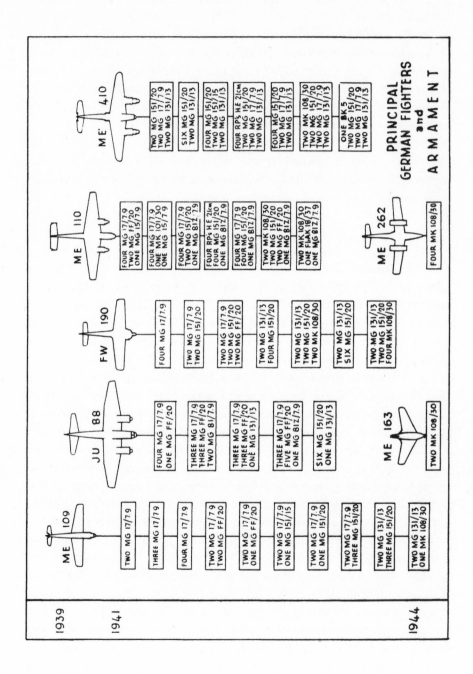

PRINCIPAL
GERMAN FIGHTERS
and
ARMAMENT

center of all communications for the Division. Each J.D. had a Signals regiment or two attached to it, and the head of the regiment or the senior officer of the several commanding officers was the Nachrichten Fuhrer (Nafu) of the J.D., a very important man. The many signals lines running to the headquarters from all the airfields, Egon and Benito positions, Observer Corps stations, Flak Headquarters, and higher units, made the Division Headquarters very sensitive to bombing attacks and when bombs fell near some of the operations were always partially disrupted.

The Jagddivision Headquarters in Action

In the Division headquarters about 150 people were immediately concerned with operational control were employed for day operations. Courses of friendly and enemy formations were plotted on a large glass map with an amazing array of epidiascopic pencils and light projectors. The procedure was very exact.

At individual desks in front of the map sat Jagerleitoffizier (Fighter Control Officers – J.L.O.) each of which was in contact by R/T with one German Geschwader or Gruppe formation in the air. The Division commander or a substitute, acting as Chief J.L.O. sat in front and gave broad directions to the various J.L.O. about how and where they should lead their formations towards the bomber formations. He usually stated that such and such a Geschwader was to contact the bombers at such and such a point, or that all Geschwader were to be brought up onto such and such a line by a certain time. The J.L.O. then gave out their directions to the various units, which had to follow them at least until contact with the enemy was made. The chief J.L.O. naturally had to do a lot of fast guessing about where the bombers were heading. The Listening Service often gave valuable hints about the depth of penetration. Analyses of past missions by GAF intelligence also helped. Unfortunately, the Listening Service and spoof service could only be controlled from Luftflotte level and the J.L.O. were not able to order special tricks during operations. Galland tried to alter this situation, but Martini, Chief of GAF Signals, resisted all attempts to invade his empire.

The broad principles of tactical employment of fighters were formulated in doctrines issued by the Fuhrungsstab and by Goring. Such principles as attacking bombers before they dropped their bombs, the concentration of fighter forces on one Allied raid a day, and the flying of second missions by fighters were set out in this manner. The Korps and the Divisions elaborated on them and varied them somewhat. The General der Jagdflieger (The General of the Fighter Forces) was responsible for turning these doctrines into more specific tactics. These Tactical Regulations were directed to the Geschwaders after perfunctory checking by the Fuhrungsstab and sometimes by Goring.

The functioning of the Jagddivisionen reached the ultimate in air to ground control and greatly subordinated the battle freedom of formation leaders. Had there been sufficient numbers of good pilots to man the ground posts, the system would have been more successful. Most J.L.O. were pilots unfit for further combat, or very good signals officers who could grasp something of air combat. Galland remembers several occasions when the Division headquarters broke down completely and operations were led from some Geschwader headquarters with meager facilities, and yet results were as good as ever.

The faults of this system were legion. It was designed to make possible the efficient strategic control of all German fighter units, and it certainly did effect the most efficient use of the available signals facilities by both day and night forces. But it was so complicated that the ordinary limits on human mental ability prevented full exploitation of its potential for tactical and operational control. The J.L.O. could see so well what was going on in the air that they assumed roles of air strategists which their experience and ground-bound position did not warrant. They usually failed to appreciate fully the vital factors of altitude, visibility, relative strength of friendly and enemy forces and sun position. The result was that they did indeed usually bring their fighters onto our bombers with their directional orders, but often their fighters found themselves in a very bad position for an attack, or worse still, were set-up for Allied fighters. Moreover, the intricacies of the fighter control system and the game-like nature of the entire trick plotting system made the whole thing seem like sport to the headquarters staffs and they readily lost contact with reality.

All the Jagdkorps, Jagddivisionen, Luftflotten and Goring, Galland and the Fuhrungstab (GAF Operations Staff) were connected during operations on a round-robin telephone circuit. Over this circuit the Division (or Divisions) over whose territory the action was taking place put out a commentary on the enemy and friendly operations, a play by play description. Any of the higher commanders, except Galland, could cut in to give such as a change in the point of attack or the massing of forces in a certain area. Goring followed operations from Karinhall or from his town house, and often interjected silly orders. A running commentary on enemy activity was also put by radio over the Rundfunk, so that every German house had its own situation room. When telephone communications were knocked out, the whole round-robin commentary went over the Rundfunk in code.

The detailed control of routes, altitudes, and points of attack imposed on airborne formations by ground fighter control officers in order to avoid contact with Allied fighters and bring the German fighters onto the Allied bombers at the right time and place was far too rigid. It robbed the fighter formation leaders of initiative and sometimes resulted in serious errors when mechanical or signals troubles developed at Division headquarters. On occasions the fighters missed the bombers altogether. Exact and rigid control was useful and indeed necessary at night and by day in bad weather, when the fighters could not see the ground and orient themselves. And as long as the Divisions had at their disposal shadowing aircraft (Fuhlungshalter) and could get a good picture of the air situation which included weather, clouds, altitudes, and so on, the rigid control was not too bad. But when after early 1944 the shadowing aircraft were withdrawn because of the heavy Allied fighter escort, the Divisions had great difficulty in grasping the air situation.

In November 1944 when the fighter arm was preparing the big blow against the heavy bombers, a special Jagddivision called J.D. z.b.v. was set up to control several Geschwader which would otherwise have taxed the facilities of J.D. 1.

Other Fronts and Fighter Organizations

From time to time special fighter commands were set up to control fighters for certain operations. When the Scharnhorst, Gneisenau, and Prinz Eugen slipped through the channel, Galland directed fighter operations from a Ju.52 which hopped along the coast to follow the flight, while another fighter controller, Ibel, sailed on the Prinz Eugen itself and controlled the fighters in the immediate vicinity of the ships.

Throughout the campaigns in various sectors such as Africa, Sicily, Italy and Norway, fighter operations continued under the control of the Jafu. If, as in Norway, the area was too large to be controlled by a single Jafu, a smaller command called an Abschnittsfuhrer (Section Leader) was organized. There was, for example, an Abschnittsfuhrer Trondheim. Those Jafu were not usually classified numerically, but geographical names were utilized instead, for example, Jafu Norwegen, Jafu Tunisien and so on.

Throughout 1941, 1942, and 1943 no Jafu or J.D.'s were needed in Russia, due to the fighter operations dealing primarily with ground support. However, American shuttle raids and Russian night bombing compelled the organization of fighter commands in 1944. Von Greim requested and received a Jafu 6 for his Fliegerkorps VI on the central Russian front. Jafu Ost Preussen was set up to protect East Prussia. There was little for these units to accomplish and the old units in the East were reluctant to relinquish complete control of the fighters. Accordingly, the fighters were left under the Fliegerkorps for all ground support missions and placed under the Jafu headquarters for missions against bomber raids.

In 1943 and 1944 the fighter defense in the Balkans had to be improved because of attacks from Italy by American bombers. It was primarily a matter of political necessity, to keep the wavering Allies from deserting. A few German Staffeln were supplied as a nucleus and German aircraft supplied for outfitting other units. Jafu were organized in Bulgaria, Roumania and Hungary. For a while there was a Hohere Jafu Balkan (Supreme Fighter CO for the Balkans) who controlled both Jafu Bulgarien and Jafu Rumanien. Jafu Bulgarien was at this time under J.D. 8, Vienna. The Jafus in Roumania and Bulgaria were at first under the GAF missions to those countries, then under Luftwaffenkommando Sud-Ost, and during the big retreat of German forces in the east, under Luftflotte IV.

Last-Ditch Changes:
The Ardennes and a Return to the Free Hunt

The Ardennes Offensive in December 1944 brought forth a rather anomalous fighter set-up. Almost all of the remaining fighter units were situated along the Western frontier, on the Rhine. Luftwaffenkommando West, the successor to Luftflotte III, was over all the headquarters of the GAF units in the west. Jagdkorps II, a subordinate command to Luftwaffenkommando West, had under its control ground attack units as well as fighters and was shortly renamed Fliegerkorps II. Under this Korps, situated from north to south, were J.D. 3 Jafu Mittelrhein, and J.D. 5. The two Divisions divided the front roughly into thirds, and thus there was a Jafu operating on the same level as a J.D. Moreover, the J.D. and the Jafu Mittelrhein were equipped with ground attack units from time to time and hence were not pure fighter units. Jagdkorps II was composed of almost all the fighter units. Jagdkorps II was composed of almost all the fighters in Germany, but it had no units experienced in repulsing heavy bomber attacks. To remedy this, the fighter Geschwaders were left under Jagdkorps II only for the missions they flew in support of the army in the West. For missions against heavy bombers, the control was switched to Jagdkorps I in central Germany, which then issued the operational orders. The changeover was accomplished by flashing the code word 'Reichsverteidigung' (Defense of the Reich). The system was not satisfactory for two reasons. First, J.K. I did not appreciate the difficult operational conditions in the West. Secondly, the fighter units were spread all over Germany after each mission against our heavies. Their home unit, J.K. II, couldn't assemble them readily enough for new missions.

In late 1944 it was decided to get away from this detailed form of control and give more initiative back to the Geschwader themselves. The so-called 'Big Blow' was to have been the last big mission when fighters were to be rigidly controlled. During the Ardennes offensive, Geschwader actually put out their own commentaries and orders from their own headquarters to a great extent. This practice was continued throughout the remaining months of the War, into 1945.

Even in Defense of the Reich, formation leaders were allowed much more latitude in picking their own courses and deciding when to attack. The fighter arm was by this time, however, so weakened and disorganized, suffering from all kinds of shortages, that it is difficult to judge the results of the new policy. A new aggressiveness was noted on the part of some formation leaders when they were given the responsibility of finding and destroying the bombers with a minimum of ground control.

CHAPTER 2

The Organization and Functions of Fighter Units

Interrogation of Generalleutnant Galland
At Kaufbeuren, Germany, 20–24 August 1945

1. Change in the Size of Units (Single-Engine Only)

a. In peace time, before the outbreak of the Spanish Civil War, German fighter units were based on the basic flight formation of three – the Kette – as was used in World War I. During and after the Spanish War and in World War II it was switched over to the element of four – the Schwarm. The size of the Staffel was twelve aircraft – three Schwarms – instead of four Ketten. This Staffel size was adequate for operations in the West up until 1943, when an expansion of the Staffel, Gruppe, and Geschwader level was undertaken. Already in 1941 the Geschwader Molders, J.G.51, had had a fourth Gruppe added to it, on Goring's order, for operations on the Russian front and had found the increased size to be very helpful.

In late 1943 it was decided to increase the size of all the units in Germany and in the West. The expansion was carried through in 1943 on J.G.2 and J.G.26 and in all other Geschwader in the West and Germany by November 1944. The expansion was delayed by high losses early in 1944, by the invasion, and by the fuel shortage. By November, each Gruppe had instead of the former strength of 40 aircraft and pilots a strength of about 80. This expansion was accomplished by adding a Schwarm to each Staffel, a Staffel to each Gruppe, and a Gruppe to each Geschwader. In some cases another Staffel was added to the Geschwader headquarters further increasing the strength.

b. There were three reasons for this expansion:
   (1) The individual inferiority of German aircraft
   (2) The pilots demanded larger formations to combat Allied bombers and fighter escort.
   (3) The operations from the Southern Front and the great number of missions flown from England necessitated an overall expansion of the fighter arm.

c. The expansion was made by enlarging old units rather than by setting up new ones for several reasons. German maintenance was so inferior that more aircraft were needed in each unit to commit any good sized force on operations. The shortage of staff officers and all overhead personnel precluded the activation of new units. When the units were expanded, the old ratio of mechanics to aircraft was maintained, so maintenance did not suffer. Very few non-flying personnel had to be added.

d. The mechanic ratio was two crew men for each aircraft, one ordnance man per aircraft, and one motor mechanic for every two aircraft. Another shortage which forced the expansion of old units rather than the creation of new ones was the lack of formation leaders.

e. Twin-engine fighter units were never expanded to 16 aircraft and pilots per Staffel, but continued with 12. The Me.262 units utilized a Staffel of 12 aircraft, consisting of four elements of three aircraft each.

2. The Staffel

The Staffel of 12 aircraft (later changed to 16) was both an operational and a housekeeping unit, but it could not operate independently due to the absence of signals and transport. It did house and mess its own personnel, though it was common for all pilots in a Gruppe to mess together if all the Staffeln were situated near each other. The Staffel had its own personnel for maintenance and servicing.

a. The T/O of a Staffel was as follows:
   (1) *Staffelkapitan (Hauptmann).* For the first few weeks of his tour of duty as Staffel CO he was known as the Staffelfuhrer, until he was confirmed in this position. If an NCO led a Staffel because of a shortage of officers, which often occurred, he was only a temporary CO and was known as the Staffelfuhrer. The Staka (abbreviation of Staffelkapitan) had the American equivalent of a company Commanding Officer and could administer company punishment.
   (2) *Offizier Z.B.V. (Zur besenderen Verwendung–for special duties).* This officer, non-flying, was a Hauptmann. He carried on the administrative duties of the Staffel and acted as counselor to the Staka, who was usually inexperienced on military routine. The Z.B.V. was usually a Reserve Officer or an old 1st Sergeant promoted to officer rank. He was usually the backbone of the unit.
   (3) *Four Officer Pilots.* Their rank was Leutnant or Oberleutnant.

Usually the officer shortage prevented a Staffel's maintaining their T/O of officers. Before the expansion there were only three allotted to a Staffel beside the Staka and the Z.B.V. These officers not only had flying duties but also had special ground duties. One was the deputy formation leader, another the Technical Officer, one the Ic. (Intelligence Officer), and another in charge of military matters such as simple discipline.

(4) *Ground Crew and Overhead.* The mechanics, in the ratio already mentioned plus the other ground personnel, brought the personnel up to approximately 130 assigned to the expanded Staffel (100 having been assigned to the old 12 aircraft Staffel). The fighter arm in 1944 was repeatedly forced to give up portions of its personnel to the paratroops, which was detrimental to maintenance. In 1945 the situation became much worse.

(5) *Twin-engine fighter units* had the same organization except that they never expanded to 16 aircraft per Staffel, maintaining the old system. The Me. 262 units, J.G. 7 and K.G. 51, K.G. 54 and other twin-engine units, utilized a Staffel of twelve made up of four elements of three aircraft.

3. The Gruppe

The Gruppe, made up of three or four Staffeln, was the smallest independent fighter unit. It was capable of independent operation, having housing, signals, transport, and repair units. The repair units could change wings and engines, and repair ordinary belly landings. It was usual for a Gruppe to operate together with all its Staffeln at one airfield.

The Gruppe Headquarters was itself both an administrative and operational unit, with at least one Schwarm of four aircraft.

a. The Staff of the Gruppe was made up as follows:
    Kommandeur – A fighter pilot with the rank of Major.
    Adjutant – A fighter pilot with the rank of Oberleutnant
    Hauptmann beim Stabe (Captain on Staff) – This Officer was an older man, usually a Reservist. He was the Stabskp (Staff CO) and functioned more or less as an Operations Officer. He did not fly operationally. One of his functions was that of adviser to the young CO.
    Medical Officer
    Civilian Administrative Official (Beamter) – for unit administration
    Intelligence Officer, Ic-Hauptmann

Signals Officer – Hauptmann, also CO of the Gruppe Signals Platoon.

Technical Officer – Hauptmann, sometimes from the Engineers Corps.

2 NCO pilots for flying operations with the CO and Adjutant.

Personnel of the Gruppe Headquarters were organized into a Stabskompanie with the following Platoons and indicated CO's:

Signals Platoon – Signals Officer

Truck Platoon – NCO or Z.B.V. Officer of Kompanie

Repair Platoon – Technical Officer. This unit accomplished echelon repairs on Staffel aircraft.

Kompanie Troup – Admin. and Overhead personnel.

This Stabskp was headed by the Hauptmann beim Stabe and his assistant, the Z.B.V. officer. In the Defense of the Reich, a meteorologist was added to the Gruppe staff, and in all units there were a few mechanics to maintain the aircraft of the Gruppe Schwarm. A Gruppe Headquarters might have attached to it one or two reserve Formation Leaders to use for replacements. For travel purposes, the Gruppe had a small number of Me.108's and Fieseler Storchs. Early in the war they might have had transport aircraft also, but these were later taken away.

b.   The Gruppe Headquarters Schwarm on operations could fly in two ways, out in front of all the Staffeln or leading one Staffel which in turn led the others. In each case the Gruppenkommandeur or his substitute led the entire formation. The Schwarm might well be made up of as many as six aircraft if the Gruppe had enough aircraft, and pilots.

4. The Geschwader

The Geschwader, made up of three and later of four Gruppen, usually had its headquarters at an airfield with one of its Gruppen. The Headquarters had a telephone or loud speaker communication system by which the Gruppen could be informed of the air situation.

In late 1944 and in 1945 the Geschwader Headquarters of units based in the West were usually so completely equipped that they could control their formations in the air, making a return to more decentralized interception tactics possible

a.   The Staff of the Geschwader was made up as follows:

Kommodore – Oberst, fighter pilot.

Adjutant – Hauptmann, fighter pilot.

Operations Officer – Major, fighter pilot

Intelligence Officer – Hauptmann.

Signals Officer – Engineer Korps (This corps was made up of civilian
Administrative Official – Beamter
Meteorologist – (A Civilian Official in uniform)

At first the Staff personnel of the Geschwader Headquarters were organized into platoons, headed by a staff platoon which did all the house-keep-
ing for the entire unit:

Staff Platoon
Signals Platoon
Truck Platoon
Maintenance Platoon – for the maintenance of the aircraft of the
Geschwader Headquarters.

(1) Later on in 1941, the introduction of radar and more complicated
    signal hook-ups forced the expanding of the Signals Platoon into a
    company, which then took over the administrative duties, as follows:

    Signals Company –   Responsible for signals and also for adminis-
                          tration and housekeeping for the Geschwader
                          Headquarters.
    Staff Platoon –   Handling operational headquarters work.
    Truck Platoon –   Furnishing transport for the Headquarters
                          only, not for Gruppen, except in emergency.
    Maintenance Platoon.
    Like the Gruppen, the Geschwader might have attached to its head-
    quarters a few surplus formation leaders in case of casualties.

(2) The Geschwader Headquarters personnel, including theKommodore,
    Adjutant, Operations Officer, and any surplus pilots, officers or
    NCO's, flew operations either in a Schwarm or, in some cases, in a
    Staffel of their own. The Kommodore usually flew a great many mis-
    sions. With his Schwarm he might lead a Gruppe, the whole
    Geschwader, or might attach it to a Staffel and lead the formation
    from that position

(3) The Geschwader Headquarters had a number of transport and courier
    aircraft for its own use. On the English Channel they had some Air-
    Sea Rescue aircraft, which could drop emergency equipment into the
    water. In Russia they had ski-fitted snow rescue aircraft, and in
    Africa, desert rescue Storch aircraft.

5. The Jagddivision

The Jagddivision, a large territorial command controlling day fighters, night fighters and Zerstorer (twin-engine fighters) varied considerably in organization. Although each had a comparable area of operations, some never had any appreciable number of fighters after they were organized in 1943. The average Divisionen (discussed here) were J.D. 1, 2, or 3, based in Germany and mainly concerned with defense against strategic bombing, by day and night. Fighter units on the Russian front were under the control of Fliegerdivisionen, and not Jagddivisionen.

a.   A Division had a Staff and a Headquarters of 6000 to 7000 people. Its main complement was Signals Personnel operating all the various Radar and fighter control sites in the Division Area. It had little to do with the building and maintenance of ground installations, which were the responsibility of the other territorial commands, the Luftgau. The Division could, however, check up on ground matters insofar as they affected operations and insure the efficiency of the Luftflotten controlling the Jagddivisionen, the Jagdkorps, and the Luftgau. Supply was similarly handled by the Luftgau and checked on by the Divisionen.

b.   The Division was mainly an operational command, concerned with the detailed planning, control, and conduct of missions. It exercised absolute military control of the Geschwader deployed within its borders. In addition, it tended its own signals system. It had almost no inspection function and depended on periodic conferences with the Geschwader and Gruppe CO for maintaining contact with its operational units. It could, with the Korps' permission, transfer units within its own borders, but transfers of units from one Division to another was a power reserved, rather stupidly, by the Luftwaffe Operations Staff and Goring. The Jagdkorps from time to time exercised this power to facilitate operations in bad weather and so on, but were severely reprimanded.

c.   Division Staff – The Division had a complete Staff with positions corresponding to the USAAF's A-1, A-2, A-3, A-4, and so on, but only the most important operational staff heads will be considered here.

   (1) *Division CO*: A General, usually an old fighter man from World War I, but in 1944 some young Geschwader CO's were given the job and attained high success. Frequently the CO had been a Jafu. In choosing men for the job, Goring laid more emphasis on dynamic personality than on fighter experience. It took at least 6 months for a CO to get enough experience to be really good, but Goring often replaced them too soon.

(2) *Chief of Staff*: Oberst and General Staff Officer. There was a great lack of fighter men with General Staff Training, which seriously hindered operations.

(3) *Day Operations Officer* (Ia Tag): Major. There was also a lack of these with both General Staff training and combat experience.

(4) *Night Operations Officer*: There were usually more of these available, because night fighting was not so heavy and there were plenty of experienced night fighter pilots.

(5) *Intelligence Officer*: Not a General Staff position.

(6) *Signals Commander* (Divisions Nachrichten Fuhrer): A very important officer, in charge of the Signals Regiment of the Division. If there was only one, he was its CO. These officers were either very good or very poor. Their main trouble was age, since Martini, Chief of Signals of the GAF, disliked to replace his old experienced men.

d. **Changes in Organization** – There were two great additions to the powers of the divisions which greatly affected the Defense of Germany. They related to Air Raid Reporting and to Flak.

(1) *Air Raid Reporting* – Before 1943 three agencies, the Jagddivisionen, the Observer Corps under the Luftgau and the Listening Service under the Chief of Signals each kept a situation map at a central headquarters. The Divisionen had control of radar, the most accurate and reliable form of reporting, but the Observer Korps under the Luftgau had the right to sound all the air raid alarms based on visual reports. Many conflicts and errors arose in this way. In 1943 the Divisionen were made the agencies responsible for formulating the final air situation picture. All Observer Corps and radar plots were channeled to the Headquarters of the various Divisionen, which correlated them ('plot fusion') and informed the Luftgau of the situation. The Luftgau then put out the raid alarms accordingly. This change at first caused much friction with the Luftgau, who had their share of empire builders. The Chief of Signals with his listening service still kept his own situation map.

(2) *Flak*: Cooperation of flak and fighters was up to the Luftflotten, which were so far removed from the scene of operational command that they never managed to effect active cooperation during missions. The result was that fighters were fired on whenever they entered the heavy flak zones. The flak authorities felt that they should be allowed to shoot down whatever flew into these zones, since IFF equipment was not

too reliable. But night operations and bad weather flying made it impossible for fighters to navigate so exactly that they could avoid these zones, so cooperation was an absolute necessity. One proposed solution was that the flak and fighters be combined under Luftverteidigungsdivisionen (Air Defense Divisions) but staff work would have been impractical because of size and friction, so it was decided to effectively subordinate the flak to the fighters and attach a flak operations officer to each Jagddivision, to direct the flak during missions. The CO's of the Flakdivisionen were aggrieved by this and sent only representatives to the fighter Divisionen in some cases. Disputes had to be referred to higher flak operations COs which were attached at the same time to the Jagdkorps, and in some cases disputes during missions were carried up to Weise, CO of Luftflotte Reich. Cooperation depended largely on the personalities of the flak officer and the Jagddivision CO and was in some cases very good. The type of fighter control exercised by the Divisionen headquarters was too exact and detained, and in late 1944 it was altered to give the Geschwader CO more authority and tactical initiative.

6. Jagdkorps

There were only two Jagdkorps, I and II, with J.K.I being the most important. It controlled the units based in Germany for the defense of the Reich, while J.K.II controlled the units based in the West, which did not assume importance until the invasion. The Jagdkorps were not set up until 1943.

a. The Korps was, like the Division, an operational command, but its powers were exercised in supervision and planning rather than actual control during missions. Only in case something unforeseen happened did they cut in on mission control. The Korps attempted to control the deployment of units in its area, but this function was usually retained by the Fuhrungs Stab (GAF Operations Staff) which otherwise would have had nothing to do with the fighter air arm.

b. The Korps carried on a running analysis for all Divisionen under it on enemy intentions, based on weather forecasts and the listening and radar services. It received the Division readiness reports and dictated broad lines of strategic fighters' employment to coordinate the work of the Divisionen. The Jagdkorps (though subordinate to Luftflotte Reich and Luftflotte III in the cases of J.K.I and J.K.II respectively) were the most important commands in the GAF. The Luftflotten were too far removed from the operational scene to know much about fighter operations.

c.   It was the duty of the Jagdkorps to marshal fighter forces against bomber raids by day and night and to supervise broadly the tactics employed. Beppo-Schmid, head of J.K.I, was not even a pilot, much less a fighter pilot, but was capable of energy and vigor. He asserted himself, grasped the situation in an amazingly short time, and was a good CO, although in Galland's view he furthered the false defensive tactics which were very detrimental to the fighter arm.

d.   The Korps had very large headquarters. J.K.II was at Chantilly and J.K.I in Holland, then in Brunswick, Waggum and last at Treuen, Brietzen, south of Berlin. The Staff was organized like that of a big Division, but there was no staff of fighter control officers to control the Geschwaders in the air. The Korps maintained a situation map and contacted the Divisionen when changes were to be made in the control of operations. One of the most important functions of the Korps was supervising the change of control from one Division to another when fighter formations passed from the range of the control equipment of one Division.

7. Luftflotten

There were six Luftflotten in the GAF. Each Luftflotte was a territorial command and controlled the Luftgau, Flak, Signals, fighters, bombers and so on.

a.   The Staff of the Luftflotten had a Flak Section, a flying Section and a ground Section. Galland always felt that the reorganization of Luftflotte Reich was imperative. He would have absorbed into it Jagdkorps I and have had in Luftflotte a fighter section, Flak section, and ground section. Thus, the Flotte CO and his three section heads could have conferred daily and solved problems of vital operational importance. As it was, fighter operations were in effect controlled from Jagdkorps level, while Flak operations were controlled from Luftflotte level. In addition, Luftflotte Reich had under it, until 1944, all training units and replacements pools, which were later given to a special unit without territorial command, Luftflotte 10. The primary responsibility of the Flotten was the coordination of operations of the various branches, without attempting much detained planning. Luftflotte 3 had been mainly concerned with attacks on England, and Luftflotte Reich was a Flak command before it had any fighters in it. Luftflotte 3 retained its Flak command and most of the actual planning and conduct of fighter operations was taken over for Germany by Jagdkorps I.

CHAPTER 3

A History of the Twin-Engine Fighter Arm (Zerstörerwaffe)

By Generalleutnant Galland, Oberstleutnant
Kowalewski, Major Nolle and Oberst I Eschenauer
At Latimer House, England, 8 October 1945

(a) General

In the German Air Force the Me.110, Me.210, and Me.410 were called Zerstörer. (literally Destroyer) The basic idea originated with General Wever, around 1935–36, for the use of such aircraft as long range fighters with the main missions of bomber escort and strategic fighter missions beyond the penetrating depth of single engine fighters. Very early (1939) the idea of fast bomber missions with the Zerstörer aircraft was introduced. In this a basic mistake was made. Only the performance of the aircraft (speed, climbing, ability, maximum altitude, and maneuverability) determined whether a Zerstörer aircraft could prevail against a SE fighter. Stronger armament, rearward armament, two engines, instruments, equipment for blind flying and radio navigation, a two man crew and finally greater range were all of minor importance in this question. Our Zerstörer aircraft Me.110 (various series), Me.210, and Me.410 were always inferior to German SE fighters at any given time. Only the Dornier Do.335 would have provided an effective combat capability and would probably, by its improved technical performance, have become a Zerstörer aircraft capable of competing with enemy fighters. *The Zerstörer must therefore at least perform as well as a fighter. Since this was not the case it could not achieve its goal in the operations conceived for it.*

In the planning at the time, the TE Zerstörer was absolutely determined upon as the long range fighter. Thus the need for an SE long range fighter with good performance (like the Mustang) was not considered in time. The proof for these contentions was provided in the Battle of Britain.

After this began the dissipation of the operations of Zerstörer units, but not of the aircraft.

The uses of these so-called Multi-Purpose aircraft now came under:

45

(1) Ground Attack .... Gen. der Schlachtflieger
(2) Fast Bomber Missions (In Army and Navy areas) .... Gen. der Schlachtflieger
(3) Fast Bomber Missions on a strategic basis (Me.410 night raids on England) (Bombers) .... Gen. der Kampfflieger
(4) Staff Staffeln of Stuka Geschwader .... Gen. der Kampfflieger
(5) Reconnaissance Missions .... Gen. der Aufklärer (Recce)
(6) Night Fighter Missions .... Gen. der Jagdflieger (Fighters)
(7) Day Missions in Defense of the Reich.............. Gen. der Jadgflieger

Thus there resulted a complete dissipation of the TE forces and nothing was left of the original intended use.

What was still more decisive, however, was the fact that *then and for the foreseeable future no fighter with good performance and long endurance for air defense and strategic operations was available.*

(b) Organization of a Zerstörergeschwader

Zerstörergeschwader had 2–3 Gruppen. Each Gruppe had 3 Staffeln and a Staff Company.

Every Staffel had 12 aircraft.

The Geschwader had a Signals Company (motorized)

This organization, similar to that of fighter units, was introduced only at the end of 1942. Until then, in accordance with the planned strategic use of Zerstörer, the units were dependent on Airfield Servicing Companies, as were bomber and Stuka units. An increase in the unit strength of the Zerstörer (as in fighter units) was never planned.

(c) Setting Up and Operations of Zerstörer Units

(1) **Polish Campaign** Here the single completely equipped Zerstörergruppe, I/Z.G.76, was in action. Its peace time base was Olmutz and its CO was Hptm. Reincke, who was later killed in Norway. It scored some successes with very small losses, since no equal opponent appeared. The successes of the Zerstörer in low level attacks are worthy of special notice. After the Polish campaign the unit transferred to Jever near Wilhelmshaven. Its job was protecting the coastal area and also the pursuit of the enemy over the ocean as far as possible. Its missions included attacks off Norway and the air warfare over the North Sea coast in December 1939. The victories of the Zerstörer were about the same as those of the SE fighters.

Demands for Zerstörer were increased on the basis of the operations planned. In January, Göring personally recruited pilots from SE fighter units for the Zerstörer Arm as an elite unit.

(2) **Norway and Denmark** One Zerstörer unit took part in this campaign, namely I/Z.G.76. The newly created unit I/Z.G.l under Hptm. Falk was given occupation duty.

In the Norwegian Campaign, after the appearance of the first British aircraft carrier fighters in the Narvik area, one Staffel of I/Z.G.76, equipped with 900 liter belly tanks, was moved up to Trondheim and escorted bomber formations from there to the Narvik area. Several victories were scored against the Blackburn Skua which appeared there for the first time.

For operational airfields I/Z.G.76 used Stavanger-Sola, and I/Z.G.1 used Aalborg-West.

I/Z.G.1 was transferred to Kirchhellen shortly before the beginning of the campaign in the West.

(3) **Campaign in the West** Meanwhile the production of the Me.110 had been further raised in order that new units could be equipped. Thus, the following units were ready for the campaign:

I/Z.G.1 at Kirchhellen

II/Z.G.1 at Buer

Z.G.26 (with three Gruppen) at Crailsheim under Oberst Huth.

III/Z.G.76 (location not known) – under Oberst Grabmann.

In the first 10 days of the campaign these units scored considerable success. They shot down many of the few Belgian and Dutch fighters in the air and proved especially good in low level attacks against airfields, anti-aircraft positions, and troop columns. After initial uncertainty, French Morane fighters resolved to attack Me.110s and discovered that Zerstörer were easily shot down. From this time on German losses increased.

Before the beginning of the Battle of Britain, an organizational change took place. I/Z.G.1 was transferred from the Zerstörer arm and, as I/N.J.G.1, founded the German night fighter arm. II/Z.G.1 was renamed II/Z.G.76 and now consisted of three complete Gruppen.

(4) **Battle of Britain** Here were used Z.G.26 (with 3 Gruppen), Z.G.76 (with 2 Gruppen), and Erprobungsgruppe 210 (Experimental Gruppe) with Hptm. Rubensdörffer as CO. Z.G.76 was at Laval and Le Mans. The missions for England departed over the Channel Islands, Cherbourg, and Caen. Z.G.26 was in the Lille area.

After about 6 weeks' combat the Gruppen went back to Germany for refreshing after losses of about 20 crews per Gruppe. About 10–12 experienced crews were left per Gruppe.

On one occasion I/Z.G.76 took part in the Battle of Britain from Stavanger. It was supposed to escort K.G.26 on a bombing raid against Driffield from Norway. On this mission bitter fighting with Spitfires resulted, south of the mouth of the Tyne, and the Gruppe lost its CO, Hptm. Restemeyer, two Staffel CO's, and 12 good crews. To replace I/Z.G.76 which had thus been torn to pieces, II/Z.G.76, which had been re-set up in Germany, came to Norway in September 1940. Here it took over the fighter and escort jobs, flying and operating in Staffeln and Schwärme. Its fields were from Bardufoss to Christiansand.

(5) **Eastern Campaign** For this campaign, Erprobungsgruppe 210 was reorganized into Schnellkampfgeschwader 210 (Fast Bomber Geschwader) under the General der Kampfflieger, with Major Storpe, as its CO. It had two Gruppen. I/S.K.10 was the former Erprobungsgruppe 210 and II/S.K.G.210 was the former II/Z.G.76, which had returned from Norway. Still another Gruppe of Z.G.26 was thrown in on the middle sector of the Russian front.

The chief functions of the Zerstörer units on the Russian front at this time were attacks on airfields at low levels, dropping 2 kg. fragmentation bombs and 50 kg. bombs, and support of the Army and of tank spearheads. Enemy artillery and A.A. positions were also bombed by them.

At the beginning of 1942, S.K.G.210 was transferred to Lechfeld to re-equip with the Bf.210 (Messerschmitt). This idea came to nothing, however, because the aircraft was not satisfactory from a flying standpoint. Thereupon, out of S.K.G.210 and four former Army reconnaissance Staffeln, two mixed Zerstörer Geschwader were set up under the General der Jagdflieger. They were Z.G.1 and Z.G.2 with three Gruppen each. After early 1942 they went into action in Russia, each having two Gruppen with the old Bf.110 and one Gruppe with the Bf.109. They were used as ground attack units. Insufficient supply of new aircraft caused the units to collapse in the winter of 1942–43.

(6) **Bay of Biscay** With the introduction of Air to Surface Vessel (ASV) radar equipment on English Coastal Command aircraft, German submarine losses in passing through the Bay of Biscay began to rise. To give the submarines some relief by day at least, on the request of the Navy, a Schwarm of Ju.88C6s was set up in July 1942 from K.G.40 (the bomber unit which operated attacks against shipping in the Atlantic). This Schwarm was built up first to Staffel strength and then to Gruppe strength up to November 1942. As V/K.G.40,

this Gruppe was led by Major Hemm. Operating in Schwärme it flew to about 16° West, and in exceptional cases it started from its airfields at Lorient to combat heavy bomber attacks on the U-boat bases, when no Allied fighter escort was along.

Initial successes against single aircraft in the Bay of Biscay were satisfactory. But with the reinforced appearance of Coastal Command Mosquitos and Beaufighters, the Zerstörer were forced to fly in double Schwärme formation. Against the Beaufighters the Ju.88's could get along fairly well, but against the Mosquitos they had high losses.

A further job of the Zerstörer was the protecting of German blockade runners. For these frequent missions, one Zerstörer Gruppe no longer sufficed and in early 1943 I/Z.G.1 was transferred from Russia to Brest. The Bf.110s scored considerable successes against bombers, but were under great pressure from Spitfires which flew down to Brest. On one mission, which extended into the ocean North of the Scilly islands, nine out of 12 Bf.110's were shot down. For operational coordination of the Zerstörer Gruppen operating in the Bay of Biscay the Headquarters of Z.G.1 was moved to Lorient, and the Ju.88 Gruppe in Lorient was re-named II/Z.G.1, in early 1943.

The deeper penetrations of Allied fighter escorts into the Bay of Biscay made the Zerstörer operations increasingly ineffective, with very high losses.

In the Winter of 1943 and 1944, the Zerstörer units were recalled from the West into Germany. I/Z.G.1 went over to the Defense of the Reich operating from Wels, near Linz, Austria, and II/Z.G.1 converted to the Bf.109 and became a Gruppe of J.G.4.

(7) **Southern Theater of Operations** In 1941, III/J.G.26 was operating here with three Staffeln of Bf.110 and one Staffel of Dornier 17, later Ju.88C6. Chief missions were:

(a) Protection of air and sea routes to Africa.
(b) Combatting of ground targets in Africa.
(c) Bombing raids on Malta.
(d) Sea and land reconnaissance.
(e) Attacks on enemy ship convoys.

This Gruppe was mostly divided operationally into Staffeln and operated from Africa, Crete, and Sicily.

The Headquarters of Z.G.26 and III/Z.G.1 with the Me.410 came into the Mediterranean area in December 1942.

Both Gruppen, especially III/Z.G.26 scored great success in combat.

Among other things, they were very effective in the attacks against Crete. The worst thing was that here the Zerstörer were never used in a consistent concentrated way for special missions, but instead they were overloaded as a 'Maid of All Work', with too many varied missions. With the increase of Allied air superiority, the Zerstörer had higher losses, without having achieved their full purpose. Everywhere, where Allied SE fighters operated Zerstörer units demanded fighter escort by German SE fighters. But the Bf. 110 was just equal to the British Beaufighter. What was achieved under these conditions is best shown by a diagram (taken from documents of III/Z.G.26, at No.2 GAF Personnel Holding Unit), at the end of 1942.

III/Z.G.26	Sorties	Low Level	A/C Dest. on ground Cert/Prob.	Vehicles Destroyed	A/C Victories
France 1940	1204	50	7/8	14	
England 1940	756	–	–	–	220
Meditr. 1941	2962	483	30/5	764	
Meditr. 1942	4443	379	5/0	440	35

During the battle for Tunisia in 1943 the Zerstörer were mainly used as escort for sea movements and air transport. At this time, however, these convoys were attacked only by enemy forces with fighter escort, so that the Zerstörer also had to have their own fighter escort. Also the air transport units, who flew poor formations, were often attacked from Africa by strong fighter forces. In such cases devastating losses occurred. When escort was mixed, the Zerstörer always flew the close escort and the SE fighters the escort cover.

After this the Zerstörer were withdrawn to the Italian mainland, one Gruppe to Naples and one to Rome. Together with fighter units they were used against American heavy bomber formations. Also attacks with RP were carried on. They scored some success worthy of mention in missions with heavy losses. Adequate fighter escort was lacking, because SE fighter units were still needed in Sicily. The Ju.88 Staffel was based at this time in Greece and proved its worth in combat further in the Aegean Sea, because here bombers without escort and therefore vulnerable were still used.

After the evacuation of Sicily, the Geschwader Staff of Z.G.26 and its two Gruppen were transferred back into Germany, reorganized, rebuilt, and set up for missions in the Defense of the Reich.

(8) **Operations of Zerstörer in the Defense of the Reich** In the summer of 1943 Z.G.26 with its two Gruppen was withdrawn from Italy into The Reich, because of the stronger and deeper penetrating American heavy bomber formations. The third Gruppe was recalled from the Russian front and the first Gruppe of Z.G.1, which had until then operated from Brest over the Bay of Biscay, came back to Germany with its Bf.110's.

The operational airfields of Z.G.26 were at first Wunstorf and Hildesheim, later Braunschweig, and finally Königsberg/Neumark. I/Z.G.1 was based in the southern Germany area and for the most part of its operational period in Wels, near Linz, Austria. The Gruppe was transferred for about three weeks to Constanza for the evacuation of the Crimea, and shot down 28 Russian aircraft for two losses, in escort missions, and then returned to Wels for Defense of the Reich. In September 1943 Z.G.76 with three Gruppen was re-formed and stationed in the South Germany area. (I/Z.G.76 came from reconnaissance Staffeln, with Me.110, II/Z.G.76 from school units and from night fighter units, III/Z.G.76 – a skeleton unit – and I/Z.G.1 under Z.G.76.) Operational airfields were Ansbach, Wertheim, Ottingen, and later Lepheim, Prague, Vienna, and Malacky in Czechoslovakia. III/Z.G.76 was again dissolved in February 1944 for lack of new aircraft.

The supply of crews came out of the two Zerstörer schools under the General der Eliegerausbildung (Gen. of Training), from Z.G.101 with Gruppen in Memmingen and Bad Aibling, and from the two OTU Staffel of the Zerstörergeschwader 26 and 76, in Braunschweig and later in Sagan.

Aircraft Equipment of the Various Zerstörer Geschwader
I/Z.G.26 – Bf.110 with 4 × 2 cm or 2 × 3 cm (MK 108) and 4 × 21 cm RP. From May 1944, Me.410 with 4 × 2 cm.
II/Z.G.26 – Me.410, with 4 × 2 cm., from early 1944 with 5 cm. cannon (BK 5), and 2 × 15 mm.
III/Z.G.26 – like I/Z.G.26 but with GM 1 boost apparatus for oxygen injection.
I/Z.G.1 – Bf.110 with 4 × 2 cm., or 2 × 3 cm. (MK 108) and 4 × 21 cm. RP.
I/Z.G.76 – Bf.110 with 4 × 2 cm., or 2 × 3 cm. (MK 103) and 2 × 15 mm.
I/Z.G.76 – Bf.110 with GM 1 – 2 × 2 cm., 1 × 37 mm. (Flak 18) and 2 × 21 cm. RP. from May 1944, Me.410 with 2 cm. and 3 cm. (MK 103) mixed.
I/Z.G.76 – like I/Z.G.76.

(d) The Bf.110 and Me.410

The flying qualities of the Bf.110 fully loaded and at the combat altitude of 25,000 feet were bad. Formation flying with it was hard for new crews, because it had to be flown with full throttle.

In flying with the GM 1, the radio man could not operate the rear MG for lack of space, so the device was taken out again. The Bf.110 with the Flak 18 37 mm. cannon was very nose heavy and turned poorly. Moreover the weapon was not cold-resistant at all, so that usually it jammed after 1 or 2 shots. In place of the Flak 18, the 37 mm. Flak 43 was tried with better results.

The Me.410 with the 5 cm. (BK 5) was likewise very nose heavy and bad in turning combat. It did have the advantage that it could be effectively fired from a range of 1000 yards with the telescopic sight (Zielfernrohr 4) and one hit usually brought about a victory. Gunnery with the telescopic sight required much practice, however, plus neat flying, and a long period of time in the shooting position. The first difficulties with the loading were mitigated by the installation of an improvised clearing device. (shell cartridge case). On the whole, however, this method of employing large calibers, forced by the High Command against great resistance from the units themselves, proved false. Rockets should have instead come into timely use.

The Me.410 was not as well liked among old Zerstörer crews as the old Bf.110, despite its greater speed, (about 80 km/hr more than the Bf.110), since it turned worse, was more sensitive to hits, and was hard to bail out of if it burned.

(e) Tactics

The operations of Zerstörers in Defense of the Reich were so conceived that they were to be used outside of the range of the American fighter escort and exclusively against four engine bombers. To make up for the lack of maneuver ability and in the hope that they would not have to engage in fighter versus fighter combat, the Zerstörer could be equipped with heavier armament. This resulted, therefore, in equipping them with the 2 cm. RP, and 3, 3.7 and 5 cm. cannon. With these the heavy bomber formation was to be shot at and broken up from outside its effective zone of defense. After that, the individual bombers were to be attacked with the 2 cm. cannon and destroyed.

These tactical concepts were correct and brought considerable success, *as long as the American fighter escort was not present.* But if it came to contact with enemy fighters, heavy losses resulted every time, because the Bf.110 as well as the Me.410 was absolutely inferior in every respect. In such cases, only a defensive Lufbery was helpful, which however required flying experience and formations of at least 12 aircraft, or armament toward the rear.

Three basic phases of Zerstörer operations in the Defense of the Reich can be identified.

(1) Operations of Zerstörer against heavy bombers without fighter escort.

(2) Operations of Zerstörer with fighter escort when enemy escort was expected.

(3) Operations of Zerstörer in a mixed formation when American fighter escort was sure to be present.

(f) Operations of Zerstörer against Heavy Bombers without Fighter Escort

The Gruppen of each Geschwader were based on airfields close to each other. Upon receiving that start order over the tactical voice radio, a take-off by Schwärme took place. The Gruppe assembled in a column of Staffeln during a wide left hand curve over the airfield, and flew on, still climbing to the Geschwader assembly point, which lay over some prominent geographical point or in bad weather over a radio beacon.

At the Geschwader assembly point the Gruppen formed into a column of Gruppen. Where formations were mixed, that is, with one Bf.110 and one Me.410 Gruppe, the Bf.110 Gruppe flew ahead of the other.

Upon sighting the enemy, the formation deployed into a line, in which the stepping up of the Gruppen was very important if 21 cm. RP were to be fired. After discharge of the RP, which took place at a range of from 800–1000 yards, the formation was closed up again and an attack with MG and cannon carried through. The range for shooting down bombers with the RP was gauged either by estimating it in the ordinary Reflex sight or with a stereoscopic range finding sight. Some crews scored up to eight victories with RP. The RP were fired on the order of the formation leader, given by radio. (Individual firing was possible.) In attacks from the front or from the side, overshooting was the common tendency, and in shooting from the rear, the tendency was to undershoot. The most practical and ballistically most perfect manner of attack was dead astern. After the attack with the MGs and cannon, the column formation was resumed and the aircraft flew home.

The operational strength of each Gruppen was, in the case of the Me.410 units, about 15 aircraft per Gruppe. With the Me.110 units, it was about

20–30 aircraft per Gruppe. Losses were about 5–10% per mission and successes in this phase of the Defence of the Reich were good.

(g) Operations of Zerstörer with Fighter Escort in Anticipation of Enemy Fighter Escort

After the increased cases of contact with American fighters towards the end of 1943, the Zerstörer were, first, moved back and, second, provided with one fighter Gruppe for each Zerstörer Gruppe, to take over the escort of the Zerstörers as their chief mission. As a result of this innovation, the Zerstörergeschwader assumed command of its fighter escort Gruppe that was attached in this combination.

During this phase, most of the Zerstörer units removed their 21 cm. RP tubes in order to be more maneuverable in case of contact with enemy fighters.

The fighter Gruppe flew close escort for the Zerstörer Gruppe with two Staffeln, which flew in Schwärme formations to the sides of and behind the Zerstörer, about 1500 feet higher, in the shape of a half cross. The third Staffel of the fighter Gruppe took over the top cover about 6,000 feet higher. The COs of the fighters and Zerstörers were in radio contact.

At first, the fighters were forbidden to attack the bombers. Only when the Zerstörers had carried through their attack and absolutely no American fighter escort was to be seen, did the fighter formation leader give the order to attack the bombers. The top cover Staffel was excluded from this.

At this time the attack from head-on was more and more used by the Zerstörers, who flew in a column of Schwärme. After passing through once from the front, the next USAAF formation following it was either attacked from the front also, or after the Zerstörer turned in and attacked it from the rear, continuously in Schwärme. Especially good cooperation between fighters and Zerstörers was demonstrated by I/Z.G.26 with the fighter Gruppe of Major Specht (I/J.G.11) as well as by II/Z.G.76 with the fighter Gruppe of Oberstleutnant Dahl (III/J.G.3). Losses in this manner remained within bearable limits and successes were good.

(h) Operation of Zerstörer in Mixed Battle Formation when American Fighter Escort was sure to be present

After March 1944 the American fighter escort came from the West as far as Stettin-Berlin-Munich and from the South up to Vienna. This condition led the Zerstörers to suffer unbearable losses, since even the fighter group which each Zerstörer Gruppe had as escort was immediately involved in air combat and had all it could do to take care of itself. On 16th March 1944, Z.G.76 in the Augsburg area lost, out of 43 aircraft in action, 26 shot down and 10 belly landed, shooting down only four heavy bombers. The attack of the fighter took place just as the Zerstörer were attacking the bomber, so no defensive Lufbery could be formed.

The fighter commands decided as a result of this to form up battle formations in which the Zerstorer Gruppen, together with the available fighter units, would be brought concentrated into the attack. This tactic proved good during the initial period following contact with the enemy, but after the first successful attacks on the bomber from head-on, the formation of German aircraft was usually spread out a little so that the Zerstörers could be attacked individually or in Schwärme by the American fighter escort. Thus in the first American raid on Berlin in March 1944, I/Z.G.26 was almost totally destroyed and I/Z.G.76 had about 10 losses. Victories scored were in ratio to losses about 1:2. These mixed battle formations were led by the Kommodore of a fighter Geschwader with his Staff Schwärme; the Me.110s hung on behind him and behind them came the Me.410 Gruppen, with the other fighters bringing up the rear. The assembly usually took a very long time and unified control in the air by radio was very difficult to achieve. The strength of the battle formation during the first attack on Berlin in March was about 200 aircraft, of which about 70 were Zerstörers.

Even after the conversion of I/Z.G.26 and II/Z.G. 76 to the Me.410 ended in May 1944, these conditions remained the same. The American fighter escort had become as much stronger as the German fighter force had become weaker. So it merely became a question of being either skillfully vectored or lucky enough to meet a heavy bomber formation, whose fighter escort was not on hand. In such a case, for example, Z.G.26 scored about 15 victories against heavy bombers for two losses during a raid on oil works at Stettin. During an attack on Budapest, in July 1944, 12 Me.410's of I/Z.G.76 shot down eight American heavy bombers for *no* losses. The greatest success was enjoyed by I/Z.G.1 in the area of Budapest-Vienna-Munich, which under Hptm. Albrecht scored many victories with very low losses. But even this unit was victim of a surprise attack by Mustangs in a raid on Wiener Neustadt and lost 13 out of 26 Me.110's. I/Z.G.76 started from Vienna with 12 Me.110's and in climbing up to an assembly point on the Danube to the West was surprised by Lightnings, losing 10 crews in all.

Z.G.26 and 76 were converted to SE fighters at the end of June and beginning of July, which fulfilled finally the long-felt wish of the Zerstörer crews themselves.

(i) Conclusions and Retrospect

This historical sketch of the Zerstörer cannot be complete and all inclusive. Documents and records are lacking. But the most important things have been noted and are summarized shortly below:

(1) The Zerstörer aircraft was in its performance so inferior to a well equipped enemy, especially when air superiority was lost, that its planned purposes could not be fulfilled.

(2) The multi-purpose use of the Zerstörer as 'Maid of All Work' meant a giving up of its own intended use and a complete dissipation of effort in the respect to tactics and technical matters.

(3) On the other hand, the idea of the Zerstörer had diverted attention from the necessity of increasing the range of SE fighters.

(4) In 1943 the Zerstörer were brought nearer their old purpose, even if only in a defensive role in the Defense of the Reich. With this the dissipating of forces to all fronts ceased.

(5) The Me.210 was a great technical error.

The Me.410 came therefore into operation one year too late.

The F.W. (Tank) Ta 154 was supposed to bring about the replacement of the Me.410, offering better performance, but it had to be cancelled from the production program shortly before the series production began.

The Dornier Do.335 would have been a useable Zerstorer. But even in the planning stage, and in the production preparation the High Command squandered the whole thing in talk of fast bombers, night fighters, reconnaissance aircraft, and Zerstörer all using the Do.335 airframe.

Finally a proposed series of very heavily armed Tank Ta 152 aircraft (the Tank 1520) was designated as a Zerstörer. The technical equipment of Zerstörer aircraft was still a matter for argument.

(6) Despite all these mistakes, the Zerstörer force achieved remarkable things, through the good morale and courage of its personnel, even in the hardest times. The high quality of the old formation leaders and crews is mainly responsible for this.

CHAPTER 4

German Fighter Pilots: Equipment and Service

Interrogations of Generalleutnant Galland
At Latimer House and Kaufbeuren, 16–17 August, and at Latimer House, 15 October 1945

Types of Equipment

Each German fighter pilot supposedly had his own chute, but they sometimes were mixed. All of the pilots used the quick release for the straps, and each pilot carried a knife in his boot for cutting the shrouds. Experiments were made with a barometric pressure release. Other experiments included a band type parachute for jumping from the Me. 262, the theory being that the great speed and rapid deceleration required a chute with less resistance and greater falling speed, but it was never popular.

Each pilot was supposed to wear helmet, goggles, and gloves. Late in the war they were all equipped with natty two piece leather suits which gave very good fire protection. Their fur boots were well built for walking and were worn all summer long by some pilots.

Dinghies were not built into German fighter aircraft (single engine) but were carried around the waist of the pilot, where they sometimes inflated at high altitudes and had to be punctured. Mae Wests were required for flights over water or along coastal areas. For winter flying in Russia pilots were equipped with snow shoes or short skis, because it was impossible to walk through the deep snow after a forced landing.

Use of the Radio

R/T discipline in units was always poor, which was a result of short training and the fact that German fliers always found themselves quanitatively inferior in battle and continually called for help. Galland stated that it was always easier to control a winning team than a losing one.

Various measures were introduced to counteract this tendency to talk too much in the air. In J.G. 26, in 1941, Galland installed an extra R/T button in all fighters so the pilots had to push two buttons before they could talk.

The monitoring of R/T and resultant punishment of some offenders helped very little. High losses caused such rapid personnel turnovers that it was hard to determine who had done the talking. The pilots did not have time to learn each other's voice over the R/T.

Fighter Pilots' Service Paths

Promotions in the Jagdwaffe were on the same basis as those of other GAF flying personnel, except that the fighters at first received more promotions for bravery than did other branches. The length of time in grade was usually much longer than that required in the USAAF.

(1) NCO pilots usually left the fighter schools with the rank of Uffz., but the front line units complained and asked that only those who were really ready for combat receive this rank. From then on men not ready for combat went to the front units with the rank of Gefr. or Ogefr. and were promoted when they proved their worth. NCO's could be promoted up to Uffz. by their Gruppenkommandeur and to Ofw. by the Geschwader Kommodore. The TO of each Staffel called for five officers and 11 Ofw. (Master Sergeants). Each NCO was usually required to spend a year in grade but promotions for bravery could freely be given out by the Kommodore.

(2) Officers were of three classes, Active, Reserve and Kriegs (comparable to our AUS). Active officers were trained as pilots in special flying schools for officers and then continued their training to the regular fighter schools. They were commissioned when they left the Luftkriegsschulen. Kriegs officers were of two types, those selected and trained as officer candidates after they became NCOs and those who passed special examinations and entered the GAF as officer candidates. From the start of the war no more active officers were commissioned, but Kriegsoffiziers could become active by passing special tests and signing up for life. Great stress was always put on political reliability. Often the officer candidates could not be spared from operational units and they were commissioned directly without going to the Luftkriegsschule.

(3) Goring frequently appeared in operational units and made spot promotions of NCOs to officers for little or no reason, thereby burdening the GAF with some unqualified officers.

(4) Early in the war, requirements for officers included the (Abitur) successful completion of a course in a Gymnasium or higher school which was roughly equivalent to a US prep-school or high school. However, later, this

requirement was reduced to only eight years of school, the usual amount taken by German youths.

(5) Galland does not believe in making all pilots officers. The German conception of an officer, idealistically stated, is a man who is given special privileges and extra duties commensurate with his superior abilities. In an ordinary fighter unit of the GAF, there were not enough extra duties to keep more than five officers happy and busy, so they were staffed with five and usually fewer.

(6) Officers of the three lowest ranks were treated with the same regard, as to promotions, whether they were Kriegs or Aktiv, but Reserves were not promoted as rapidly. For promotion above the rank of Major, active officers were preferred. It was common to promote young officers to higher grades simply because they held a high TO position, but Galland believes it would have been better to have had dual ranks, one based on seniority and the other based on position, wherein a young officer of ability could have the pay and honor of a high position and still not promote him too fast. He could have a special title which went with his position, for example, Kommodore or Kommandeur.

(7) Officer promotions were usually made on the basis of a seniority list. These positions on the list were determined first by grades received on the officer candidate's examinations and later his fitness and efficiency reports.

(8) Before a man could be promoted, his superior officer had to certify his political reliability as a National Socialist. Poor indorsements in this respect were rare and good indorsements were automatic in most units.

(9) Very early in the war, many able young fighters were promoted very rapidly and later proved to lack leadership ability. This practice was later discontinued.

Staff Training for Fighter Pilots

Fighter pilots were not held in high esteem by the Luftkriegsakademie. This school was composed chiefly of bombardment personnel who were not sympathetic toward the fighter arm. In 1942 the Luftkriegsakademie pronounced seven fighter pilots unfit to be staff officers. As a result of this, no fighter officers were sent to the school for about a year. In 1944 the fighter arm again began sending officers to a short staff training course of about four months' duration.

Decorations and Awards

Early in the war most of the higher decorations were given out by Hitler and Göring. It was then much harder to get the Eiserne-Kreuz II (Iron Cross 2nd Class) and the Eiserne-Kreuz I (Iron Cross 1st Class) than it was later. In the last years of the war, they were given for about one and five victories, respectively. It was first intended that the Ritterkreuz (Knight's Cross) would be the highest decoration, but the Eichenlaub (Oak Leaf), Schwerte (Swords), and Brillianten (Diamonds) added new superlatives. No fighter pilot ever got the Golden Eichenlaub (Gold Oak Leaf), the highest award, which was set up only in the last few months of the war, except Rudel, who was a ground-attack expert.

It soon became apparent that some medals were needed in between the Eiserne-Kreuz I and the Ritterkreuz, so the Deutsche Kreuz in Gold (German Cross in Gold) was invented. The Deutsche Kreuz was actually an anomalous medal which could be awarded at almost any point in the series after the EK I and was often awarded to people who were not deemed worthy of going one step higher. German medals could not be awarded more than once to the same person. Only the next higher medal could be given, which caused some trouble and forced the introduction of stiffened requirements to avoid the cheapening of the medals themselves. This, however, came at a time when victories were much harder to score against toughened Allied air forces and hence morale was badly affected. Hitler and Göring thought the fighter arm had more than its share of medals and made it more difficult for them to get decorations. Unfortunately, this happened just as the air war became much harder for the fighters.

Other steps in the line of medals for combat were the Ehrenpokal (Cup of Honor), a loving cup awarded by Göring, and a silver framed picture of the Reichmarschall himself. No special pay was ever given for awards or decorations. Another distinction was a mention in the OKW communiqué, which Galland won three times.

Awards were also given for a number of combat missions, and only missions for which the enemy was contacted counted for this decoration, the Frontflugspange (Front Flight Wings) in bronze, silver, and gold. This was the only distinctive decoration by which branch of service (i.e. fighters, bombers, etc.) could be determined. The Fighter Spange had an eagle in the middle of it while other branches used an eagle's head, bombs, and so on.

Early in 1944 the point system for fighter decorations was introduced, and Galland set it up at Göring's order. It made bombers in formation count more than bombers out of formation or fighters and so on, and it varied from time to time. Victories on the Eastern Front counted less than victories on the Western Front or over Germany. All the medals were made a bit harder to get.

Honorary medals for office workers and administrative officers were in the form of the Kriegsverdienstkreuze II, I (War Service Cross – similar to the Bronze Star or Legion of Merit) and Ritterkreuz. Commanding officers of high units could also be awarded the regular combat decorations if they were exposed to enemy action; for example, Kesselring got the Diamonds for his transport flights across the Mediterranean in the face of heavy opposition while he commanded the Luftwaffe forces in Africa. General Staff officers often did tours of operational flying to gain a few medals necessary for prestige and promotions. Hitler sometimes violated his own rules and awarded combat decorations to men who had never left their desks. This sat badly with the front units. It became common to award all decorations up to the Ritterkreuz for such chairborne activity.

Despite the stiffening of awards late in the war, Galland believed that the fighter arm continued to be stimulated by the race for decorations and no great changes in policy would have been needed even had the war lasted a year longer.

Discipline

Disciplinary problems in the fighter arm were almost non-existent.

[. . .] Galland believes that the use of military brothels did not minimize VD, but they did minimize homosexuality, which has always been a problem in Germany.

In general, the youth of fighter pilots tended to make life in each unit fairly lively.

Fighter training units had little time for recreation and the conduct was more strictly controlled in these units.

Gollob on Quality of GAF Pilots and Commanders

The quality of pilots and commanders at the beginning of the war in 1939 was good. There were plenty of experienced leaders – at least, there were plenty to fight the war which was planned.

The reasons for the decline in quality of pilots and commanders were:

(1) Inadequate training

(2) High losses

(3) Lack of staff training for commanders

(4) Decline in morale due to the overwhelming power of Allies

Gollob stated that no positive measures were taken to counteract the decline in quality because of the serious and continuous reverses in the war. There was very little aerial gunnery training.

CHAPTER 5

Mobility of Fighter Units

Interrogation of Generalleutnant Galland and Oberstleutnant Bär

At Kaufbeuren, Germany, 4 September 1945

In general, fighter units maintained their mobility throughout the war. The smallest fighter unit which could subsist and operate independently for any length of time was the Gruppe (40 a/c early in the war and increased to about 80 in 1944). The Gruppe had its own signals organization, supply and motor transport. Fighter units, with their entire personnel, were fully motorized and could move anywhere.

(a) Throughout the war there was a struggle between two different schools of thought about aircraft maintenance and mobility of fighter and other units. The High Command of the Luftwaffe always favored a system whereby each airfield would have a regular complement of signals, maintenance, and supply personnel which would service whatever unit happened to be based at that field. The fighter units, on the other hand, favored a system whereby a unit was independent. Bomber units and twin-engine fighter units (Zerstorer) did use the station complement (Flughafenbetriebskompanie) system, but single engined units of the fighter arm were able, throughout the war, to resist the introduction of the station complement theory into the fighter force. It would indeed have simplified the purely physical problems of moving units, but the maintenance problem for fighters would have been vastly complicated. The station complement mechanics were never as well acquainted with maintenance problems as the unit's own mechanics, and fighter aircraft were more susceptible to minor peculiarities than bombers. Moreover, bomber units did carry some mechanics in their own aircraft during transfers, and the aerial engineer and radio operator in a bomber assisted in the maintenance of their aircraft.

(b) Although most fighter units were fully motorized when originally organized, they were not always able to repair their vehicles and became partially dependent on civilian transport which they confiscated from time to time. SS and Army units in turn confiscated transport from fighter units during retreats in Russia and France after the invasion. The gasoline shortage was another limiting factor.

(c) As fighter equipment became more complicated, the need for special transporation arose, for example, special tankers for the GM I and Methanol boost equipment, special weapons repair trucks for the heavier caliber guns, fuel trucks, etc.

(d) Some units were organized in Germany as permanent units without transport, but they usually managed to confiscate a few trucks and by the time they had to retreat in 1945, they were motorized, though poorly.

(e) In transferring from one base to another the theory was that operations were to continue without interruption. An advance party (Vorkommando) was sent out several days in advance of the transfer to the new airfield to prepare it for the arrival of the Gruppe. On the day of transfer, the Gruppe would fly a mission and land at the new field. The main body of ground personnel would follow by truck or rail, while the advance party would service the aircraft at the new field and prepare them for another mission. The advance party was large enough only to service the aircraft with great effort. At the old airfield, a rear party remained to clean up and followed later. In some moves during the French Campaign, the advance party and the main force were transported by air, along with supplies.

(f) A few Gruppen early in the war managed to get enough transport aircraft so that they were almost entirely airborne. This system worked very satisfactorily in the Polish and French campaigns but ended soon after that for lack of fuel, transport aircraft and trucks.

The transportation difficulties on the Russian Front were so acute that ground equipment was overrun time and time again, and units had to evacuate their best ground personnel in fighter aircraft. The Me.109 could carry two passengers in addition to the pilot. The F.W.190 could carry three passengers. This performance was also accomplished in the evacuation of fighter units from Tunisia to Sicily. Despite the difficulties in Russia, it was clear that motorizing fighter units was the salvation of the fighter arm, which without its trucks would many times have been overrun and completely wiped out.

(g) It was often possible in Russia to transfer a fighter unit by attaching only its aircraft and pilots to another unit. The otherwise impossible maintenance problem attending such a unique transfer was solved by the fact that the aircraft strength of units on the Russian front was usually so low that the mechanics of one Gruppe could easily service the aircraft of two Gruppen. Ground losses of servicing equipment in Russia usually was a more serious detriment to operations than the loss of ground personnel.

(h) The supply of units was also ideal for rapid movements. In certain campaigns, such as Poland, France and Africa, gasoline, parts, and ammunition were transported by aircraft. Otherwise each Gruppe had its own motor transport to haul supplies from supply dumps which were to service every 6 to 10 airfields on any front.

(i) Although the mobility of fighter units was often impaired by fuel and truck shortages, it was proved right in principle time and time again.

Part 2
The Offensive War

At the start of the war the German fighter force was the only one of the major combatants that had taken to heart Trenchard's demands from the Great War: 'Use scouts offensively.' Because of the lessons of Spain, and the fact that the German Army was committed to fighting on other countries' territory, the German fighter force had retained an offensive orientation while the bomber-destroying interceptor mission had shaped the other major combatants' tactics.

The chapters in this section form three pairs, dealing with three of the key German fighter missions during the years in which they were on the offensive: the fighter sweep, escort missions, and naval cover. Each of these three topics is covered by Galland's interrogations, supported by those of many of the other contributors. The specifics of each mission are shown in a follow-on chapter. Bär shows how typical escort missions would have been carried out during the Battle of Britain and a free hunt mission later in the war. The naval cooperation chapter is followed by Galland's 1942 directive for such operations. Of his operational successes, Galland was most proud of his organizing and then directing the fighter cover for the 'Channel Dash' of three major German warships to Germany from Brest in 1942. This document was drafted for that operation. Joint war-fighting is a difficult task at the best of times, and in the Second World War the Germans often found themselves unable to coordinate the different services, so Galland's success is particularly significant.

CHAPTER 6

Escort Tactics

Interrogation of General Leutnant Galland
At Kaufberen, Germany, 3 September 1945

Escort Missions for Bombers

In peace-time doctrine and in maneuvers, bomber formations were used almost always without fighter escort. The range of SE fighters did not fit into the plans for strategic bombing. About the years 1937/38, it was resolved to build twin engine fighter units for these purposes, called Zerstorer units.

In Spain, the necessity was recognized of furnishing fighter escort for bomber formations by day wherever enemy fighter action was to be reckoned with. The introductions of the so-called fast bombers, the Do.17 and the He.111 did not alter the situation. The Russian and other Republican forces at the time also used fighter escort for their bomber missions, by day.

In Luftwaffe circles in Germany at the time arose a mental conflict, because in maneuvers the Do.17 and the He.111 were being used, while the fighters were still using the Arado 65 and 68 and the Heinkel 51, which were old slow fighters. In this way the impression arose that the bomber of the future would apparently be faster than the fighter of the future. Experience in Spain with the introduction of the Me.109 soon corrected this wrong impression. As a result, steps should have been taken to bring the range of the SE fighter aircraft up to that of the bombers and thus to conduct the strategic air war as a cooperation of bombers and fighters by day. This step was, however, not taken. It was maintained instead that the twin-engine fighter (Zerstorer) was an aircraft equal to or better than the modern SE fighter, to compete on even terms. In practice, the Me.110 was able to perform adequately in Poland and France. In the Battle of Britain they suffered the already frequently predicted defeat.

Starting in the Battle of Britain the conduct of escort missions was accordingly the exclusive function of the SE fighter, whose inadequate endurance and range worked decisively against it. It was still believed that the deficiencies of the twin-engine fighter could be remedied by better technical performance. This thought led to the construction and series production of the Me.210, which later was developed into the Me.410. Entirely apart from their

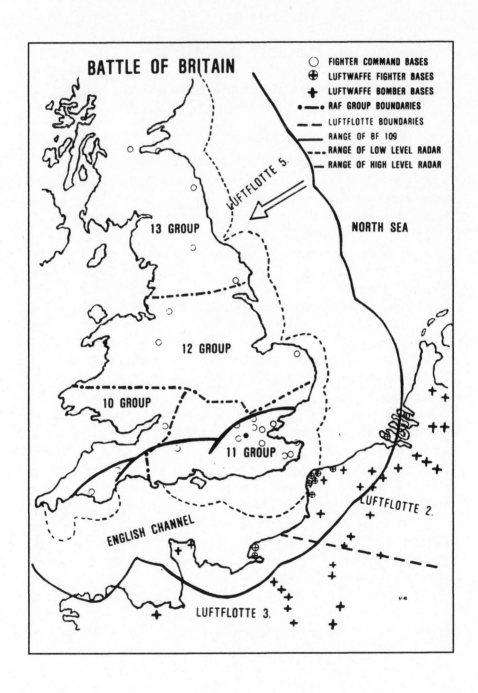

failures in design and in construction the performance of these aircraft would never have been sufficient against modern SE fighters. The only possible result should have been the raising of the range of the SE fighter. Until the introduction of the drop tank, nothing was done along these lines. On the contrary, the range of the Me.109 on its interior fuel tanks continually declined from the greater consumption of the continuously improved and more powerful engine.

Escort tactics

Operationally, the following types of escort are:

(a) Close Escort
(b) Escort Cover
(c) Sweeps to clear the approach and target areas.
(d) Combined escort by SE and TE fighters

(a) **Close Escort** was conducted by SE and TE fighters, whose units were assigned to protect certain bomber formations. Fighters were divided into Rotten (two's) or at least into Schwarme (four's). They protected the bomber formation against close attacks from ahead, behind, above, right and left. It was strictly forbidden to let air battles tempt the fighters away from the immediate vicinity of the bombers.

The difficulties and weakness of this type of escort lie in its purely defensive character. Where enemy attacks are energetically led, this type of protection cannot be effective, because the available time and tactical possibilities for the escort are always less than for the interceptors. A further difficulty lay in the slow speed of the heavily loaded German bombers, which was much lower than the best maneuvering speed of the fighters. The result was that the fighters had to follow the bombers by continually turning and changing altitude.

Nevertheless, even this type of incomplete escort always satisfied the bombers. Anything that took place out of his immediate vicinity did not interest the bomber man, although a roving escort was a prerequisite for keeping enemy fighters at a distance. The demands and complaints of the bomber men thus always materially injured the carrying out of the escort mission.

In this discussion it is not forgotten that only a part of the fighter units concerned carried out their difficult jobs with the necessary exact discipline. The cooperation was especially good when certain bomber units could work for a long time together with certain fighter units so that both could work out and compare their opposed interests and demands.

For a considerable time – before the Battle of Britain – the TE fighters were able to conduct successfully this close escort alone. Later the weakness of the TE fighter and the recognition and exploitation of this weakness by RAF fighters became so serious that the TE fighters could no longer escape from aerial combat but were forced always to take purely defensive measures, like the defensive circle (Lufbery). From this time onward the TE fighter (Zerstorer) could no longer be counted on for escort missions; instead the TE fighter itself required fighter escort and increased the escort burden of the SE fighters.

When individual damaged bombers left formation because of technical trouble or because they were shot up, it was the job of the close escort to provide special cover for the imperiled aircraft. It is clear that close escort as a purely defensive tactic cannot be successful against a strong and energetically led fighter attack. Close parallels can be drawn between the conduct of German escort in 1940 and the first missions of American fighter escort over Europe. After repeated demands of German formation leaders it was decided to use simultaneously a close escort and an escort cover.

(b) **Escort Cover** was conducted by Staffeln or weak Gruppen. During the escort of the bombers the escort flew about 3000 to 6000 feet higher, off to the side. Their mission was to attack approaching enemy fighter formations before they were in an attack position. The escort was supposed to combat enemy fighters until they were at least temporarily unable to attack the bombers effectively. They were then required immediately to resume contact with the bombers and continue escort cover. They were also required to help the close escort should enemy fighters effect a surprise and break through to the bombers from front or below. In any event, the escort cover had to remain with the bombers on the way in to the target and out again.

The strength relationship between close escort and escort cover varied according to the strength of the bomber formation to be escorted, and the strength and formation size of the fighter opposition expected. It was usually about 1 to 1. Bombers, close escort and escort cover were linked by a common R/T frequency. This was first achieved in the Battle of Britain by retrofitting radio equipment into aircraft already operational. Very signals and smoke signals have not proved of value except to show the colors of the day.

In special situations the escort cover can be released on the way home and strafe ground targets. This can only be done when it is known with confidence that no further contact with enemy fighters is to be expected. The success of a close escort mission or of an escort cover mission depends exclusively upon how well the bombers are protected, that is to say, upon the losses suffered by the bombers. The escort fighters' victories are less important and of secondary interest. This should be taken into consideration in evaluating the success of missions.

(c) **Sweeps to clear the approach and target areas** are desirable if sufficient fighter strength is on hand. This can be especially successful if the strength and conduct of the enemy fighter defense is known with some exactness. The sweeping force must be on the approach route and over the target at the proper time ahead of the bombers, engage every enemy fighter formation, break it up, or at least keep it away from the bombers. In such cases, the escort cover can frequently enter temporarily into the fight. The formations of the sweeping forces must try with determination to press on into the target area despite intervening air combat. The departure from the target area can only proceed after bombs are away and a rear cover is provided for formations of pursuing enemy fighters. The mission of the fighter sweeping force is to shoot down the enemy and keep as many enemy fighters as possible away from the bombers. In practice this type of mission is the most fruitful and therefore the most popular.

This type of operation was completely mastered from the middle of 1944 by American Mustang fighters on escort duty. German escort fighters in the Battle of Britain in 1940 suffered seriously from their short endurance and resulting short range. Rendezvous with the bombers could take place only right on the Channel coast and had to be completed in a very few minutes; no delay could be allowed the bombers and the flight to the target could only be effected over the shortest possible route. If anything irregular happened, the fighters could not return after the mission to their place of start, but had to land on the beach or in the water for lack of fuel.

Jettisonable fuel tanks were not introduced until after the Battle of Britain. This temporary limitation on the use of fighters resulted in preventing the forming of large bomber streams; instead the bomber Geschwader had to fly in to the target or targets in small string formations. This was repeated in every mission. Variations and resultant surprises for the RAF did not exist. The points and times where the various bomber formations crossed the coast and rendezvoused with their respective fighter formations were so close together in time and place that the fighters frequently rendezvoused with the wrong bomber formation, with the result that other bomber formations were covered insufficiently or not at all. This became especially frequent when the weather began to get bad in autumn 1940 and rendezvous points and times could no longer be held on top of the clouds. Moreover, the defensive firepower and resistance to hits of the Do.17 and the He.111 would not stand comparison with the qualities of four engine American bombers. Radar navigation and fighter control procedures were not yet available for the German side. The cumulative effect of all these circumstances, and *not* a weakening of the German fighter formations, led to greater bomber and fighter losses. The advent of bad weather also caused excessive losses. When it was decided to attack important targets which were completely beyond the range of the fighters, the Luftwaffe had to resort to night attacks.

On the southern front and especially in the Battle of Malta the German fighter forces were numerically so weak that the effective conduct of escort missions according to the above points was not possible. A compromise of the various types of escort was therefore improvised as the situation and possibilities permitted. At the same time that the attacks on Malta resulted in more and more losses because of the ever stiffening fighter defense, the fighter escort for transport aircraft over the Mediterranean was doomed to failure in the face of meager fighter forces and heavy enemy fighter action. No new tactical points were brought up here anyway.

The air war on the Eastern Front developed in the course of the years to an ever higher standard of technical achievement and tactics. The increased use of the German forces for strategic bombing operations would no doubt have speeded up this development. As it was, fighter escort for bombers was carried out in the most primitive form. A few fighters would attach themselves to the bomber formations as they passed over the fighter fields and escort them to the target and back, as far as the front, when the fighters usually broke off and engaged in fighter sweeps. The Russian fighters usually refused to attack even the lightly armed German bombers, mainly because they had not mastered the tactic of a disciplined attack. Usually the German bombers were attacked only by courageous Russian lone wolves, who dived daringly and cleverly onto the bombers. The German fighter escort was therefore a combination of close escort and escort cover, and fighter sweeps were flown after a completed escort mission.

For attacks and raids on the tactical area (battle area), the number of escort fighters was usually less than that of the bombers. Only raids of great penetration range were flown with a number of fighters equal to the bombers. Radar service and fighter control were not at first available in Russia, and the later introduction of these things did not bear much fruit because of the repeated retreats. Only the Listening Service always furnished useful service on the Eastern Front. The supply and support missions of the Luftwaffe for surrounded areas and cut-off forces (Stalingrad Demyansk, Crimea, Cholm, etc.) put the fighter arm to very difficult tasks. If supply landing fields were available, part of the fighter escort landed with the transport aircraft, in order to furnish cover as soon as the transports started back. For the most part, however, four-fifths of the fighter combat on the Eastern Front took place over the battle area in support of the Army.

Escort for Dive Bomber Formations (Stukaverbande)

Ju.87 dive bomber units were largely manned by fighter personnel when they were set up. They therefore took on a special character which was always more closely related to the fighter arm than to the bomber arm. Outmoded in performance, slow in level flight and also in dives, inadequately armed both from the front and rear, the Ju.87 soon had to quit the Battle of Britain and the anti-shipping war. When German air superiority in Africa was lost the Ju.87 could not be employed without heavy losses even in the presence of fighter cover. On the Eastern Front, use of the aircraft was possible until the end of the war, with the losses from Russian fighters being less than those from ground defenses. In some respects the Ju.87 was the counterpart of the Il-2 used by the Russians.

The most conspicuous weakness of the Ju.87 formations lay, however, in their impossibly low formation flying speed of about 250 km per hour. The operational altitude of the Stuka in the Battle of Britain was about 16,000 feet and lower. In Russia they flew at about 6500 feet. Pull-out altitudes were set according to targets and ground defenses. The minimum pull-out altitude was about 1900 feet. On the Eastern Front the Stukas almost always went over to ground attack tactics after their bombing dive.

The single basic difference in the conduct of escort for Stukas (Ju.87's) compared to ordinary bombers is the special need for protection during the dive and during the re-assembly after the pull-out.

In practice this was accomplished by a part of the close escort. This was best done by the escort cover arriving at the pull-out altitude shortly before the Stukas and patrolling there. This pull-out altitude must be determined in advance in the field order. In case it is altered, all elements must be notified by R/T. The other part of the close escort dives with the Stukas, but because of greater diving speed this escort must resort to turning to hold position. A special danger exists from the time of the pull-out until the re-closing of the Stuka formation. It is not possible in this period for the fighters to protect each individual Stuka. Therefore it is the Stukas' responsibility to keep formation at least in Ketten (3s) and to get as quickly as possible into closed formation. When they had to dive through cloud, or when the pull-out altitude was clouded in, this coordination did not work and losses resulted.

Ju.88 Formations

Influenced by the concepts of pre-war times, German medium bombers like the Ju.88 and Do.217, even the heavy bombers like the He.177, had to be fitted for dive bombing attacks. Greater accuracy was supposed to be obtained by this. The disadvantages of this requirement were, with the exception of dive bombing against shipping, so great that the concepts must be now regarded as false. For the fighter arm, however, it did mean an aggravation of the job of escorting, first because of the diving itself and second because of the weak defensive armament of the bombers. As early as the Battle of Britain, the Ju.88 formations gave up dive bombing and went over to high altitude level bombing. As long as dive attacks were conducted, the fighters flew escort according to the principles laid down. Because of the inferior maneuverability of the Ju.88 compared to the Stuka, the dive and pull-out of the Ju.88 formations were even more spread out and the re-assembly took more time than with the Ju.87's. The Do.217 and the He.177 were practically never employed by day on dive bombing missions.

Bär's Comments on Escort Missions for Stukas

One important fact for the escort of Stukas is that the Stuka is very slow and vulnerable, therefore, rendezvous with the escort must be carried out with great certainty. In Africa, where during most of the campaign the threat of enemy fighters behind the German lines was not great, the following method of rendezvous proved to be good: For example, the Stukas flew over the fighter field at 6000 feet at 1500 hours. The fighters were ready in their aircraft on cockpit alert (Sitzbereitschaft) at 1455 hours. As soon as the Stukas appeared over the field, the fighters got the order to start. The Stukas flew on to the front and the fighters caught up. In this way, rendezvous was both sure and economical as far as fighter fuel was concerned. This type of rendezvous is, however, only possible where enemy forces are not strong enough to fly over the front. At the target it was important that a portion of the fighter escort dive with the Stukas (or fighter-bombers, or ground attack aircraft) to cover their most vulnerable moment as they pulled out of the dive. Radio communication between the fighters and the bomb-carrying aircraft proved well worth while. Radio silence is extremely important, especially when other formations are sighted. It is easily possible that a false sighting of enemy fighters will take place and the bomb carrying aircraft will jettison their bombs unnecessarily. Only the most experienced pilots and formation leaders should be allowed to announce the approach of enemy aircraft.

For missions of tank-destroying aircraft it is often advisable during the attack for the fighter escort to shoot up A.A. installations in the vicinity, to remove this greatest danger for the tank-destroyers.

Escort for Ground Attack Units
(Schlachtverbande or Schlachtfliegerverbande)

In Spain, ground attack missions at low level were flown exclusively without fighter cover. If fighter opposition developed, the He. 51 formations were able to defend themselves. The Legion Kondor fighter Staffeln, however, often entered the front area at the same time as the ground attack Staffeln and gave indirect escort by flying fighter sweeps in the general area. For operations against enemy airfields farther to the rear, a common time of arrival over target was given both fighters and ground units. No case is known to Galland, however, where actual immediate fighter cover was furnished for ground attack units in Spain. In the Polish campaign ground attack units with the slow Henschel 123 bi-plane operated completely without fighter escort.

In the French Campaign, in 1940, similarly, no fighter escort was flown for ground attack units. Fighter units were regularly sent in to sweep clear the combat area for the ground attack formations. Only one ground attack (Schlachtflieger) unit existed at this time, II/ (Schlacht) Lehr Geschwader 2, which was attached to Fliegerkorps VIII (Richthofen's tactical air force) and was equipped with the Henschel 123 bi-plane. After the campaign in France, this Gruppe re-equipped with the Me. 109 fighter-bomber and was in combat together with Kampfgruppe 210 in the Battle of Britain. The missions which these two Gruppen flew in the Battle of Britain were not ground attack missions, but fighter-bomber missions. They were, of course, flown under fighter cover, because of the strong RAF fighter defense.

The Campaign against Russia was begun in 1941 with the single ground attack Gruppe, II/(Schlacht) Lehr Geschwader 2, which at the time had variously three Staffeln of Me.109's and one Staffel of Hs.123's, or two of Me.109s and two of Hs.123's. In any event, the Gruppe needed no fighter cover, furnishing its own cover with the Me.109s. One other Staffel of the Gruppe was at this time being equipped with the Henschel 129, which was used more and more. Later these Hs.129 Staffeln specialized as tank-destroyers with the MK 101 cannon.

The setting up of two more ground attack (Schlacht) Geschwader in early

1942, with Me.109's and Me.110's, brought new demands for fighter cover. In II/ (Schlacht) Lehr Geschwader 2, fighter cover was still furnished by the Gruppe itself. Even the tank-destroying Hs.129's, attached to the newly created Schlacht Gruppen, were covered during missions by fighter aircraft, Me.109s and Me.110s.

It frequently occurred that for concentrated offensives twin-engine bombers, Stukas, and ground attack units operated in uninterrupted succession, in the same area, for example, where a break through had occurred. For this period of massed activity, the area concerned was covered by an air umbrella of all fighters available not being used for the immediate escort of the bombers and Stukas.

Later, some Henschel 129 tank-destroyer Staffeln were attached to fighter Geschwaders to provide a striking force with heavy fire power for use against Russian tank breakthroughs. Because of the lack of Hs.129's this experiment was stopped. In addition, in Summer 1943 an operational concentration of all the Hs.129 tank-destroyer units was attempted. The use of the tank-destroyers en masse resulted in several successes. During this period, fighter escort for the Hs. 129's was furnished by a fighter Gruppe especially subordinated to the tank-destroyers for this purpose. This was one of the few cases in which a sub-ordination of fighters for such cooperation was successful. For this special purpose it was worthwhile.

Starting in 1943 the ground attack units (Schlachtverbande) converted to F.W.190's. Right after this the Stuka Gruppen began their conversion from Ju.87's to F.W.190s and became not only nominally but also actually ground attack units (Schlachtgruppen). Fighter cover was not provided for them, however, except in special cases. For the purpose of protecting these ground attack units from enemy fighters, the chief method employed was the sweeping clear of the battle area by regular fighter units. Only the few remaining Stuka units required an actual fighter escort. No further alterations or developments occurred until the end of the war.

Southern Front

In Africa there were first one and later two ground attack units with F.W.190's. Operations were only possible with a ratio of escort to escorted aircraft of 1:1. With increasing Allied air superiority in Tunis, Sicily, and Italy their operations became more and more difficult and losses heavier. A single Hs.129 tank-destroyer Staffel which was in the Southern theater could not be used operationally at all and was transferred to the Russian front.

In June 1944 one ground attack unit was used on the invasion front, and it required strong close escort. Allied air superiority soon made the use of ground attack units impossible. No operational order could be carried out on time, since the Allied fighter umbrella hung almost continually over the fighter bases. Assemblies and rendezvous in the air were knocked to pieces or never even allowed to start. At the latest, on the way to the target area the formations of ground attack aircraft and fighter escort were engaged in combat with numerically superior enemy forces. Under such an oppressive enemy air superiority every type of planned mission was brought to a halt. Only in those surprise missions like the attack on Allied airfields on 1st January 1945 could anything be accomplished by the personal initiative of the immediate formation leaders. In conjunction with the air superiority of the Allied fighters and their good fighting spirit and ability, the Allied radar and fighter control organization deserves special mention. They succeeded in grasping every German air operation immediately.

CHAPTER 7

Typical Orders for Fighter Escort to a Geschwader (Battle of Britain)

Interrogation of Oberstleutnant Bär

At Kaufbeuren, Germany, 19 September 1945
Note: The Geschwader designations used below are fictitious

Jagdkorps to J.G. 4: '100 Do.17's and He.111's will be over Calais at 0950 hours at 6000 meters. Target: Port installations east of London. Bombers climb to 7000 meters to 7500 meters. Approach: Dover – London. Return: London – Thames Estuary – Dunkirk. Geschwader will protect bomber formation and will be reinforced by I/J.G. 3. Fighter sweeps ahead by J. G. 1. Extended fighter cover by J. G. 2 and two Gruppen of J. G. 3. Establish contact with returning bombers over Thames Estuary.'

Geschwader to Gruppen: (It is assumed that Geschwader is stationed in Calais Area). The above mission orders are transmitted. *In addition*: Assembly of Gruppen individually over Calais at 6000 meters to be accomplished by 0945 hours. Gruppen take ordered positions independently as follows: I. Gruppe left, same altitude as bombers; II. Gruppe right, also same altitude as the bombers; III. Gruppe right above, somewhat stepped up to the rear (i.e. for the approach with the sun in back). I/J.G. 3 in the rear of bomber formation in slightly stepped up formation. Important: Keep exact position, because other Geschwader will meet and carry on with extended fighter cover. Main job of J.G. 4 is direct protection of bombers, up to the limits of fuel supply and then return to their home A/D's. Formation leader of Gruppe I will 'weave', when all Gruppen have joined up with bombers (RT). Formation leader of bombers then proceeds on his course. When weather is bad over target, 'weaving' of fighters means for the bombers to turn back. Primary assignment is protection of bombers and air combat only when bombers are directly attacked. Attention is directed to the fighter cover meeting them at the Thames Estuary.

After the mission: Mission report: Time of take-off, landing time, No. of A/C, special events (meeting up with bomber formation, flying formation of bombers, enemy intelligence), claims, losses, special observations (increased fighter defense, flak, bomb hits), No. of A/C ready for next mission.

CHAPTER 8

Fighter Tactics: the Free Hunt

Interrogation of Generalleutnant Galland and Oberstleutnant Bär

At Kaufbeuren, Germany, 17–20 September 1945

Fighter Sweeps (Free Hunt).

This was the most original, most natural and best loved type of fighter combat mission. Here the fighter could determine and utilize all the advantageous factors of battle. Fighter sweeps were not an end in themselves, but always a means to an end, i.e. they are subordinated to some purpose, for example:

a) Fighter sweeps over the front area to combat and keep down enemy combat recce aircraft or artillery observation aircraft.

b) Fighter sweeps over the battlefield and the tactical area to combat enemy fighter-bombers and ground-attack aircraft.

c) Fighter sweeps in conjunction with operations of friendly fighter-bombers, dive-bombers, ground-attack aircraft and bombers; to lure up the enemy fighters to battle, clear combat areas, secure the flanks in the air, and draw enemy strength upon friendly fighters.

d) Fighter sweeps over the airfield areas of the enemy fighter force, to engage the enemy's defenses and weaken them.

e) Fighter sweeps in the defense of Germany to engage the enemy fighter escort in battle and divert it from its escort mission.

f) Fighter sweeps against ground targets.

The fighter sweep was hardly mentioned in GAF peace time tactical regulations, although it had been the chief mission in World War I.

In Spain, more than 50% of all missions were flown as fighter sweeps. Even the ground attack Staffeln with the Heinkel 51 had great success with fighter sweep missions in defined areas behind the enemy front against targets of all kinds.

In Poland and in the French campaign of 1940 many fighter sweeps were flown, first to force up the enemy fighter force and secondly to have forces in the air during the enemy's main periods of aerial activity, since the aircraft warning system was too bad to permit scramble starts when the enemy appeared.

The Battle for Britain was begun with a period of fighter sweeps for the purpose of so reducing the RAF fighter defense that the subsequent strategic bombing by German bombers would be as safe as possible. The later use of fighters with small formations of decoy bombers to lure up RAF fighters was a degenerated form of fighter sweeps.

In Russia the fighter sweep was especially popular and successful. Sweeps were always flown when strength and escort missions permitted.

On the Mediterranean and African fronts, fighter sweeps were the exception, because there fighter strength was already far overloaded by the great variety of required missions. Galland's unit, J.V.44, operating with Me-262's, flew fighter sweeps, right up to the end of the war.

Goring and his staff usually had little understanding of the employment of fighter sweeps. Instead they required fighters to fly 'definite objective missions'.

In general the fighter command (Division, Jagdkorps, Jafu or other unit) gave orders for units to fly fighter sweeps without specifying strength, areas, and time in great detail. (Exceptions were the big fighter sweeps over Britain at the beginning of the Battle of Britain.) Fighter sweeps were permitted only when no defensive missions were to be flown.

The operational order was usually sent out from the Geschwader after the fighter command had given permission for sweeps to be flown. The Geschwader determined the strength, times and areas, but usually did not specify the altitude. The operational order was usually communicated to the Gruppen by telephone or by courier. The Gruppen in turn reported back through the same medium its time of take-off, landing time, and success.

Strength of formations varied according to available strength, enemy activity, weather, and the depth of penetration. In Russia fighter sweeps were flown in strength of the Schwarm on up; in the French campaign usually in Geschwader or half Geschwader; in the Battle of Britain, Gruppen; in Defense of the Reich, Gruppen; and in the Ardennes offensive, Gruppen and Geschwader.

The briefing of flying personnel was done by the Gruppe CO and the Staffelkapitan and was short and simple. The missions were so planned that almost all advantageous factors like position, sun, launching of attack and breaking off, were left up to the formation leader in the air.

One thing only was vital for the operation: which force first discovered the other. The relative strength of the foes played a minor role when technical performances of the aircraft were approximately equal and the training of the pilots about the same. The most certain advantage was surprise, then in this order: position, technical and tactical flying ability of formations, gunnery experience and ability, cohesion of formations, and relative strength.

In Russia, for example, the relative strength of formations was almost always to the disadvantage of the Germans: nevertheless, fighter sweeps were successful for them up to the last of the war. In Russia, German air superiority consisted of technical advantages, better tactics, and in the strong feeling of superiority enjoyed by German fighter pilots. In the Battle of Britain the Germans also had the better tactics and experience. Nevertheless, position played a very important role at the time and helped the British win. In Russia it was required (by Richthofen of Fliegerkorps VIII for example) that the fighters on sweeps first drop a bomb on some worthwhile target behind the enemy lines or at least after the mission strafe until their ammunition was gone (Russian fighters were so slight a threat that the flight home could usually be made safely without ammunition).

Start and Assembly was begun basically from the circumference dispersal areas except from fields where a runway had to be used because of bad surface conditions. (Runways were unpopular with pilots of conventional German fighters.) Assembly of a Gruppe had to be completed after one circuit in about three minutes after start. In general, at least four aircraft started simultaneously; on good fields, whole Staffeln. Formation leaders of small formations always started first, and with larger formations they usually did so too, a matter of taste. The formation for fighter sweeps was widest open of all, with considerable stepping upward as soon as more than four aircraft flew in one formation.

In the approach to the target, altitude was gained in slightly closer formation. The battle area was so entered that all possible advantages were used. With 10/10th clouds, if the ceiling was not more than 1500 feet or if sweeps were ordered under the clouds, the formation usually flew on the deck. Ground defenses prevented this maneuvering over front line areas and over the enemy rear zone.

In attacks the element of surprise was always striven for. If this was not successful, having the altitude advantage was very important. When a turning fight began, enemy fighters turning in the opposite direction warranted especial notice. Superior climbing ability was absolutely used to advantage in a turning fight. Rotten (two-ship) and Schwarme (four-ship) formations must not break up. The top cover had the mission of joining in effectively soon after the beginning of the turning fight, and at the latest upon the first appearance of weakness in the friendly formation. The top cover usually retained its superior altitude after the attack in order to attack again with the advantage. Moreover, it prevented enemy fighters from entering the fight from superior altitude.

Break off and return usually followed after the order of the formation leader. Arbitrary breaking away in air combat, diving away or split-S-ing and breaking up of formations was fatal, but occurred more and more in the German fighter arm. Galland explained this only by the insufficient training of pilots and by the deterioration of their formation leaders. This lack of discipline in battle was always a sign of an inferior fighter force, inferior in numbers, achievement, training and morale. This inferiority could not be successfully combatted with orders and punishments alone. Successes always gave the fighter arm its self confidence.

Thus, in the last months of the war, every German fighter formation broke up. At most, Rotten and Schwarme (two-ship and four-ship) held together. As a result the return flight of aircraft after each mission took place with little organization and much straggling. In the West and in the Defense of the Reich, landings after long missions were often made on many scattered airfields.

Inferior in numbers, technical performance, flying training and gunnery, unaccustomed to fighter combat and led by inexperienced leaders overloaded with many missions and insufficiently specialized, demoralized or at least depressed by a bad victory-loss ratio, the Jagdwaffe finally accomplished nothing more in purely fighter combat. An exception to all this was the fight against the Russian air force.

CHAPTER 9

Typical Fighter Sweep

Interrogation of Oberstleutnant Bär
At Kaufbeuren, Germany, 12 September 1945

Telephone call: Ia-Fl. Korps to Geschwader Kommandeure: Geschwader free today for 'Fighter Sweeps'. Time for missions 1000 hours, 1100 hours and 1500 hours to 1600 hours in sector A-B-C-D. The mission will be flown in Geschwader formation.

From Geschwaderkommandeure: Commitment of Geschwader at times and place specified above. Assembly of Gruppen 0940 hours over Geschwader a/c. Order of assembly: Kdre. I Gruppe joining up to the right, II Gruppe to the left and 500 meters above, III Gruppe to the rear on the right side and 1000 meters above. All Gruppen will fly in stepped-up formation. If no enemy contact is made until 1050 hours, ground-attacks on worthwhile targets will be made, each Gruppe attacking separately. Orders will be given by the Kommandeure. Second in command will be Kommandeur I Gruppe. Assembly over Geschwader a/c at 1000 meters turn left. Combat altitude at the beginning will be 6000 meters. Having a good flight leader, cover flight (Deckungsschwarm) is furnished by III Gruppe.

Gruppenkommandeur: calls all Staffel Kapitans (Stakas) and pilots for briefing. He announces area, time and kind of mission (fighter sweeps). Order of formation; Gruppen staff, 1st Staffel joining up to the right, 2nd Staffel to the left, 3rd Staffel joining to the rear, all stepped up (500 meters for the whole Gruppe).

Time of take-off: 0925 hours, Order of start: same as order of formation.

Other briefing subjects include: whether in target area, emergency L.G.'s, short instructions on low level attacks and approach to them is given, along with security reminders (Identification-cards and classified documents). 0920 hours: Whole Gruppe in readiness.

Staffelkapitan: assignment of a/c to pilots, Schwarm leaders, and Rotten leaders. Alert-time for technical ground personnel designated by chief-mechanic. Deputy Kommandeur's Reminder of flying discipline in Rotten formation.

In the air: At 1020 hours contact with 15 a/c, probably enemy, left ahead.

Order to II Gruppe: Investigate and attack. Enemy a/c same altitude II Gruppe approach out of sun and attacks from slightly above. 3 Staffel remains on top as cover. Air battle between 6000 meters and low level in Rotten (two-ship) formation. If battle extends beyond time set for mission, Gruppenkommandeur orders Gruppe to disengage and to assemble at specified location.

Interrogation and critique by Kommandeur: Defects in formation, in combat, claims (shot down and probables), losses.

Special observations: painting or markings of enemy a/c and enemy tactics.

Report to Geschwader: Take-off and landing time, duration of air-battle, claims and author of claims, losses and names (certain losses and missing). These reports are collected by Geschwader and transmitted to Jagdkorps in similar form.

CHAPTER 10

Fighter Escort for
Ship Convoys and Naval Units

Interrogation of Generalleutnant Galland,
Oberstleutnant Bär, Oberstleutnant Dahl and
Oberst Petersen
At Kaufbeuren, Germany, 10–12 September 1945

1. **Norway.** The conduct of air operations in the Norwegian campaign was under Fliegerkorps X. For escort purposes, two Geschwader were available: a Zerstorer Geschwader with Me.110's and a fighter Geschwader with Me. 109E's. The locations of these Geschwader at the beginning of the campaign were in Schleswig-Holstein, and later in Aalborg and several fields in North Jutland and later in Christiansand, Stavanger, Trondheim, and Bodo. In the course of operations the range of the Me.110 proved to be too short. The aircraft was therefore fitted with a drop tank (called Dachshund-belly). Although no experience or regulations were available for such undertakings, the missions were in general successfully carried out. Most of the attacks on the convoys were made by Blenheim bombers and torpedo aircraft and were repulsed by the fighter escort.

2. **French Coast.** In late Autumn 1940 came the preparations for Operation 'Sea Lion', the landings in Great Britain. J. G. 26, Galland's unit, was supposed to be the first to transfer to England. Preparations were not taken seriously. Loading plans were made up, and small loading and landing maneuvers with fighter cover were conducted on the Dutch and Belgian coasts.

Beginning in 1940 and increasing in 1941, 1942, and 1943, the Navy demanded fighter cover for small coastal convoys, individual ships and for tankers. From Autumn 1941 ships were moved during the hours of darkness and laid over in ports during the day. The strength of fighter units permitted continuous fighter escort only in the most pressing cases. The usual procedure was that the Navy informed the fighter command (in this case the Jafu 2 or 3) of the Navy's intentions, the times and the locations and asked for fighter cover. This insured the readiness of fighter escort if it were needed, but did not always mean that each Navy unit had continuous fighter cover. When, on the basis of the Radar Service or Listening Service, warnings indicated the imminence of enemy operations, the fighters were ordered to scramble and protect the Naval units.

From the middle of 1942, the conduct of sea transport in the Channel was impossible as a result of English air superiority. Along the Dutch and Northwest German coasts the use of convoys was still possible when fighter cover was available. Great attention was given to the bringing in of single blockade runners. Zerstorer Geschwader 1 with two Gruppen of Ju.88's, a Gruppe of Me.410s (used temporarily) and a Staffel of Arado 196s were based in Brittany and assumed the fighter cover far at sea. They engaged in heavy fighting with Mosquitos, bombers, and torpedo aircraft, as well as with American long-range fighters. The missions undertaken by the Ju.88s had especially heavy losses. This operational responsibility was usually relieved in the vicinity of the coast by a Gruppe of drop-tank carrying F.W.190's of J.G.2.

In general, the many demands of the Navy could not be fulfilled, since the fighter forces required were lacking. The Russian campaign began in Summer 1941 and forced the withdrawal of all but two fighter Geschwader (J.G. 2 and J.G. 26) to the East. Alternative counter-measures were found in making ship movements by night and in bad weather and the equipping of ships with concentrated A.A.

3. **Cooperation with Motor Torpedo Boats** (Schnellbooten) was prepared by direct conferences and conversations with the young and daring Flotilla leaders and C.O.'s. The mutual understanding of requirements and possibilities hereby attained was at all times very helpful for cooperation. The MT boats were mainly harassed by English fighters and fighter bombers. The fighter escort was conducted, in the critical times, in low level flights and upon the appearance of enemy aircraft the escort rose to medium altitudes. After common undertakings the conduct and the experience gained were discussed by the Naval officers and fighter men involved.

4. **U-Boat Cover in the Bay of Biscay**. The responsible command for this work was the Fliegerfuhrer Atlantik, and Z.G.1 was the flying unit involved. The mission was to safely escort single U-Boats and larger U-Boat formations, and to protect them against low-level attacks by aircraft equipped with cannon and bombs. The missions were similar to those used for blockade runners. Anglo-American air superiority, technical superiority of Allied aircraft, and superior quantities of Allied radar equipment made these missions

progressively more difficult. Nevertheless, the fighters and Zerstorer accomplished much, often through self-sacrificing missions. The mutual understanding between fighters and U-Boat personnel was good.

5. **The Channel Break-through of the German Warships**. The *Prinz Eugen, Scharnhorst,* and *Gneisenau* had to be removed from Brest to the North Sea. Galland was personally entrusted, by Hitler, with the job of preparing and conducting the mission, for the Luftwaffe, of covering this. The Navy bestowed all of the responsibility to the Luftwaffe and demanded complete security against all air attacks. Extreme secrecy, surprise, and deception were the most important conditions for the success of the mission. The planned conduct in all its details was settled with the Navy.

This was the first great undertaking in cooperation with the Navy. In addition, very few fighters were available. For the transition periods from night to morning and from evening to night, night fighters with Zerstorer training and experience were made available. In detailed and exhaustive form and in cooperation with the Navy, a *Memorandum for the Conduct of Fighter Escort for Sea Forces and Large Naval Forces* was prepared and circulated. On the basis of the experience gained in the actual carrying out of the mission, only minor changes in the doctrine had to be undertaken. An important operation of this kind was never conducted again.

The fighter escort itself was organized into:
a.   Close escort against low level attacks (Enemy aircraft armed with torpedoes).
b.   Close escort for attacks from medium altitudes.
c.   Escort cover for low level attacks (patrol a distance from the convoy).
d.   Escort cover for higher attacks. (patrol a distance from the convoy).
e.   Fighter sweeping forces against anticipated attacks.

Standing strength of the fighter escort was 40–50 a/c. During the time when one patrol was being relieved, a 15–20 minute overlap period was allowed during which the cover was twice as strong. Reserves were ready for scramble starts against anticipated attacks in strength of 40 a/c. or more.

A fighter control station was set up on one of the ships for immediate control of the fighters by R/T against recognized attacks and for the control of the ships' A.A. and friendly fighters.

The committing of the fighter forces and the relieving of one unit by another was controlled from the land by another fighter control station (Galland's) which moved along the coast. This control was airborne to keep up with the ships. Galland had a special Ju.52 transport fitted with fighter control apparatus which he used to control operations from the ground.

The second part of the operation was conducted with the participation of night fighters who operated in this case as twin-engine day fighters. The day and night fighter forces available transferred with the fighter command as they proceeded along the North Sea Coast, toward North Jutland and Southern Norway. In Norway the control was turned over to the Jafu Norwegian, who, with its own fighter forces, took over the fighter cover from Trondheim onward. For the entire operation, twin-engine fighter units were especially valuable. On the whole, the escort mission for the warships was successfully handled by the fighter arm of the GAF.

6. **Mission in Norway**. Protection of naval bases, operations of German naval forces, supply and oil convoys, all presented great demands on fighters for escort in Norway. The available forces were extremely small. In the years 1940, 1941 and 1942 only one Gruppe of J.G.5 was there. From time to time it was reinforced by another Gruppe from the same Geschwader on the Murmansk front. The Jafu Norwegian controlled the missions, from either Stavanger or Trondheim. The great distances and the bad signals conditions permitted only a geographically limited control. The same geographical difficulties made the improvement of the radar and fighter control system a very difficult undertaking.

Along with the Jafu Norwegian, the Fliegerfuhrer Nord-West and Nord-Ost at Lofoten and near Murmansk, respectively, took part in control of the fighter organization and their operations. Special difficulties were caused by drawing the boundary between the responsibility of Luftflotte Reich and Luftflotte 5 (the Luftflotte which controlled Norway). This boundary was never satisfactorily settled. All this time the Luftflotte, Reich or Oberbefehlshaber Mitte had to use the fighter control center in Jutland, Abschnittsfuhrer Jutland. Subordinated to it were the escort missions in the North Sea, along the coast of Jutland and in the Skaggerak up to the operational transfer of control of Jafu Norwegian. There was therefore adequate and well staffed fighter control commands, but there was a lack of fighters.

The conduct of the escort for the naval units was rendered easier by the fact that the attacking RAF aircraft always flew without their own fighter escort. This explains why the Germans with unusually small forces were able to achieve astonishing successes. The Zerstorer Staffel used in Norway, in addition to its fighter bomber missions on the Russian front at Murmansk, flew successful escort missions on the West Coast of Norway.

7. **Baltic Sea and Lake Ladoga (Russia).** Escort missions were flown here only in exceptional cases, such as the supply and evacuation of the Baltic area and the Siebel ferry undertaking in Lake Ladoga. These missions were controlled by Luftflotte I and flown by J. G. 54. At the same time the fighters flew offensively against Russian supply lines and gun boats, using strafing, bombing, and rocket projectile attacks with some success.

Naval maneuvers in the Baltic were protected, upon demand of the Navy, by OTUs and school units because of the lack of operational forces.

8. **Black Sea Operations.** Escort missions became necessary in the Black Sea as a result of the German supply routes and final evacuation of the Crimea. These missions were flown partly from the Crimea peninsula and partly from Roumania. Twin-engine fighters (Zerstorer) proved successful because of their long endurance. Lack of forces prevented a complete victory against the Russian attacks which were flown by much larger formations.

9. **Missions in the Mediterranean.** Escort missions in the Mediterranean began after the beginning of the English air activity. The Allied air superiority was such that for these escort missions, demanded by the German and Italian Navies, more Geschwader would have been needed than were available in the entire theater; the German fighters failed by the greatest margin to fulfill the many and varied demands for operations. The Italian fighters participated temporarily in these operations, but with small forces and in an undependable manner. A German Zerstorer unit was used here and there, but could not specialize in the escort of shipping because it was needed again and again in Africa for the support of tank units. The Italian Navy in general did not conform to the combat orders as to times, strengths, and courses.

In the supply of Africa the routes were so long that the necessary continuous escort and cover could only be furnished reliably in very small numbers. There could therefore be no question of an *effective* defense against *powerful* attacks on convoys or individual ships, especially tankers. This was not even achieved during the great crisis in Africa when almost all fighter forces were assigned to defend convoys. Allied air superiority, especially with the long range fighters, also decided this battle to the disadvantage of the Luftwaffe. A scramble start against attacks on convoys in the Mediterranean was not successful because it necessarily always came too late. During the battle in Tunisia an additional demand was placed on the fighters to escort air transport aircraft and Siebel ferrys. Fighter operations were controlled by the Fliegerfuhrer Africa, later Jafu Tunis, Jafu Sizilien, Jafu Italien, and Jafu Agais.

10. **Protection of Naval Bases** was undertaken as far as possible by the fighters being used in the Defense of the Reich. During the lay-over of the warships in Brest in 1941, J.G.26 was used there temporarily, but RAF attacks occurred only during the hours of darkness. In Norway, the use of fighters for protection of naval bases was conducted according to the demands of and in concurrence with the Navy, from the bases at Trondheim and Tromso. Italian naval bases were protected exclusively by Italian fighters.

11. **Cooperation with the Sea Rescue Service** was developed at the beginning of the campaign against England in the late Summer of 1940, and was later important in Norway and in the Mediterranean. The effectiveness of it declined with the increase of Anglo-American air superiority but was better preserved in those sectors not usually frequented by Allied long range fighters.

Missions of the fighters in such cooperation were to discover and announce sea crashes by place and type, to maintain contact, to lead the sea rescue boats to the scene, and to provide cover during the approach, the rescue and the trip back. Cooperation was good on the basis of close contact and assistance.

CHAPTER 11

Protection of Naval Forces and Convoys by Fighter Forces

Tactical Regulation for the Channel Breakthrough by Generalleutnant Galland, spring 1942

I. Operational Principles

(1) The fighter escort mission is that of protecting naval forces and convoys from attacks by enemy torpedo aircraft, bombers and fighter bombers, as well as repulsing enemy shadowing aircraft and destroying them. It is necessary in all ocean areas where attacks of enemy aircraft are to be reckoned with. Lacking aircraft carriers, the limits of fighters escort depend on the range of our fighters.

Of greatest urgency is protection against torpedo aircraft.

(2) Escort can be conducted by:

    (a) *Close Escort.*

        It furnishes the best security against air attacks by continuous cover directly over the ships, but requires nevertheless strong forces.

    (b) *Cover Escort (Striking Reserve).*

        It is used when strong fighter forces are available over and above the close escort to combat the approach flights of enemy formations.

    (c) *Alerted Escort.*

        Used when only weak forces are available. Fighters make a scramble start only after the recognized approach of enemy formations.

        It provides no sure protection for shipping.

(3) The use of fighter escort is dependent upon weather and time of day.

    (a) For day operations visibility of at least 5 km. and ceiling of about 1500 feet are operational minima.

    (b) Twilight requires usually the strongest fighter cover, because it is the favorable time for torpedo attacks. Operations are only possible when visibility is 6 km., so that; (1) enemy and friendly aircraft can be distinguished from the ships (taking into consideration the difficulties attending recognition signal exchange) and (2) so that fighters can recognize enemy fighter bombers in time.

(c) By night – including by bright moonlight – and for operations which require night take-offs or landings, only TE aircraft (night fighters or TE day fighters) can be used.

(4) The relieving of the close escort is to be so arranged that an overlapping of ten minutes at least occurs over the ships. In this period a double protection should be over the objective, insofar as pressing reasons do not make necessary the immediate return of the relieved close escort. If an enemy attack occurs during the changing of the escort, the relieved fighter formation must take part in the combat up to the limit of its flying endurance.

(5) Independent breaking off by the fighter escort may only take place:

(1) at the limit of endurance.

(2) in bad weather or in twilight when too low visibility no longer permits the carrying out of the mission. In both cases a simultaneous report must be made to the ships by visual signals. Report will be by radio only when radio silence has not been ordered.

Fighters will not break off when the weather becomes temporarily bad. The fighter formation will move away in the direction of the enemy in order to avoid the bad weather area and will resume the escort after the bad weather has passed along. Upon approaching the ships again, visual recognitions will be exchanged.

A breaking off on the desire of the ships can be ordered by them by radio or visual signals.

II. Cooperation in Preparation and Conduct of the Fighter Escort

(1) Frictionless cooperation requires early liaison activities between the Air Force and Naval commands concerned. For large operations, the mutual appointment of liaison officers is useful.

(2) For the planned conduct of fighter escort for ships, a mutual exchange of information between the controlling commands of the Navy and Air Force about the momentary location of the ships and of the fighter formations forming the fighter escort is decisive.

The reports about the fighter escort being sent out or withdrawn must include time of take-off, number, and aircraft type.

(3) At the Headquarters of the controlling Air Force command, the position of the ships must be continually marked on a sea situation map. The pilots are to mark on their maps before take-off the last announced position and course of the ships to be escorted, so that when announcements about the enemy are made they will be able to form a picture of the situation and to bring the reported enemy approaches into correct relationship to the ships.

(4) If in addition to the fighter cover, a form of immediate protection is used. (This immediate protection – eng Sicherung – is a naval concept and means close support for ships, rendered either by small naval units or by naval aircraft.) In the case naval aircraft are referred to, mutual notification by Air Force units and ships must take place, in order to avoid confusing them with enemy aircraft and to prevent mutual interference. The duties of the immediate protection force cannot simultaneously be taken over by the fighter escort.

Around the ships and in their vicinity the seaplane, Arado 196, must be reckoned with; it is used for immediate protection and in some cases as an emergency fighter, starting from aboard ship against shadowing aircraft. Notifying the fighter cover about the catapult aircraft of this is not possible because of radio silence on the ships.

(5) *A vital condition for the planned conduct of operations at sea is the keeping of strict radio silence by the ships and fighter units until contact is made with the enemy.*

The giving up of radio silence may only take place on the part of the flagship or the fighter formation when it can with certainty be assumed that the enemy has already ascertained the location of the ships (through presence of enemy shadowing aircraft, or from an imminent enemy air attack). Radio silence can at any time be reimposed by the flagship by radio or short code signals.

Even changing relief or breaking off of the fighter escort is not to be reported from the aircraft during radio silence.

(6) As soon as the fighter cover is within sight of the ships, it may be committed to combat by the fighter control officer (naval) on the flagship against any attack formations or shadowing aircraft detected and recognized as enemy with certainty by eye or with radar. In such cases the following facts are to be reported to the fighter escort by radio:

    (a) Bearing of the enemy aircraft from the ship. Announcement takes place according to the aircraft reporting rose (clock face) oriented with the course of the ship at the time,

    (b) approximate range,

    (c) approximate statement of the aircraft's course, in case they are not directly approaching the ships,

    (d) any major alterations in course intended during the attack by the fighter escort.

(7) Complete use of the strongest anti-aircraft protection of the ships must take place, even if it makes difficult the job of the friendly fighters.

The fighter formations must therefore seek to combat enemy aircraft outside the anti-aircraft area. Target indicating shots of the ships' anti-aircraft artillery should make it easier for the fighters to locate the enemy.

Ship's anti-aircraft is to only fire on enemy fighters when an attack is suspected from the manner of approach.

Heavy anti-aircraft will cease as soon as friendly fighters are in an attack position which promises success, but in the field of fire of light anti-aircraft, the fighters must give way in all cases.

The endangering of friendly fighters by ship anti-aircraft must be reckoned with in critical situations and it does not relieve the fighters of their mission.

(8) Target indicating shots of the ships' anti-aircraft or regular batteries consist of a chain of several explosions fired in the direction of the target. AA fragmentation shells and under some conditions AA flare shells with parachutes are used. At the same time the attention of the fighter escort is called to the target indicating shots by one or more Morse smoke signals from the deck of the ship giving signals (flagship). Target indicating shots and smoke signals are only to be fired within the field of vision of the fighters.

III. Close Fighter Escort

(1) The fighter forces are to be stepped up, in cloudless weather not over 12,000 feet, and under solid clouds up to the ceiling. Where clouds are dispersed and the possibility of attacks through holes in the clouds exist, a weak force (about one Schwarm) is to be used above the clouds.

The main effort of the fighter escort lies always in low level protection. It flies in Schwarm (4-ships) and stays below 3000 feet. For example, when 16 fighters are available, three Schwarm will fly for low level protection and one Schwarm will fly as top cover between 3000 and 10,000 feet.

(2) The top cover and low level cover must always fly so they can

    (a) keep the ships directly in sight,

(b) combat attacks as quickly as possible

(c) not be surprised by the enemy

(d) not fly over the ships even in approaching or going away during changing of cover and during attacks against enemy aircraft.

It is useful to have two Schwärme fly on the side towards the enemy according to visibility, and these Schwärme fly back and forth in opposite directions in long stretches parallel to the course of the ships. One Schwarm can meanwhile be used on the side of the ships away from the enemy. In such cases the ordered altitudes are to be maintained and approaching closer than 6000 feet to any ship, including the screening force, is to be avoided.

If only weak forces can be used, they will fly in Rottes (2-ships).

(3) *Regardless of all other principles, combat with fighters is to be avoided.* Only enemy fighter-bombers which threaten the ships with bombs or strafing are to be attacked.

For recognized bomb or torpedo attacks, it is necessary to destroy the enemy before he drops his load, to hinder him in aiming or in emergency to ram him to turn him away from his target.

In such cases it is vital, that

(a) *regardless of unfavourable position for attack*, even from head on, the enemy must be attacked as quickly as possible, *before he reaches the Anti-Aircraft zone or, above all, the ships.*

(b) All weapons be used for as long as possible before dropping of the bombs, regardless of self-protection or the tactically correct carrying-out of the attack.

Enemy aircraft on their way back may only be attacked when no further attacks are apparent. Pursuit out of sight of the ships is forbidden to the close escort.

(4) The top cover too has the mission of combatting bombers and torpedo aircraft first of all. Furthermore it should try to improve the position of the low cover when the enemy is first contacted by effective attacks from good positions. When attacked at great altitudes it cannot count on support from the low cover.

(5) After warding off an enemy attack, fighter forces are to reassemble and resume their formation and altitude. The mission must as far as possible be carried through with all forces until the ordered time. Only urgent technical trouble in the aircraft or in all weapons give single aircraft the right to break off.

(6) The relieving fighter force is always to reach the ordered combat altitude from a still greater altitude, i.e. in cloudless weather from an altitude of about 10,000 feet, and in weather forming a ceiling from just under the ceiling. As far as possible recognition signals are to be fired on approaching.

IV. The Cover Escort (Striking Reserve)

(1) Escort cover is only justifiable when sufficient forces are available and support of the close escort is required. It is to be used as soon as the air raid reporting service or the radio listening service report an intended attack or when the close escort must have relief from continuous unexpected attacks.

(2) The fighter forces designated for escort cover are to be kept in sitting readiness and after take-off they will be so led onto the enemy that they find and destroy him as early as possible. Their primary mission is the combatting of the *approaching* enemy and they can only go over to pursuit when this mission has been fulfilled. If they arrive too late to repulse the attack, they can only pursue on receipt of a special order.

(3) The forces of the escort cover may also be employed as close escort by the order 'stay with the object'. Before every mission therefore the assigning of the Schwärms must take place to insure frictionless taking over of the close escort.

(4) If in the protecting of an especially important naval force a diversion of a part of the close escort against shadowing aircraft cannot be effected, emergency Rottes (two-ships) of the escort cover can be used to combat them. The vectoring onto the enemy must take place from the flagship by the fighter control officer (naval).

V. The Alerted Escort

(1) Where only small fighter forces are available, fighter escort for convoys along the coast must be provided by alerted escort and scramble starts. In some cases fighter forces already committed on other missions can be diverted.

A sure protection for convoys cannot be guaranteed by an alerted escort. It must be taken into consideration that convoys can be attacked in a short time before friendly fighters can disturb the conduct of the attack or drive away the enemy.

(2) Operations resulting from timely recognition of enemy intentions or

upon request from the convoy. Anticipatory mutual determination of convoy routes makes possible the careful deployment of fighter forces on airfields near the coast, so that all points along the convoy can be quickly reached. According to the forces and airfields available, one fighter unit (Gruppe says Galland) should lie ready for every 100–150 kilometers.

(3) The fighter units designated for alerted escort are to be held in the most advanced state of readiness for scramble starts.

Because of speed and combat efficiency, only single engined fighters are suitable for these operations.

Formation strength should not be under one Schwarm (4 aircraft).

When the distance to the convoy is short, belly tanks and fittings for them can be dispensed with to achieve greater speed.

Part 3
Air–Ground Operations

The chapters in this section are primarily by Hubertus Hitschhold, Galland's air-to-ground counterpart as General der Schlachtflieger and, like him, a cooperative subject of the APWIU's work. Galland also contributes, for while he is usually associated with air-air combat, he started the war off in air-ground missions, flying Hs 123 biplanes in Poland in 1939, so he was aware of both the importance and the limitations of the Luftwaffe fighter force's air-ground missions.

One of the key distinctions seen in this section is the difference between fighter-bomber and ground attack units and tactics. While the terms are often used interchangeably in English, reflecting USAAF and RAF practice in the Second World War, the Germans saw these as distinct missions and aircraft. Fighter-bombers also fell under Galland's inspectorate responsibilities (which is why he writes about them and Bär provides his usual description of a typical fighter-bomber mission), while the specialized ground attack units were Hitschhold's concern. There was, of course, considerable overlap between the two, and fighters would also carry out ground attack missions, as seen in the chapter by Gordon Gollob and in Galland's repeated regrets that the fighter reserves he built up by 1944 were fed into the fighting in France after D-Day and lost without influencing the ground battle.

The air-ground mission required fighter aircraft; aircraft such as the Ju 87 Stuka dive-bomber that proved highly effective in the opening years of the war became increasingly non-survivable. As a result, there is little in this section about the early 'Stuka years' of German air-ground operations. These accounts do show that, far from being tied to the Army, as often portrayed in English-language sources, Luftwaffe air-ground operations were highly independent.

CHAPTER 12

Fighter-Bomber Tactics

Interrogation of Generalleutnant Galland
At Kaufbeuren, Germany, 3 September 1945

As a result of the experience in World War I, fighter aircraft were, during the building up of the present fighter force, fitted to carry small caliber bombs (10 kg. fragmentation). In regulations and in maneuvers, ground attacks by fighter formations in the combat area and against forward airfields were planned.

In Spain, fighter Staffeln with outmoded fighter aircraft specialized in ground attack missions, while the fighter units equipped with more modern aircraft, the Me.109, attacked only targets of opportunity. As a result of this experience, special ground attack formations called Schlachtflieger (Battle flyers) were formed in the Luftwaffe in 1938. It had been shown that special tactical and flying training was necessary if the most effective action possible for the immediate support of the army was to be effected. Moreover, the first series of the Me.109 were not equipped to carry bombs.

The Schlachtflieger units (ground attack units) now embarked on their own course of development, related to the fighters, having the same elementary fighter training as a basis and subject to the Inspectorate (both were at first under the General der Jagdflieger). In October 1943, however, the Schlachtflieger were rightly combined with the Stuka units to form an independent branch. This did not, however, alter the fact that from fall 1940, pure fighter units continually engaged in fighter bomber attacks paralleling those of the Schlachtflieger. These fighter bombers are called Jabos, a contraction of Jagdbomber – fighter bomber.

In the Polish Campaign and French Campaigns, German fighter units were not technically equipped to drop bombs, since the Me.109 was not fitted with bomb racks. Nevertheless a great many planned strafing attacks were carried out by fighter units and even more unplanned attacks on targets of opportunity. The frequent fast retreats of the enemy produced a mass of good targets. In addition, the destruction of the enemy air forces in the air was quickly effected in both campaigns, leaving more time for ground attacks by fighters.

Pre-requisites for effective cooperation with the Army are recognition of friendly front lines, knowledge of the intentions of the Army and its requirements for air support and the recognition of friendly troops; therefore the low level attacks by fighters can only be conducted in very clear situations. Operations right on the battle front and attacks against targets hard to recognize, especially in indistinct situations and during rapid situation changes, are to be flown only by the Schlachtflieger.

Targets especially suited for attacks by fighters are: road and rail movements, troop assemblies in defined areas, airfields and installations, river crossings and so forth. Especially important is the just and adequate rewarding of successful low level attacks with medals, promotions and so forth, in comparison to the often easier and cheaper air victories. This is important because otherwise the fighter will hunt air targets until the end of his aircraft's endurance and will overlook the best opportunities for effective low level attacks.

Entirely new possibilities came in the Fall of 1940 with the bomb carrying fighter (Me.109 Jabo). Of necessity, this aircraft became, until the advent of the F.W.190, the standard ground attack aircraft for the Schlachtflieger. Fighter units now could carry out low level attacks as well as high altitude bombing.

Fighter Bomber Tactics During the Battle of Britain

Fighter bombers had to be assigned fixed targets, geographically well defined and clearly visible. The state of training of fighter pilots permitted successes only against area targets (as distinguished from point targets). The fighter bomber attacks could be flown as high level attacks, dive bombing attacks, or as low level attacks with strafing after a high altitude bombing run.

Fighter bomber attacks during the Battle of Britain were conducted almost without exception as high altitude attacks. The approach to the target area took place almost at maximum operational altitude, about 22,000 feet. The formation used was the usual one for fighters, only a little more closed up and with less stepping up. The bomb-carrying fighters were surrounded with a fighter escort, set off higher and to the sides. The dropping of the bombs was carried through after a short dive losing about 3000 to 6000 feet in order to have some slight possibility of aiming. These attacks could only be used effectively against large area targets. Even against such targets the effect was only harrassing and not destructive in view of the low bomb load and the small bombs. Against area targets like airfields, low level attacks with bombing from 1000 to 1500 feet had to be employed.

In 1940 such attacks were flown mainly by two special Gruppen, II/(Schlacht) Lehr Geschwader 2 and Kampfgruppe 210. Often regular fighter Gruppen carrying bombs were put in formation with these special Gruppen, all covered with a close escort. Kampfgruppe 210 was a fast-bomber experimental group, which was supposed to be equipped with the Me.210, but which got Me.109s. The various twin-engine fighter units, called Zerstorer Geschwader, which had been unsuccessfully used in the Battle of Britain as long range fighters, were fortunately not equipped to drop bombs, although this change was discussed.

J.G. 26 was delegated to cooperate with II/(S)LG 2 (Galland had himself been a Staffel C.O. in this latter unit in the Polish campaign). J. G. 26 furnished cover for almost all the missions of this Gruppe (II/(S)LG2). In most cases the fighter-bombers flew together and in somewhat closer formation than the fighter escort, which was positioned to the right, left, and high rear. When the English fighters later concentrated only on the fighter-bomber, the trick was tried of dividing up the Gruppe of fighter-bombers among the three escort fighter Gruppen. It became harder to tell which of the Me.109 aircraft were carrying bombs. Area targets like London, cities and harbors, and smaller targets like oil depots and fighter airfields, were attacked in this manner. The approach took place usually at about 23,000 feet. Area targets were bombed from high altitudes after a shallow dive. Smaller targets were attacked from low levels after a long shallow dive begun from a great distance to gain speed. In such cases the cohesion of the fighter-bomber formations was easily lost and the escort job was thereby appreciably toughened. After bombs were away the fighter-bombers had sufficient speed for a get-away and didn't need cover so badly. Fighters were thereby released to engage the RAF fighters. The losses of the fighter bombers were bearable.

The High Command of the GAF soon demanded more use of fighter-bombers, which previously had been undertaken by the fighter units themselves. Training for such missions was non-existent. Fighter pilots had little interest in fighter-bombing. It must also be noted that at this time they had behind them three months of intensive missions against England. When the weather had permitted, they had flown daily at least two and often three and four missions across the Channel.

The required modification of equipment was that one third of each Geschwader's aircraft be used as fighter-bombers. In various Geschwader this order was carried out in one of two ways, either by converting one whole Gruppe to fighter-bombing, or by converting one Staffel in each of the three Gruppen to fighter-bombing. The second solution seemed to be the better. Its advantage was that no large fighter-bomber formations were created which would immediately have demanded fighter cover, and that each Gruppe continued to conduct itself purely as a fighter outfit and just inconspicuously carried bombs along. A disadvantage was the greater technical and maintenance effort and equipment which now had to be on three airfields instead of on one.

A few fighter-bomber missions were still flown against shipping in 1940 but had little success because of the inadequate training in bombing.

The fighter bomber attacks which figured in the last stage of the Battle of Britain were not terminated because of high losses, but because of the beginning of poor weather, which prevented the fighter bombers from seeing their targets. Moreover, the fighter bomber missions were not much liked by the fighters. Nevertheless there was, from this time on, an order from Hitler that all fighter aircraft must be manufactured and maintained in condition to drop bombs, and that pilots must be trained in bomb dropping. This order remained until the end of the war but fighter training for bomb dropping was naturally scanty.

Fighter Bomber Tactics in the West, 1941–42

In the West in 1941 a Staffel of J.G.2 and in 1942 one of J.G.26 specialized in fighter bomber attacks. The Staffel of J.G.2 was especially successful against ships along the south coast of England and against harbors and coastal targets.

The special formations II/(S)LG2 and Kampfgruppe 210 were more in need of fighter-cover than the fighter-bomber formations. These special units had not mastered aerial fighter combat and were inexperienced in fighter warfare as it was in the Battle of Britain. In exhaustive conferences the conduct of missions between fighters and fighter-bombers was clarified and defined.

In 1941 and 1942 several fighter-bomber attacks in Staffel strength were flown without fighter cover, as pure surprise attacks, with some success against shipping targets. Most of these were by J.G.2 and were absolute surprise attacks. To avoid the English radar service the approach flight was made at sea level, a few meters above the waves, and absolute radio silence was observed. These formations only ran into English fighters over a convoy, or RAF patrols to intercept German fighter-bomber thrusts.

From this type of attack developed the so-called Revenge and Retaliation raids (ordered by Hitler and called by the RAF the Baedecker Raids, because they concentrated on English historical and artistic monuments as listed in the German Baedecker Tourist Guide Books). For this purpose, fighters were again converted to fighter-bombers. On some missions as many as 100 Jabos were sent over en masse. Conduct and planning of the missions were based on surprise and deception. Accordingly, the approach flight was made at low level up to the coast of England, when it was changed to medium altitude, and after bombing the return flight was made at a very low level. Usually only weak close fighter escort was sent along, while stronger fighter forces drew onto themselves the RAF fighters after a high approach flight. In every instance, the Germans successfully got to the target without being intercepted. On the return flight, however, they were usually cut off by RAF fighter standing patrols and engaged in combat. This caused a serious problem because the GAF fighter, the Me.109, had a limited range and short flying time. Losses of the fighter bombers were heavier from light A.A. than from RAF fighters.

These attacks were carried out partly at tree-top level, and for the rest at high altitudes with fighter escort, and with screening and feints by subsidiary fighter forces. In all cases, the much strengthened English fighter defense forced the GAF to take advantage of the element of surprise. The missions continued successfully with low to bearable losses.

Fighter-Bombers in Russia

For the Russian campaign the special Schlachtflieger Geschwaders were available. Still, on many occasions fighters with bombs, and even more often fighters merely with guns, were used in low level attacks.

The necessity for technical alterations for bomb dropping as well as the necessity of supplying airfields with bombs resulted in the fighter units not being ready for fighter bomber operations at the desired moment. In the Winter of 1941/42, therefore, two Schlachtflieger Geschwader, each with one Gruppe of Me.110's and two Gruppen of Me.109's were set up for the second offensive planned for early 1942. These Geschwader, together with the regular fighter Geschwader, carried through in 1942 a great number of successful low level attacks.

The Schlachtflieger units were partially equipped with a special ground attack aircraft, the Henschel 129. This aircraft, mounting the MK 101 with tungsten steel armor piercing ammunition, was used to equip special tank-destroyer Staffeln, set up in Fall 1942. The tank-destroyers operated either with a simple fighter escort or together with bomb carrying aircraft of the Schlacht Geschwader, who were supposed to keep down and neutralize ground defenses for the tank-destroyers.

The End of The Fighter-Bombers

At the time of the invasion of Normandy, fighters were given the mission of taking part in the ground combat with a third of their force as fighter bombers or as RP firing aircraft. These types of missions were forced to stop fourteen days after the beginning of the invasion by the oppressive air superiority of the USAAF and RAF.

The last great effort, to throw in the fighter force for the decision on the ground, was made during the Ardennes offensive. The then current training of the fighter pilots was wholly concentrated on combat against heavy bombers and was thus completely inadequate for ground attack. Because of enemy numerical air superiority, augmented by the extremely concentrated A.A. which confronted the Jagdwaffe, the attempt failed.

The large ground attack mission against Allied fighter and other bases on 1st January 1945 was, in all details, a project and plan of the bomber man, Peltz. Despite careful preparation the planning was too complicated, and in many respects clearly demanded too much. The timing should have placed the attack at the beginning of the Ardennes offensive. The same massed use of air power would have, in any event, brought about a perceptible relieving of the Eastern Front, or led to the 'Big Blow' against bombers.

Ammunition and Bomb Load

The Me.109 carried one 250 kg. bomb or 4 × 50 kg. The F.W.190 carried a 250 kg. bomb, a 500 kg. bomb, or 4 × 50 kg. bombs in the fighter version. Instead of the heavy bombs, containers with a number of small anti-personnel bombs could be fitted. From 1943 on, the Me.109 and F.W.190 could be fitted with two rocket tubes for the 21 cm. army rockets. Ammunition for the MGs and cannon was the same as in use for regular fighter missions.

Carrying of drop tanks was only possible when bombs were not carried, except in the case of a special model of the F.W.190 which had fittings onto which both bombs and tanks could be attached.

Missions with RPs were more popular with fighter pilots than bombing missions, because RP firing better suits the mentality of the fighter pilot.

CHAPTER 13

Fighters in Ground Attack

Interrogation of Oberst Gordon Gollob,
General der Jagdflieger
At Latimer House, England, 18 September 1945

Gollob stated that in the Polish campaign the GAF had little or no opposition from either air or flak. Me.110s and Me.109s were used against airfields and roads using machine guns only.

The GAF in Poland used the one-directional attack, all Gruppen coming in from the same direction one after the other. They approached low – pulling up before their objective – or approached high – diving out of the sun in a 20 degree or 30 degree dive – attacking and departing on the deck. Machine guns and cannon were used against aircraft on the ground. Bombs were used against armor, bridges, etc., but very rarely. One Gruppe was equipped for bomb-carrying while other Gruppen were acting as pure fighters.

In Russia, the GAF used Me.109's against airfields. Using machine guns and bombs, they attacked the aircraft on the field and cared very little about the installations. The GAF tried to get information about the airfields but little was to be had.

In Russia, there was little defense from the ground. Although there were Russian fighters in the air, they were not aggressive, and offered little or no defense. The Russians fired anything they had at the Germans, even pistols. This caused the Germans to change their approaches from the low to a high approach, but it was never necessary for them to get over 3000 to 4000 meters.

The Germans dispatched aircraft to attack flak positions, previously assigned or ones they saw on previous missions.

Germans did not use rockets on Me.109's on the Russian front. They used 2 cm. cannon with armor piercing ammunition or 50 kg bombs against tanks and always approached low, out of the sun if possible, and from the rear.

Ju.87s came over at 3000 meters, dived to 700 to 1000 meters on bridges, armor, communications and occasionally other pin-point targets. Throughout the whole Russian campaign, they did not change their tactics.

Later on, Me.109's rarely used bombs against bridges. During the retreat of the Germans, Me.109's, Me.110's and F.W.190's were used against troop concentrations as well as cover for troop columns on the move.

The GAF had control only in a few cases because they lacked the necessary equipment. Occasionally, they had an Air Liaison Officer in a tank located at the head of the armored columns.

Large numbers of small formations were employed throughout the battle, and they usually utilized sun, cloud and any other cover available.

CHAPTER 14

A Typical Ground Attack
Mission by a Fighter Geschwader

Interrogation of Oberstleutnant Bär
At Kaufbeuren, Germany, 16 September 1945

Assumed Location: Western Front at the time of the Ardennes Offensive or the Normandy Invasion.

1600 Hours: Order to Geschwader: Tomorrow ground attack mission by Geschw. in front sector B. Strong concentration of MT and tanks observed there. Start about 0900 hours. One Gruppe will carry bombs, one Gruppe R.P.'s and one Gruppe will furnish fighter escort. Load: 250 kg. explosives (without delay) and 21 cm. smoke shell rockets.

Geschwader to Gruppe: Transmits above order to Kommandeur, also orders to attach bomb-racks and to clear a/c. Bombs will be in readiness alongside the respective a/c. Order to lead will be issued early. Pilots will receive detailed briefing in navigation to and within front sector B.

At the Gruppe: The Geschwader order transmitted to the Staffelkapitane. Stakas initiate immediate attachment of bomb-racks, checking of fusing system, transport of bombs to individual a/c. Detailed briefing of pilots on front with aid of 1 : 100,000 map. Short refresher instructions for pilots on bombing procedures and ground attack tactics (approach, sun, break-off). When all this is done, the 'all clear' report is given to Geschwader. The same procedure as above in the 2nd Gruppe, except that instead of bomb-racks the attachment of R.P. apparatus is ordered.

Next morning: Start orders for the Geschwader at 0900 hours. Attack area B, main target: concentration of M.T. Exact front-lines (conspicuous land marks) from A over B and C to D. At the same time J.G. 10 will be committed in this sector as additional fighter cover in altitudes from 5000 meters to 7000 meters.

From Geschwader to Gruppe: The above order for the mission, also: assembly at 0915 hours over L at 1000 meters curving left, in the following order: II Gruppe – R.P., I Gruppe – Bombs. Both Gruppen in open, slightly stepped up formation. III Gruppe 500 meters in the rear and above ready for combat as close fighter protection. Altitude of approach 4000 meters. Wide envelopment to the South will be made to attack out of the sun. Leveling off at 4000 meters. Return after the attack to the rear of front line. When contact with enemy fighters is made, III Gruppe engages enemy, so that formation can carry on mission undisturbed. If no contact with enemy fighters during approach and over target area, III Gruppe carries out a ground attack right after II Gruppe and resumes immediately thereafter fighter protection of the homing bomber A/C.

Mission report from Geschw. to next higher echelon: Includes the following information.

Start time, landing time, no. of a/c, targets encountered, bombs and r.p. used, results observed, losses, A.A. defenses.

CHAPTER 15

Organization
of Ground Attack Units

By Generalmajor Hitschhold

At Latimer House, England, 20 October 1945

a. Aircraft

Day ground attack units were organized into Geschwaders of three Gruppen. Each Gruppe had three Staffeln. Each Staffel had 12 aircraft. If it had been possible to enlarge the size of ground attack units, no new Gruppen would have been added, but instead the number of aircraft and pilots in each Staffel would have been raised to 16.

The existing organization of the units would thereby have been better used. By a slight additional increase in servicing personnel, so the required operational readiness standards could have been maintained. Furthermore, this enlargement would have been necessary on operational grounds.

Weak formations no longer achieved much success in the face of increasing defense, like stronger formations could have. A strong formation was helped by its very appearance and could fight longer and more effectively.

A further increase of the unit strength would have been impractical.

Quick operational turn-around would not have been attainable. Take-off and landing of formations would have lasted too long. This would, with the short endurance of German ground attack aircraft, have reduced penetration and time in combat so much that the units could not have been used to full advantage.

Geschwader and Gruppe staffs had six ground attack aircraft, so that each could put its own Schwarm up in combat and did not need to draw any pilots from any of the Staffeln.

Anti-tank ground attack units had usually about 16–20 a/c and pilots. During 1944 there were independent anti-tank Staffeln in SG 1,2,3, and 77, being the 10th Staffel in each Geschwader. Four other Staffeln were combined into an anti-tank Gruppe. The High Command thus planned to use this one Gruppe almost together for main efforts. With the other 10th

113

Staffeln, they planned to have at least one anti-tank Staffel available on all sectors of the Russian front.

This one anti-tank Gruppe, IV/Pz. S.G. 9, was however usually committed in Staffel strength on various parts of the Eastern Front and was seldom used together. In order to score at least halfway effective victories over tank forces, it was necessary that these Staffeln had at least 16 aircraft each.

The following reorganization of anti-tank ground attack units was in process of completion at the end of the war.

With the conversion of the anti-tank units to the F.W.190, three purely anti-tank Gruppen were to be formed with three Staffeln each. In addition, the third Staffel of every regular ground attack Gruppe was to become an anti-tank Staffel. The use of one or two anti-tank Gruppen *en masse* in an area of main effort was expected to produce good and lasting success.

All anti-tank Staffeln were organized so that parts of the Staffel could use bombs to suppress ground defenses, so that the Staffeln were not bound down by the necessity of relying on other units to suppress air defenses. In the 10th Staffeln of the various Geschwader, outfitted with Ju.87 with 2 × 37 mm cannon, one third to one fourth of the aircraft were bomb carrying (the normal version of the Ju.87). The Henschel 129 carried, in addition to its cannon, a 50 kg bomb under each wing. Thus, even the Hs 129 units could combat ground defenses independently.

The FW 190 anti-tank aircraft were equipped at first with 12 Panzerschreck (Tank-terror) RP. The rockets were fired in threes from mounts fitted to a wing bomb rack. Later the FW 190 were fitted with 12 Panzerblitz (Tank lightning) RPs. Then the bomb racks had to be taken off each wing and a special rack for 6 Panzerblitz RP built under each wing. The FW 190 anti-tank aircraft could always carry along a bomb under the fuselage and instead of the Panzerschreck rack, bombs could be carried on the wing bomb racks.

Night ground attack Staffeln in the east had 20 aircraft. Two or three Staffeln were combined into a Gruppe. Since no effective night fighter defense existed on the Eastern Front, all types of aircraft could be used. The missions were usually by single ships or small formations.

The quality and performance of the night ground attack units were not up to standard as far as pilots were concerned. Concentrating the night attack Staffeln of each Gruppe onto one airfield was necessary in part because of the inadequate signals net. It was planned, after improving of the quality of the pilots, the state of training, and the serviceability of aircraft, to increase the number of aircraft to 20 per Staffel and to operate each Gruppe from a group of two or three airfields in a small area.

b. Pilots

The supply of new pilots for day ground attack operations was good. Those pilots not entirely suitable were detected in time in the schools or in the OTUs. It proved to be very profitable for COs of primary schools who had themselves been ground attack pilots to have influence on the selection of men for ground attack forces. By skilled instruction, the good pilots could be inspired with a love of ground attack work so they would volunteer for that branch. The shoving off of poor pilots with the designation of 'suitable for ground attack work' was thereby avoided.

But the supply of new pilots alone could not cover the needs of operational units. School units simply did not get sufficient pupils for the ground attack force. Therefore the pilots from other branches had to be grabbed. In general only the pilots relieved from other branches were available. Fighter pilots who had been relieved because of lack of suitability and achievement failed just as badly in the ground attack arm. Only those fighter pilots who were relieved because of altitude trouble and who were otherwise good became good ground attack pilots. Reconnaissance units continually made available surplus officer pilots but only pilots from SE reconnaissance units were of use. These pilots in general proved good in ground attack operations, since they brought with them as a result of their reconnaissance experience a tactical understanding of ground attack missions.

Former bomber pilots did not usually prove good ground attack pilots. Even the conversion from TE aircraft to the FW 190 proved difficult. They lacked the practical eye for recognizing targets in the air and on the ground, and the necessary maneuverability for flying formations. Their main advantages lay in their good operational morale and willingness and in their stubborn determination to go ahead at any cost. Usually they were shot down the first time in air combat.

The ideal number of officers for a Staffel was, besides the Staffel CO, three or four young pilots who were mainly used as Schwarm leaders. The rest of the pilots were NCOs. In the last months of the war, these figures were rarely reached because of the bad officer supply situation, which caused serious difficulties.

The pilots of night ground attack units which were not outfitted with the FW 190 were worthless, unsuited for day fighter or day ground attack operations. The night ground attack units were supplied with relieved pilots so far as they had no character deficiencies, some from transport units and some from liaison units. Since enough of these pilots were available, the need could be covered after careful selection. These pilots who could not measure up to the new operational requirements when their units converted from the Ju.87 to the FW 190 usually became good night ground attack pilots. Finally old instructors from primary schools proved very good night ground attack pilots, those who were too old to be used for day fighter or day ground attack work. The FW 190 night ground attack pilots had to be well trained, good quality pilots, and replacements could not be made from surpluses of not fully capable pilots.

The quality of officers in night ground attack units was decidedly worse than that of day ground attack units, because many old officers who had long been on staff work were used in the night units. The Staffel COs had to be very good officers, however.

For anti-tank units, good pilots who had a good knack for gunnery and liked anti-tank work were chosen.

c. Various Staff Positions

Schwarm COs. Schwarm leaders needed to have sufficient experience in formation flying, in recognition of ground situations, and in recognition of targets on the ground and in the air. He had to have much tactical knowledge to be able to lead a Schwarm on missions.

Staffel COs Officers were appointed as Staffel COs only when they had had enough combat experience and when they had proved themselves capable. Thus it was often the case that young officers were used as Staffel COs while in the same Gruppe several old officers were merely used as ordinary pilots and Schwarm leaders.

Gruppe and Geschwader COs. These were recruited from among old proved and tried Staffel and Gruppe COs. In the ground attack force, the matter was handled as far as possible according to the following principles: a Staffel CO or Gruppe CO who was in line for promotion to a higher position was withdrawn from operations from six months to one year. He was used during this period as Gruppe or Geschwader CO in a training unit. Here he had an opportunity under direction of a Geschwader or Division CO to get acquainted with his new position. When he later took over his operational unit, he brought with him, especially administratively, the necessary knowledge for his new job. Furthermore he could thereby rest up for more missions and make available the latest front experience for the training units. This planned scheme was not always possible to carry through because of the lack of officers for the usual command positions. Officers who were no longer available for operations were put into good positions at the pilots school and officers schools and could from there still help out the ground attack arm by influencing the giving over of good recruits to the ground attack arm.

Technical Officers. At the beginning of the War, the TOs (technical officers) were always flying officers who in part had been at special T.O. courses. It was then regarded as essential that every formation leader should have some knowledge of technical matters and that the prerequisites for this knowledge were courses and some experience as technical officer. In most cases it was so that the TOs didn't like to stay off missions, flew along too often, and worried too little about their chief job. The inadequate number of flying officers led to the situation that flying officers were no longer trained as TO and could not be used long enough as TOs to gain experience. The use of old chief mechanics and grounded officer pilots, the latter after a short technical course, proved to be very good. Only to this is attributable the high serviceability of ground attack units (70%).

Adjutant. It was really planned that only flying officers could serve as adjutants. Activity as adjutant was for every officer a good basis to later become a Gruppe CO. Because of the high rate of loss of officers, the adjutants' jobs could not any longer regularly be filled with flying officers. For this purpose, grounded officer pilots or suitable reserve officer pilots or suitable reserve officers were used.

Operations and Intelligence Officers. Experienced officer pilots, who were grounded, or suitable reserve officers were used as operations and intelligence officers. Former reconnaissance pilots were found best suited for intelligence work. For ground attack units, intelligence officers were first introduced toward the end of 1944. In the west, intelligence officers were necessary for Geschwader and Gruppe Staffs. On the Eastern Front one intelligence officer sufficed for one Geschwader. It proved to have been a mistake to have omitted intelligence work in the units.

Meteorologists. There were only weather men at the individual night ground attack Gruppen, where they were very important. They were superfluous with the day ground attack units. It sufficed for day units to have the weather reports and forecasts reported from higher headquarters, since missions rarely went more than 150 kilometers anyway.

d. Maintenance Personnel

Strength of maintenance personnel was usually the same as that in Fighter units. The only differences were that there were more bomb personnel and less ordinary ordnance personnel. The strength of technical personnel was so set that the unit could send off an Advance Unit (Vorkomando). This unit was able to prepare a new airfield for the unit and, with the aid of the other key personnel which would come in with the unit's aircraft, to perform maintenance on the aircraft for operational serviceability. The use of women in Ground Attack units was never carried through, although orders to that effect were given out.

e. Equipping with Technical Equipment

Outfitting with technical equipment was kept down to a minimum, usually just like fighter units. Since oxygen was rarely ever needed for ground attack operations, oxygen equipment was at a bare minimum. On the other hand proportionally more bomb loading equipment was on hand for bombing up. The equipping of Ground Attack Units was in general so carried through that operations could be flown without dependence on any ground units at all.

f. Equipping with Signals Apparatus and Signals Personnel

Telephone equipment was supplied so that the unit could have a telephone net connecting all operations rooms, dispersal areas, dwellings, and radio stations. The radio telephones often improvised by the units themselves proved good. They gave good connection between the HQ and dispersal areas, and there were no wires to be damaged. When an airfield was newly occupied, the radio telephones furnished adequate connection until wires were laid down. Its range was sufficient for the normal distance from Hq to dispersal areas. Teletypewriters were available only for Geschwader Hqs. On some occasions independently operating Gruppen were assigned teletypwriter operators by Geschwader HQ. Within the Geschwader, no teletypewriter traffic took place.

The Geschwader staffs were so equipped with radio that they could hook into the command net of the next higher command and also conduct a field order system within their own Geschwader. The Gruppen were correspondingly radio equipped in order to complete this system. The Geschwader and Gruppen both had radio telephone stations. Only the Gruppen had the Tornado radio beacons. At the end of the war, all Ground Attack units (with the exception of some few night unit, were equipped with the FüG 16 (The GAF VHF radio telephone sender transmitter, for air and ground).

A part of the night ground attack units, especially those in the west, and in Italy, were equipped with Egon control procedure personnel. The actual assigning of these personnel to the units proved to be a good idea.

g. Mobility and Transfer Organization

In advance and in retreats the ground attack units lay closer to the front than any other flying units, because of the short ranges of ground attack aircraft and because of the desire to keep high the number of sorties flown by cutting down on the distance flown. In wars of movement, transfers were quite usual. Ground attack units were transferred sometimes on the ground and sometimes in transport aircraft. Complete mobility of the ground personnel and equipment was insured by giving them enough trucks. All ground equipment except that of the motorized repair platoon could be transferred by air. Therefore the ground attack units had in addition to the motorized repair platoon, a flying repair platoon, with equipment that could easily be loaded into transport aircraft. Because of the small amount of air transport space allotted to the various commands, the flying units were allowed only enough space to transport their key personnel. Since these transfers often took place over long distances and were usually intended by the high commands only to last for a few days, the result was that the flying units often had to carry on operations with only their key personnel and serviceability accordingly dropped greatly.

The demand of two transport aircraft for every Gruppe was recognized as justified but could nevertheless not be fulfilled because of the general lack of transport aircraft.

The equipping of ground attack units was in general such that they could with their own personnel and equipment without any support from ground units, except the bringing of bombs and fuel to the airfields, guarantee full serviceability and at the same time maintain an advance or rear party at some other airfield. For transfers over long distances, external tanks had to be given to ground attack units to keep them from having to make constant intermediate landings.

CHAPTER 16

Principles for the Control of Operations of Ground Attack Units

By Generalmajor Hitschhold
At Latimer House, England, 2 October 1945

The purpose of operations of air force units in the tactical area is to help the army in combat in every possible way. For this purpose, reconnaissance aircraft, fighters, bombers, and ground attack formations are used. Of these formations the ground attack units are the ones which attack enemy ground troops as their chief mission. They are best suited to help the army, especially in the area around the front and in attacks against small but important targets. For their operations, certain principles of command and control have been developed out of experience and are explained below:

I. Requirements for successful ground attack operations.

(a) According to the fighter strength of the enemy, at least air superiority and, better still, control of the air (air supremacy) must be won by friendly fighter forces. If continuous air superiority cannot be achieved, then at least air superiority for the duration of ground attack operations must be insured by the furnishing of adequate fighter strength to support these operations. Otherwise the ground attack operations will not bring about their usual complete success.

(b) Only when signals facilities are adequate is quick support of the army insured. Close co-operation with the army must therefore be made possible by use of the necessary signals organizations and their dependable work. The army and air force listening services must be capable of rapid evaluation of intercepted enemy signals. The same map material with same scales must be used by the army and by the commands and units of the air force, and, when possible, photo maps with practical grids and designation of important points should be used.

(c) Basically only those targets are to be attacked which the army cannot strike or only strike with medium and heavy artillery.

(d) The command organizations of the army must establish a priority list from the great number of demands for support which they desire fulfilled. Operations which are not absolutely necessary must be struck off by the army headquarters themselves. The final decision if and where the attack will take place concerns in all cases, however, the responsible Luftwaffe headquarters. If an attack is to be conducted, it should be done with large forces in order to make sure that it will succeed.

Operations by weak forces are a waste. They bring decisive success at no one point and in the final analysis are 'morale operations' which are only justified in a few cases.

(e) Of great significance for a proper and practical control of ground attack operations is the continuous surveying of the tactical area by reconnaissance aircraft. These have to supply ground attack units with necessary targeting material. If such continuous reconnaissance is not possible, the ground attack arm becomes at best a form of mobile long range artillery, and is degraded to a branch of the army, which combats only targets found by ground reconnaissance. Its many-sided operational possibilities would be so employed only to a small extent.

(f) Since German ground attack units possessed a short penetrating range, about 150 km., their operational airfields had accordingly to be placed near the front. This close movement to the front – as far as enemy air defense permitted it – brought the following advantages: the number of ground attack missions could be raised because of the short flights in and out and the practical duration of the flight over the battle area was not appreciably cut down by the small amount of fuel carried in the aircraft. Furthermore, the signals communications between the fighting troops on the ground, the commands of the army and air force, and the airfields of the units themselves were shorter and therefore more dependable.

Behind advances, suitable emergency landing fields had to be prepared as quickly as possible. At the time of transfer of flying units a sufficient A.A. protection ready for action was needed because of the great danger of strafing attacks. Adequate supplies, especially of bombs and bomb containers, also had to be provided.

II. Operational possibilities

Ground attack units attacked chiefly the following targets
    (a) Ground troops in assembly areas, in positions, moving, in march, and during loading and unloading.
    (b) Heavy weapons, MG, artillery, rocket, cannon, A.A. and RR artillery.

(c) Vehicles of all kinds, especially tanks.

(d) Field fortifications.

(e) Headquarters, houses and settlements.

(f) Bridges, especially military bridges.

(g) Airfields, aircraft on the ground, and in the air.

(h) RR installations, RR trains, especially locomotives.

(i) Shipping targets.

The choice of suitable bombs was mainly the job of the unit itself, but the command organizations had to keep a watch over it and sometimes interfere. This matter is touched upon in the following paragraphs:

(a) **Against ground troops.** Ground troops in open country and in positions which offer no cover against air attacks were effectively bombed with small fragmentation bombs of 1, 2, 4, and 10 kilograms, in large containers if possible. Less effective were the 50 and 70 kg. fragmentation bombs, even with *projecting fuses to make them explode above the ground.* These latter bombs had to be used often because of the supplies on hand. Their small effectiveness was continually confirmed, while the smaller bombs dropped in large containers had a bomb carpet effect and still considerable destructive power. A special belting of ammunition – loading the rounds in belts – was not used. The belting usually was: 2 HE, one HE incendiary, followed by 2 armor-piercing incendiary or ordinary armor piercing.

(b) **Against heavy weapons.** These targets were bombed to destroy personnel with the same bombs used under (a) above. If the cannon stood in the open, without cover (being transported or simply dispersed), then the 50, 70, and 250 kg. fragmentation bombs, all with projecting fuses, are suitable. Strafing attacks were flown against the personnel and the lighter weapons, but they were useless against heavy apparatus. On the other hand, Russian rocket batteries mounted on trucks were destroyed with the greatest effectiveness by strafing attacks. Armored trains and rail-road guns were only successfully bombed with heavy bombs of 250 kg. or more.

(c) **Vehicles.** Horse drawn and motor vehicles were bombed with 1–70 kg. bombs. The same goes for lightly armored vehicles. Tanks could be destroyed with 3, 3.7, and 7.5 cm. cannon, with hollow charge RP, and with 4 kg. hollow charge bombs. Bombing with 50–500 kg. bombs was not successful because the tanks presented too small a target. Destruction with such bombs was only accomplished if the bomb hit within 15 feet of the tank.

(d) **Field fortifications**. Field fortifications of all types could only be attacked with heavy bombs of 250 kg. or more. Attacks on modern prepared fortifications brought no success.

(e) **Headquarters**. Parts of towns and houses where headquarters or troops were quartered were attacked with bombs of 250 kg. or larger. Wooden houses, especially with straw roofs, were most practically ignited with incendiary ammunition.

(f) **Bridges**. Bridge destruction was a difficult job and usually brought little success. Stone or concrete bridges were only damageable with direct hits from heavy bombs and then only temporarily. Complete collapsing of such a bridge was almost impossible.

Steel bridges were most invulnerable, because the blast effect usually dissipated through the steel work. Only in cases of some lucky hits was the destruction of such bridges possible.

Military bridges were attacked with a mixture of 10–500 kg. bombs. Even so, only temporary interruption of traffic was achieved. Repairs were especially easy for pontoon bridges, if a continuous observation and bombing of the repair work was not possible.

In certain tactical situations, like pursuits, last escape routes out of surrounded areas, flank threats, and bringing up of reserves, the bombing of bridges was of decisive importance and had to be carried on without regard to the success to be expected.

(g) **Attacks on airfields**. These served as indirect support for the army. The main point of such attacks was the destruction of dispersed aircraft, which were bombed with small bombs of from 1 to 10 kg. Fixed installations were attacked only at the beginning of the war, because as a result of the ensuing dispersal such attacks were usually uneconomical.

(h) **Railroad bombing**. This was a worthy target for ground attack units, especially during the movement of troops in the tactical area. Main points of attack were tracks in and out of stations, and easily blocked sections like bridges and cuts. Attacks on open stretches of track and on unoccupied stations brought no lasting effect. Most practical for these purposes were bombs of 250 kg. and more. Trains in motion were wrecked with heavy bombs and the troops streaming out of them were strafed and bombed with small fragmentation bombs.

Special locomotive-busting missions were especially satisfactory in areas where repair facilities were meager. For destruction of the locomotives, hits with cannon of 3 cm. caliber or greater or with RPs sufficed. Hits with smaller weapons or with bomb fragments only damaged the locomotives, but even this was evidently a great handicap in areas lacking repair facilities.

III. Cooperation of Air Force and Navy

The principles set out for the cooperation of army and air force are also valid for the cooperation of the navy and the air force. The holding of air superiority and availability of sufficient signals communications are decisive for success of missions. On operations where the friendly shipping force expected contact with enemy air power, special ground attack control headquarters were set up on ships. Similarly the navy coastal commands on shore were assigned liaison and control parties from the ground attack arm.

For attacks on ships, usually the larger ships were attacked because their larger size and poor maneuverability made hits easier to score. Still, only hits by bombs of 250 kg. or over would sink them. Smaller ships, like motor torpedo boats, were attacked with cannon or RP. Small fragmentation bombs were also effective, but the possibilities of hitting were small.

IV. Defensive Situations

Attacks are flown as concentrated attacks on enemy assembly areas, artillery and tank concentrations. Rolling attacks are flown mainly after the beginning of an enemy attack against tanks, artillery and reserve troops, and also against attack spearheads to rob them of their impetus. These attacks are as far as possible continued at night by ground attack units, especially with 2 kg. fragmentation bombs against troop concentrations in defiles.

V. Retreat and Defense against Enemy Breakthroughs

During disengaging movements and in retreats the enemy is combatted with rolling attacks to gain time and space for friendly troops and to give them back their battle initiative.

For tank breakthrough, the main effort in defense is the use of anti-tank units against tank columns. Rolling attacks were flown against spearheads (which in most fluid situations had to be sought out by the units in the air), against supply columns and choke points around defiles, like bridges, river crossings, etc.

At night the night ground attack units combatted the enemy in rolling attacks in heavily occupied towns or woods, and also supply lines in defiles.

CHAPTER 17

Ground Attack Operations

By Generalmajor Hitschhold
At Latimer House, England, 5 October 1945

Command Principles for Operations of
Day Ground Attack Units

Weather and terrain conditions were factors to be taken into account in operations of ground attack units.

Operational minima for weather were considered:

Ceiling 4500 feet for missions over the front and 6000 feet ceiling for missions deep into the tactical area. In all cases A.A. defenses were to be taken into consideration.

In crises ground attack units operated in worse conditions, with a minimum ceiling for front missions of 600–900 feet.

A first principle was that the size of the formation was dependent on the weather. The worse the weather, the smaller the formations, in order not to restrict the maneuverability of the formation. In extremely poor weather flights were restricted to very small formations of especially experienced pilots.

For bad weather operations radar control was planned and provided. The ground attack units were vectored over the clouds or between cloud layers to the vicinity of the target, but they were to carry on the attack themselves independently after going down through the clouds and sighting the earth. (In general, ground attack units attack only targets which they can actually see and recognize.)

Terrain conditions are important for locating targets. Open country makes the finding of targets easy, while obscure country, like wooded areas, makes target locating harder. In very difficult country and in wooded areas, ground attack operations are to be discouraged, because the success to be expected bears no relation to the effort required and the attack can be entirely ineffective.

From the command standpoint the following types of ground attack missions are distinguishable:

    a)   concentrated attack

    b)   rolling attack

    c)   free sweep attack

a) **Concentrated attack**. For the conduct of a concentrated attack, ground attack units were combined. They were operated at a determined time against clearly defined targets. The time for beginning and ending the attack was ordered to the minute. Forces used were apportioned according to the size and type of the target.

Concentrated attacks were primarily flown in direct support of the army, usually just before the beginning of a ground offensive (like infantry preparation) as a surprise measure. Therefore the duration and time of the attack was determined by the army. Concentrated attacks were flown with bombs and with strafing by ground attack units. The mission was to destroy the enemy or to injure his morale so that after that the ground troops would have little or no defense to contend with.

This was only possible when the Army, immediately after the concentrated attack from the air, took advantage of its effect by launching an attack of its own. Similarly such concentrated attacks make easier the disengaging movements of friendly troops.

Secondly, concentrated attacks were ordered not for direct army support, but as indirect support against special targets which appeared, like heavily occupied airfields, RR stations, troops unloading, and so on. An attack carried through with the element of surprise increased the effect considerably.

From the command side, concentrated attacks were carefully thought out and planned using target photos and photo maps on which the smallest targets were recognizable as well as large scale maps and other necessary documents. Of special importance was the choice of bombs and fuses. Even though this was primarily the business of the flying units themselves, it was worthwhile in some cases that the command organizations insured that the right measures were taken, so that a carefully prepared attack did not become a fiasco because of bad choice of bombs and fuses.

b) **Rolling attack**. Rolling attacks serve as continuous support for ground operations in progress. The targets to be attacked were clearly ordered, or small target areas were determined, in which every recognized enemy was to be destroyed. For this purpose, formations of Staffel size or larger were used. In these rolling attacks it was sought by the quickest possible use of formations to paralyze every movement of enemy troops against friendly troops and to destroy every enemy concentration of forces. The time of attack was therefore not strictly laid down. Short operational readiness, short time of flight into the battle area, and occasionally the diversion of a formation already in the air were possibilities for rapid conduct of missions. Only at the beginning of a ground offensive could the times of attacks be closely fixed. Bomb loading was usually finished before the operational order was received and was according to the types of targets expected. The decisive goal was to destroy the enemy as quickly as possible, before he had the chance, by dispersing and camouflage, to protect himself against air attack or to become effective against friendly troops.

c) **Free Sweep attacks.** Free sweep attacks were usually carried out in the course of flowing ground combat. The objectives of free sweep attacks were broad and bold, like continuous support of a tank spearhead or flank cover for a break through wedge. In practice free sweep attacks were a kind of hunting of individual targets, which was to accomplish a suppression of the enemy and at the same time insure a continual watch over the enemy. If, in the course of the engagement, stronger enemy forces appeared on the ground which could only be successfully combatted with more air forces, additional forces were thrown into the free sweep attack.

Free sweep attacks were flown by small units (Rotte up to Staffel) which was only possible in cases of friendly air superiority. By close cooperation with ground attack control stations or by control from forward headquarters the immediate combatting of enemy targets which appeared and the keeping down of enemy resistance were possible.

The choice of targets always remains up to the formation leader. The formation leader must have good tactical knowledge in order to attack at the right place on the battlefield. By good cooperation with the ground attack control stations, the conduct of his mission was made much easier. Bomb loading was usually mixed according to the types of targets expected.

Operational Principles of Anti-Tank
Ground Attack Operations

Missions for anti-tank units were flown only on special centers of resistance on the front, and long rest periods repeatedly arose for them. Anti-tank flying units with their special weapons were used against tanks and armored vehicles which had broken through. For use against tank assembly areas they were not suitable, because these areas were usually heavily protected with A.A. In pursuit, their use against parts of split up tank units was good.

For operations of anti-tank units, ground and air defense were specially considered, but weather conditions were of less importance. Even in very bad weather with very low ceiling anti-tank units could carry out effective and successful raids.

Because of the mobility of tanks, finding them in a short space of time was often hard. Especially in fluid situations, exact reports and locations about the appearance of tanks were seldom available. The operations of anti-tank units therefore usually took place like a free sweep attack, in which the aircraft first had to find the tanks in a large target area. Therefore, training in recognition of tanks was especially important for the anti-tank flyers.

Operational Possibilities for Ground Attack Units in Various Phases of Ground Combat Movements

1. Preparation for an attack.
2. Attack.
3. Breakthrough and pursuit.
4. Defense.
5. Retreat and defense against enemy breakthroughs.

1. **Preparations for Attack.** For preparation of a large ground offensive, ground attack units were employed in a planned manner against such targets as were found by aerial reconnaissance and which could considerably hinder the attack planned. In case the army offensive was to be a surprise, the operations of ground attack units must be omitted in order not to attract the enemy's attention too soon.

Such attacks launched in support of a planned offensive were usually flown against targets deep in the tactical zone, such as, for example, heavy artillery, important bridges, enemy supply organizations. Attacks against air force installations belong in this class.

At night, to ease friendly preparations and deployments for attack, rolling missions could be flown against enemy artillery, and at the same time the noise of friendly tanks moving up into position could be drowned out. Furthermore, enemy supply centers, like RR stations and villages, could be attacked in concentrated attacks, especially if the A.A. defense by day were too strong.

2) **Attacks.** Immediately before the beginning of an attack, missions were flown against everything which could hinder the friendly advance directly. Targets were the enemy troops in the field and other fortifications, strong points, heavy weapons, headquarters, and signals facilities. At the dropping of the last bombs on the forward enemy positions, the friendly troops began their attack.

Adolf Galland as the archetypical fighter pilot, with well-worn flying jacket and crushed cap and his Knight's Cross with Oak Leaves and Swords suspended from his neck on one of his girlfriends' garters. (US National Archives RG 242)

Galland as 'Brylcreem basher', as his RAF counterparts were termed: the fighter pilot as matinée idol. He was, at 30, the youngest German general. (US National Archives RG 242)

A Galland who did not survive: younger brother Wilhelm-Ferdinand 'Wutz' Galland, who served with his brothers in JG 26. A 55-victory ace, he fell to USAAF P-47s during the first Schweinfurt raid of 17 August 1943 while leading a formation into position for a massed attack on B-17s. (US National Archives RG 242)

Gordon Gollob after a mission. A 160-victory ace, he commanded JG 3 in 1941–42 and JG 77 in 1942–44. He was the first pilot to achieve 150 victories. He was Galland's successor as General der Jagdflieger. Galland disliked him intensely due to what he perceived as his fanatical Nazi politics and underhand personal dealings. (US National Archives RG 242)

(Above) Werner Mölders meets Hitler, December 1940. Mölders, Galland's predecessor as General der Jagdflieger and his friend and rival, was responsible for implementing many of the tactical innovations from Spain throughout the fighter force. He was the first pilot to score 100 victories. (US National Archives RG 242)

(Left) Walter Oesau, a 123-victory ace shot down by P-38s on 11 May 1944, was a keen tactician and trainer as well as a combat leader. Commanding JG 1, he was able to form his unit into effective multi-Gruppe formations. (US National Archives RG 242)

Heinz Bär. He succeeded Galland as commander of the Me 262-equipped JV 44 after Galland had been shot down. As an FW 190-equipped Sturmgruppe commander, Bär reportedly had his pilots swear to bring down a bomber on every sortie, even if it meant ramming. Galland knew him well and respected him as a leader and pilot despite his flamboyant and impulsive personal style. He scored 220 victories, 16 in Me 262s, making him the war's leading jet ace. (US National Archives RG 242)

Dietrich Peltz – one of Galland's bêtes noires. He was a bomber general who, Galland felt, was ineffective as a fighter leader and squandered resources that he, Galland, was trying to use for his cherished 'big blow' against the bombers. Peltz planned Operation 'Bodenplatte', the massive counter-air strike of 1 January 1945 that lost many of the remaining fighters trying to defend the Reich. (US National Archives RG 242)

Walter Nowotny, a 258-victory ace hand-picked by Galland – who had known him since he had been through pilot training with Galland's younger brother Paul – to command the first ever jet fighter unit, Kommando Nowotny. He was the first fighter pilot ever to score 250 victories. Galland saw him shot down and killed on 9 November 1944. (US National Archives RG 242)

Colonel Dr Thomas Kupfer, 'Hitsch' Hitschhold's predecessor as General der Schlachtflieger until killed in a crash in 1944. Like Hitschhold, he had led Stuka dive-bomber units in 1939–42 before moving to ground attack work. (US National Archives RG 242)

(Left) The 'view from the cockpit' of Johannes Trautloft. He was Inspector of Day Fighters in the West. A friend of Galland, he supported the latter in his confrontations with Göring. He was a keen tactician, and drafted the first Luftwaffe fighter tactics manuals to embody Mölders' innovations. Unlike Galland, he joined the Bundeswehr in the 1950s. (US National Archives RG 242)

(Below) Edgar Petersen talks with night fighter aces Werner Streib (left, 65 victories) and Hans Jabs (center, 31 victories). (US National Archives RG 242)

The 'men in black' who made the Luftwaffe fighter force operate: groundcrew rearm a Bf 109. (US National Archives RG 242)

Where the Luftwaffe fighter force began: an He 51 biplane fighter of 1935. (US National Archives RG 242)

The Ar 68 was operational as a night fighter as late as December 1939. (US National Archives RG 242)

The start of the ground attack arm. Galland flew these Hs 123s in Poland, and they were also used in France and Russia. (US National Archives RG 242)

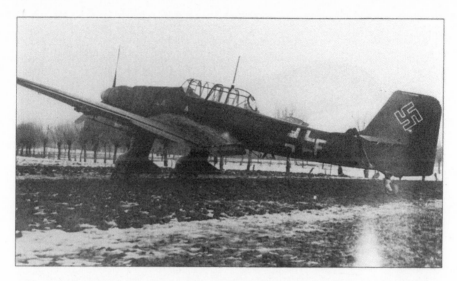

The Ju 87 Stuka started out as a weapon of the Blitzkrieg but, because its dive-bomber tactics made it vulnerable to fighter and anti-aircraft fire, it became more relevant as a ground attack aircraft in 1942–45. (Wilhelm Landau via James Crow)

A wartime propaganda photograph of an early Bf 110B. Göring saw the twin-engine fighter force as an élite group, committed solely to offensive combat, unlike the Bf 109s. (US National Archives RG 242)

The standard Luftwaffe single-engine fighter of 1939–41 – the Bf 109E. (US National Archives RG 18)

A result of the absence of the defensive air–sea co-operation that Galland stressed: a merchant ship sunk by Allied aircraft off Livorno, 1945. (USSBS)

The business end of an FW 190. This is the view seen from a USAAF bomber at the closest point of a head-on German attack before the fighter rolled away to avoid collision. (US National Archives RG 18)

Ju 87G Stukas were converted from Ju 87Ds when dive-bombing became too dangerous, and armed with a pair of 37mm underwing anti-tank guns. (US National Archives RG 242)

The FW 190A – in this case, an FW 190A-8 – helped to hold numerically superior RAF fighters at bay in 1941–42, but against a later generation of fighters in 1944–45 it was often inadequate. (US National Archives RG 18)

The Bf 109G-6 introduced the characteristic 'bumps' to cover the breeches of its 13mm nose-mounted machine guns. Many also carried underwing armament, being the first version designed from the outset to accept this. (US National Archives RG 18)

A 'long-nose' FW 190D-9 runs up for a test flight. This version started to re-equip FW 190A units in October 1944. While the aircraft was intended mainly to engage escort fighters, many were committed to Operation 'Bodenplatte' on 1 January 1945. (US National Archives RG 18)

The Me 410 played an important role against USAAF bombers, though the decision to arm it with an unsatisfactory 50mm weapon undercut its effectiveness. It also served as a bomber and reconnaissance aircraft (the photograph is of an Me 410A-3 reconnaissance version). (US National Archives RG 18)

An Me 163B of JG 400. Galland had advocated the forward deployment of individual Staffeln for point defense, but when he was replaced by Gollob this policy changed to one of concentrating all Me 163 operations at a single base, which, because of the aircraft's limited range, the USAAF was able to avoid. (US National Archives RG 18)

An Me 262 in flight. After being dismissed as General der Jagdflieger, Galland took command of JV 44, a fighter group equipped with Me 262s, in 1945. Galland was one of the strongest advocates for developing the Me 262 and putting it into mass production as a fighter, despite its unreliable engines. (US National Archives RG 18)

The He 162 Volksjäger light fighter was considered, by Galland, to be a waste of resources and a diversion from the need to supply Me 262s to keep the German fighter force viable. Only a few saw action in the last days of the war.

The Dornier Do 335. Just entering service at the end of the war, this aircraft met Galland's need for a twin-engine fighter that could carry a heavy armament against bombers without itself requiring fighter escort. (US National Archives RG 18)

Directly after the beginning of the attack and during the progress of the attack the following missions took place:

a) Rolling attacks against determined targets, especially effective enemy artillery and reserves coming up.

b) Free sweep missions against all such targets as might hinder the fluid continuance of the battle. Such targets were MG nests, new enemy artillery positions, single tanks, and so on. Purpose of such attacks was to hold down the enemy and to destroy pockets of resistance so that friendly forces could continually go forward. Movement on the battlefield must be made impossible for the enemy. At the same time, the flanks of friendly attacking forces were covered.

At night, concentrated attacks could be flown by night attack units against the enemy assembly areas which were recognized by day reconnaissance. Friendly ground operations at night could well be continually supported by night attack units in cooperation with ground control stations, the aircraft flying in Rotten or Schwärme.

3) **Break-through and Pursuit.** In break-throughs and in pursuit of enemy forces, the rolling attack was more important. Especially retreating troop columns, strong points still holding out, approaching reserves, and massed troops at defiles were good targets. The more the battle became one of pursuit, the more the free sweep attack took precedence. In such cases the retreating enemy was attacked especially in restricted areas, where his retreat reached a bottle neck. All other targets which held up the pursuit or threatened from the flanks were destroyed.

In such situations, the anti-tank flying units had a great number of successful missions, because the enemy tank forces were split up, the A.A. defense was weakened, and furthermore, enemy air opposition was weakened because of the necessity of the retreat of enemy airfields.

At night the main effort was made against recognized forward or rearward movements simply to harrass the enemy.

CHAPTER 18

Ground Attack Tactics

By Generalmajor Hitschhold

*At Kaufbeuren, Germany, and Latimer House,
England, 20 September–4 October 1945*

1. Chief Missions of Ground Attack Units in Operations

Basically it is to be recognized that German ground attack units possessed the ability to attack pin point targets. Special medium bomber units for the support of the Army were lacking in the GAF, therefore the twin engined bombers intended for strategic bombing were used for this purpose, although from the beginning of 1943 most of these bomber units did engage in strategic bombing. Since then, the operations of medium bombers were almost completely lacking over German battle areas. Medium bombers are able to combat area targets for the support of the Army. A ground force attack must consist of units which can combat area targets as well as forces which can bomb and strafe pinpoint targets.

On the German side, the chief missions and targets of ground attack units were:

a. For the support of the Army.
   (1) Fighting troops on the ground, troops in positions, and troops on the march.
   (2) Material – medium and heavy weapons, MG nests, anti-tank guns, artillery, rocket guns, A.A. guns, tanks and tank columns.
   (3) Transport – horse-drawn vehicles, locomotives, railroad, shipping, trucks.
   (4) Signals facilities – radio stations, wire communications (by attacks on entries and exits to villages) bridges, ferries, troops in villages, houses, and troops in woods.

b. Coastal Area – ships and water vehicles of all kinds, warships, landing places, etc.

c. Air combat – destruction of enemy aircraft in the air and on the ground.

2. Types of Missions and Attacks

a. Day Attacks

b. Anti-Tank Missions

c. Night Attacks

d. Day attacks as follows:

Ground attack missions were usually carried out in Gruppe, Staffel, Schwarm or Rotte strength. Only in exceptional cases where great forces were massed did attacks in Geschwader strength take place. In the Fall of 1943 seven Gruppen had the F.W. 190 and the other 14 or 15 had the Ju.87 Stukas. By the end of the war all but one of these Ju.87 Stuka units had been converted to the F.W.190.

Radio control from the ground (Egon Procedure) was planned for the units but was not to be introduced until a time several months after the war actually ended. It was planned to use the Egon Procedure to lead the aircraft to the target in bad weather only. After being led directly to the target, they then conducted the attack after sighting the ground.

Ground attack units conducted their attacks as dive (80–60°), shallow glide (50–20°) or low level attacks.

Armament of the F.W.190 ground attack model was 2 × MG 151 2 cm. and 2 × MG 131 13 mm., one 500 kg. bomb rack under the fuselage, and 4 × 50 kg racks under wings.

The choice of the mode of attack (dive, shallow dive, or low level) was dependent on the enemy's anti-aircraft and fighter defense, weather, and the type of ammunition and bombs to be used. If the enemy anti-aircraft and fighter defenses were disregarded, the most successful modes of attack were the shallow dive for dropping bombs and the low level attack for strafing. Very often it was the job of the ground attack pilot to seek out the most important targets over the battlefield, and some of these targets were very well camouflaged. This forced him to fly at altitudes from which only a direct shallow dive or low level attack was possible. The shallow dive attack brought about the best possibility of hitting, and the type of bomb and fuse determined the dropping altitude. This was especially true with the type of bomb container from which a great number of small bombs were strewn (cluster bomb units) and which required a certain dispersion to be effective. (For ground attack aircraft like the Ju.87 and other aircraft with computing bomb sights, the dive attack is the most practical.)

If the anti-aircraft fire could be kept down or nullified, the ground attacks were flown as shallow dives or as low level attacks. It was often necessary to use part of the unit to hold down the anti-aircraft fire with a suitable bomb load (containers with 1 kg. anti-personnel bombs), in order that the greater part of the formation could carry through an effective attack with as little interference as possible from ground defenses. If the suppression of the anti-aircraft fire was not possible, dive attacks had to be flown. (It repeatedly proved good to have friendly artillery keep down enemy anti-aircraft fire, when ground attack units were attacking targets near the front line.) If the anti-aircraft fire was too strong, a massed, closed-up dive attack had to be carried out in formation. In this manner the anti-aircraft gunners had only a short time to combat the attack and could not concentrate their fire on individual targets. Approach altitude and the beginning of the attack dive were, if possible, so arranged that they lay outside the effective range of the anti-aircraft fire.

3. Escort for Ground Attack Units

Besides anti-aircraft defense, fighter defense rendered difficult the conduct and effectiveness of ground attack missions. It was proved on the Western Front and in Italy that ground attack missions were impossible when the attacking side did not have air superiority, at least over the battle area during the time of the attack. Otherwise the losses of the ground attack aircraft were too high in relation to what was accomplished. The ground attack pilots had to be able to carry out attacks unmenaced by enemy fighters. If fighter opposition was absent, the ground attack unit could carry out their attacks very much opened up and dispersed in the air, but if fighter opposition was present, the ground attack formation had to be kept closed up over the battle area.

On the Eastern Front it was usually sufficient if part of the ground attack formation took over the fighter escort for the rest of the mission. It was even possible to use bomb-carrying F.W.190's as fighter escort. This was done in the following way: at the beginning of the attack, one part of the formation stayed at altitude and furnished fighter cover. This part was then relieved by another part of the formation which had already dropped its bombs. The top cover then went down to conduct its own ground attacks. In case of contact with the enemy, bombs had to be jettisoned, with fuses armed if over enemy territory.

If the enemy had air superiority, fighter escort furnished by regular fighter units was advisable. Strong fighter opposition forces the ground attack formation to make greatly concentrated mass attacks (usually with approach at great altitude for a dive attack, or on occasion a low level attack with the element of surprise). Effective strafing attacks could not then be flown, because the effectiveness of the ground attack units was thus already cut in half. The most effective weapons of the ground attack F.W.190 were its 2 cm. cannon MG 151 and its heavy MG 131 13 mm. Bombs were less effective.

It was the goal of every ground attack mission to combat the enemy to the last round of ammunition, to destroy all recognizable targets on the ground, and then by a prolonged stay over the battlefield to render impossible every movement of the enemy. (This opportunity was to be utilized by the army for attacks, redeployment, retreat, etc.)

The weather in part decides the type of mission to be flown by ground attack units and also the size of the formations, i.e. the worse the weather, the smaller the formation. A minimum ceiling of 6000–8000 feet is required for dive bombing attacks. Shallow dive attacks can be flown with a ceiling of 1500 feet and low level attacks with still lower ceilings. Attacks under low ceilings usually result in higher losses, because the anti-aircraft fire cannot be adequately combatted and because the ground attack aircraft are too easily sighted by enemy aircraft.

Anti-Tank Missions

It was necessary to use special anti-tank ground attack units against modern tank formations. In cases of lucky tank break-throughs, the army was often not in a position to throw in enough of its own tanks or anti-tank guns to stop the advance. In the Spring and Autumn in Russia, the ground was so muddy and roads so bad that moving tanks for defense against enemy tank break throughs was so slow that the only possibility of combatting them was to use these special anti-tank ground attack units.

It was apparent that ordinary ground attack units were not able to destroy enough tanks with their guns, cannons and bombs, but the special anti-tank units with armour piercing cannon and special anti-tank rockets were very successful. Anti-tank aircraft were the Henschel 129 with the MK 101 3 cm., later the MK 103 3 cm.; the Ju.87 Stuka with 2 × 37 mm. cannon, and the usual F.W.190 ground attack model with rocket tubes fixed to its bomb racks.

These aircraft were successfully used against tanks which had broken through on the battlefield or all the way into rear areas. The missions against tank assembly areas were a great mistake because these were always protected with many anti-aircraft guns and resulted in high losses compared to completely unimportant accomplishments. For attacks on tank assembly areas it was better to use formations which carried a great number of containers of 4 kg. hollow charge armour piercing bombs, which can be dropped from halfway outside the effective anti-aircraft fire. Enemy tanks which have broken into friendly troop areas can only be safely combatted by special anti-tank ground attack units, without endangering friendly troops.

Troop columns which have broken through can be defeated if the anti-tank units fight the tanks and the regular ground attack units attack the more thinly armoured vehicles which follow the tanks. In good weather, tank break-throughs were, however, protected with a strong fighter cover. The beating down of this fighter cover was a pre-requisite for a successful employment of anti-tank ground-attack units. If bad weather was used for tank break-throughs the anti-tank units can fly anyway, since they usually fly in low level attacks.

Next to the neutralizing of the enemy fighter cover, the beating down of anti-aircraft defenses is another condition for the successful use of anti-tank flying units. After a long series of successful missions against tanks, the enemy started to give the tanks anti-aircraft protection and always increased it, and at the end of the war, every nation had some sort of mobile anti-aircraft gun which could protect the tanks. The use of anti-tank units with regular ground attack units to keep down the A.A. fire became necessary. When the ceiling was low so that ground attack units could not effectively act against anti-aircraft defenses, the anti-tank units had to be used with the element of surprise and the attack was carried through in the shortest possible time before the anti-aircraft tanks, not ordinarily ready for combat, could unlimber their guns and start to shoot. Experience and practice in immediate recognition of tanks and shooting them up in the first attack brought about good successes without important losses. In the last year of the war, the Russian tank troops had accustomed themselves to the anti-tank flyers and the tanks were well camouflaged wherever possible. At the approach of anti-tank units they immediately sought cover near houses, tree clumps, or hay stacks. Often the tanks could only be found from their tracks and the Russians usually erased these by dragging branches behind the tanks.

Anti-tank units fought in Rotten, Schwärme and, at most, in Staffeln formation. Larger anti-tank units used simultaneously over the battlefield hindered and confused each other. The attacks with armor piercing cannon were conducted like ordinary strafing missions. To ensure hits, the pilots had to approach as close as possible. The best range was 100–150 yards. The gunnery run had to be very even and calm, and the direction of approach was determined by the ground situation and with the 3 cm. and 37 mm. weapons aimed at the vital points of the tanks.

Night Attacks

The mission of the night ground attack units was to combat or harass the enemy on the front and in rear areas exactly as the day ground attack units did it.

This idea arose from the use of the Russian harassing aircraft, the U-2. At first the German used harassing (Starstaffeln) Staffeln, using normal training aircraft like the Arado 66, Gotha 145, Heinkel 46, and the Bucker 181.

At the end of 1943 German ground attack units in Italy could not operate by day without difficulties and heavy losses because of great Allied air superiority. Some Ju.87 Stukas were used experimentally against the Nettuno (Anzio) bridgehead by night. The employment proved practical. There followed in 1944 the conversion of night ground units to the Ju.87 and the F.W.190. These units were able when used in sufficient numbers to disturb the enemy continually in the night, to hinder materially night marches, to hold down artillery fire and to hinder attacks. In this way considerable relief could often be given German troops.

The targets for night ground attack missions had to be small area targets; the combatting of point targets (as by day) was only possible to a limited extent. Good targets proved to be firing artillery, lighted transport columns, defiles, bridges, villages, and areas and geographic points of importance recognizable at night as troop concentration areas. Best of all were missions against lighted targets, such as tracks and firing artillery. Dark targets had to be illuminated with flares dropped from the air to the ground or through target markers either dropped or shot from the ground. The lavish use of 2 kg. fragmentation bombs (especially early in the night) was good to restrict the enemy's use of roads during the night.

An effective employment of forces was the rolling attack – a series of hard blows one after another. Such rolling attacks continuing throughout the entire night on the Russian front greatly hindered the preparations of the enemy for attacks on the following day.

Usual tactics of the night-ground attack units were dive and shallow dive attacks. Horizontal attacks were conducted only rarely and by very low ceiling, and where large area targets were in question.

Ordinary weather requirements for missions were a ceiling of 3,000–6,000 feet, visibility of 4–5 kilometers. Moonlight made the mission easier because the targets were easier to see. Average anti-aircraft fire could, even by night, be held down effectively by repeated bombing. Strong anti-aircraft fire made the mission harder. Night fighter defense against night ground attacks was not present in the East, but was very effective in Italy. Radar control (Egon)

proved good in Italy and in the West and was a great help in combat. A close
co-operation with the Army in the battle area would produce great results.
This was not achieved, since the continual retreats of the Army made cooperation of Army and Air Force harder and harder. It was proved, however, that night ground attack units, well directed from the ground, though
partly equipped with antiquated aircraft, could achieve considerable results
and effectively support the Army.

CHAPTER 19

Tactical Execution of Ground Attack Missions (FW 190)

By Generalmajor Hitschhold and Major I. G. Jacob

At Latimer House, England, 15 October 1945

A. Important Points to Note in Preparation for Ground Attack Missions

In addition to the usual points which concern all types of units, the following points are especially important for ground attack units:

(1) The *operations room* must be as close as possible to the landing field in order at all times to be able to overlook the field and dispersal areas and to supervise the start and landing procedures. If the enemy has air superiority and frequent strafing attacks on the field take place, this practice can be left out. The disadvantages of lengthening the readiness times and the increased uncertainty of the wire signals network are the results.

(2) Especially important were the immediate and adequate *developments of signals facilities*. A telephone exchange and radio station were essential for every Gruppe. The telephone exchange must have the following connections, directly if possible:

    (a) to the superior unit

    (b) to all inferior units

    (c) to the radio room

    (d) to the units' radio beacon D/Fing station and the Egon control station

Besides this, the units' headquarters were combined or linked with its own radio station for communication with the formations in the air and with any unit of the ground which kept an air situation plot (like a fighter Gruppe); if possible the headquarters was physically connected with these facilities, not just by wire.

On airfields which were not yet outfitted with signals facilities, a radio-room equipped Ju.52 transport aircraft was used, obtained from Fliegerkorps or Luftflotte.

All wire communications were supplemented by radio or courier communication for certainty of contact.

(3) **Intelligence Service**. The main effort of the work here lay in a painfully exact *keeping of the enemy situation* and in the immediate receiving and evaluating of the smallest reconnaissance reports.

In addition the supplying of the unit with sufficient maps, air photos, photo maps and map sketches of the local frontline area is an important function of the intelligence officer.

(4) **Operations Officer.** For the operations officer the main job was keeping the friendly situation map. He had to strive especially hard to keep up with the latest developments as to the locations of the front lines.

(5) **Meteorological Service.** For ground attack units, the *local* weather situation and the short range prediction were of special interest. The large weather picture and long range predictions were unimportant. Since the facts needed for ground attack missions could usually be supplied by the meteorologists of the airfields or from superior units, the meteorologist originally with the staff of the Geschwader was superfluous, and his place in the TO was therefore cancelled. It was *different*, however, with the *night ground attack units*. These units were, as a result of their usual equipment of radio and navigation devices, both in the air and on the ground, especially dependent upon a short exact weather forecast. Since they were usually not based at good airdromes, but on small field landing grounds with poor wire connections to higher units, every night ground attack unit had a weather man. It was his job to keep close track of the weather during missions and warn the aircraft on operations of sudden fog, or other worsening of the weather.

B. Operational Orders for Ground Attack Units

(1) Wherever possible, a preliminary order with statements of bomb load and times of readiness (for example, short readiness of 20–30 minutes, or one hour readiness, etc.) was given. When short readiness was ordered, the Staffel CO's usually stayed in the operations room to be informed as soon as the final operational order came in.

(2) The order was relayed verbally with the use of a map. It contained as a rule the following items:
    (a) Friendly and enemy situation on the ground and in the air.
    (b) Friendly intentions.
    (c) Mission.

While the items (a) and (b) remained standing without additions, the item

(c) Mission was enlarged upon by the unit CO as follows:

Bomb Load with fusing
Take-off Sequence
Assembly
Formation
Flight in to the target (route, altitude, point for crossing the front)
Time and duration of attack
Conduct of attack (dive, shallow dive, low level, bombing and strafing)
Assignment of targets (The aircraft which were to keep down enemy A.A. and to take over fighter escort if no special escort was provided)
Flight Back – (manner of assembly, route, and altitude)
Radio (call signs, conduct of internal communications, for example, 'radio silence on the whole approach until the front is crossed'. Cooperation with ground control.
Fighter Cover – (If it is provided, rendezvous point and manner of flying which is arranged by the unit CO with the fighter CO)
Navigation (Dividing up the route according to time and space; navigation aids, traffic with Egon stations or radio beacons)
Weather situation
Naming of deputy CO

Out of this mass of items, those which usually repeated themselves could be omitted, since they were common knowledge. On the other hand, in the preparation for concentrated attacks, and for first missions in new zones, a very exact treatment of the operational order was required.

(3) The operational order was first given by the unit CO to the Staffel CO's, who then left and passed on the information to their pilots at the Staffel dispersal areas around the airfield. Certain points could be omitted and other things important for the Staffel would be added, like time to start engines, sequence for taxiing, composition of the Rotten (two-ship) and Schwärme (four-ship) Flights.

(4) The *speed* as well as the *exactness* of the dissemenation of the order was decisive. Since the Staffel CO's were already at the operations room when the order arrived and could be informed at once, the time required to prepare for take-off was not usually more than 15–25 minutes. (Time required to brief the Staffel CO's, ride of Staffel CO's from operations room to Staffel dispersal areas, briefing of the readied crews by the Staffel CO's, marching of pilots to aircraft, starting, and taxiing to take-off).

C. Conduct of Missions

(1) The mission begins with *starting the engines and taxiing to take-off*. The principle was not to permit any traffic jams at take-off because massed aircraft at start presents a very good target for enemy air attacks, and moreover, lubrication and cooling of the F.W.190 engine (BMW 801) were bad at low RPM.

It was therefore necessary to observe even in taxiing the sequence of take-off and formation laid down in the operational order. As far as possible aircraft taxied in Rotten from the dispersal areas and took-off at once. A special appointed take-off officer had to see that take-offs took place quickly and smoothly.

(2) **Assembling** Uninterrupted taking-off of one Rotte after another was a prerequisite for quick assembly in the air. The quicker the formation assembled, the less vulnerable it was to enemy air attacks.

The assembly usually took place in a large curve around the airfield. On missions which were to go to the limits of the endurance of the aircraft, they had, however, to set out on course at once, and the leading aircraft throttled back so the rear elements could catch up. This last type of assembly took longer and was only possible when enemy fighter attacks were not to be expected.

The ordered formation is assumed during the assembly.

(3) **Flying Formation**. In the formation the following basic demands must be satisfied:

(a) The formation leader must be able to oversee his entire formation.
(b) No lagging behind, keep the formation closed up laterally and vertically. The fulfilling of requirement (b) insured at the same time the maneuverability inside the formation, the observations of the entire air space, and protection against enemy fighters. Even if enemy A.A. opened up, the effect of the fire could be escaped by evasive flying.

The formation most frequently used was the Gruppe 'vic'. Between the individual aircraft the following distances were observed in each Schwarm:

Lateral interval – 5–6 wingspans
Front to rear – ½ aircraft length
Vertical interval – ½ aircraft height

The last Schwarm in every Staffel was stepped up about 150–300 feet and took over for the time being the fighter cover for the Staffel.

The observation jobs in a formation were assigned as follows:

(a) Schwarm leader: Observation of the ground and orientation.

(b) Pilots on each flank of the formation: Look-outs for enemy fighters (must be especially good pilots).

To make easy the assembly and the keeping of formation, the Staffeln were designated by colors (Staff-blue, 1st-white, 2nd-red, 3rd-yellow). These colors were used on the numbering on the fuselage of the aircraft, from 1 to 16. Staffs were indicated with chevrons or dashes before the numbers, and the propeller spinners were painted the same color. The special unit insignia like coats-of-arms and so on which were used early in the war were later forbidden on grounds of security in ground attack units.

At low levels, the column of Schwarms was sometimes preferred. The following is a detailed breakdown of the average type of formation shown schematically.

Schwarm formation, schematic, for F.W.190 ground attack units.
As Viewed From Above.

```
                    1
                           3
          2
                             4
```

As Viewed From the Side.

```
              4
        3
              2
        1
```

Staffel Formation As Viewed From Above.

```
    1st Schwarm
                        2nd Schwarm
      4th Schwarm
      150–300 feet higher
                             3rd Schwarm
```

As Viewed From the Side.

3rd Schwarm
2nd Schwarm
1st Schwarm

Gruppe 'Vic' Formation, Schematic.
As Viewed From Above.

Staff Schwarm
With C.O.

1st Staffel

2nd Staffel

3rd Staffel
600–1200 feet higher

As Viewed From the Side

2nd Staffel
1st Staffel
Staff Schwarm with C.O.

As Viewed From Head On.

3rd Staffel

2nd Staffel

1st Staffel

Staff Schwarm with C.O.

(4) **The flight in to the target.** Important points are: (a) course; and (b) altitude.

(a) *Course*: Usually a direct course was flown to the target from the airfield or from the place of rendezvous with the fighter escort. In very obscure country, especially prominent landmarks were flown over. Over already conquered territory infested with partisans the course often led along the safe railroads or roads. When targets were hard to find, points in the vicinity of the target which were easy to see were first approached.

In the determining of the course, the enemy defensive situation, in the air as well as on the ground, had to be taken into consideration. As far as possible enemy fighter airfields, fighter areas, and known A.A. concentration points were detoured. Further, repeated changes of course were used to confuse the enemy observer corps.

All such deviations from the basic course from airfield to target and back to airfield further limited the already small range of German aircraft and thus were not always possible, especially when the target was already just about at the limit of the F.W. 190's range.

(b) *Altitude:* As a matter of principle, a high approach flight was favored. By high approach is meant all altitudes above the effective range of light A.A. guns, or about 4,500 feet. For missions in the vicinity of the front, an altitude of about 4,500 to 7,500 feet was adequate, while for deeper penetrations greater altitudes were desirable. In the final analysis the decisive things in determining altitude were the type of attack intended and the strength of enemy air defenses. In areas with strong fighter protection, an altitude of 15,000 feet or a flight just under the ceiling was necessary to prevent surprise by enemy fighters from above.

To insure surprise, flight at tree top levels was sometimes effective. In this way, enemy A.A. was limited in its effectiveness and early detection by enemy radar was prevented.

A very important factor for the determination of the course and altitude as well was the weather. 'The weather is the terrain of the flyer.' Skillful use of weather was the duty of every formation leader. Especially liked was medium cloud of 4/10 to 6/10 at altitudes of about 6000 feet. Such weather permitted a relatively well covered flight in, but permitted at the same time a certain orientating by looking at the earth. Closed cloud layers under 3000 feet often forced the aircraft to fly at tree top levels, in order to cancel out ground fire, which was especially effective against aircraft silhouetted against a low ceiling.

(5) **Conduct of Attacks.** (a) Dive Attacks; (b) Shallow dive attacks; (c) Low level attacks; (d) Leading formations; (e) Radio traffic; (f) Anti-tank raids; and (g) Attacks against shipping.

(a) *Dive attacks*: Upon approaching the target, the attack formation is assumed. Within the Staffel the attack formation is usually the battle column (*Gefechtsreihe*).
Battle Column:

```
              T
                T
     T
                    T
        T
              T
     T              T
           T
                T
     T
                    T
```

This formation is purposely vague, to allow plenty of jockeying around to get on the target and to present no regular target to A.A. Each Schwarm leader stays ahead of his Schwarm, but otherwise position goes by the board The Rotten (2s) try to keep contact too.

Within the Gruppe the formation of the Staffeln is arranged according to the type, size, and area of the target.

Where ground A.A. is very strong and targets fixed and easy to recognize, the dive is started directly from the altitude of approach. The direction of the dive was determined by the wind and the form of the target. If possible an attempt was made to utilize the clouds and sun for cover and to so carry out the dive that directly after the dropping of bombs, the pull out and flight away would take place over undefended areas in the direction of home.

It was important that the attack be carried out in the shortest possible time. (With formation well closed up to prevent the A.A. from bringing guns to bear on stragglers).

The formation leader had to have his formation strictly under control. He determined the entire details of the attack, i.e. start of dive, dive angle (80–50°), pulling out, and the get away. Formation leading with the help of radio was not necessary except in special cases.

Attacks on moving or inconspicuous targets were begun from medium altitude. Where the approach altitude was high, the formation sacrificed altitude toward the target and reached the final altitude by curving dives or short repeated dives, to reduce A.A. effectiveness. During this loss of altitude, the formation leader assigned targets by radio.

The dropping altitude was set according to the defense, the type and especially the size of the target, and the necessary radius of the pull-out curve, determined by the speed of the aircraft, resulting from the angle, length, and speed of the dive. Usually the dropping altitude was about 3000 feet.

If the attack was to be carried out in a single dive, the bombs were dropped in salvo or one after the other, according to the nature of the target. The bombing technique is especially laid down in OKL Tactical Instructions, #4 of 13 May 1944.

(b) *Shallow Dive Attacks*: Shallow dive attacks were carried out when the permissible altitude was no longer sufficient for a dive attack, because of ceiling, visibility of target, or when the target was only weakly protected. The dive began usually from about 3,000–6,000 feet, and the angle lay between 50° and 20°. Attack formation and direction of attack were determined by the same factors as in dive attacks.

The dropping altitude was determined by bomb type and fuse type, and basically bombs were dropped from as low as possible to insure more hits. As far as ground defenses allowed, attacks were repeated several times. In such cases, the bombs were dropped by each aircraft in pairs or singly.

During shallow dive attacks the possibility of simultaneous strafing arose, fire was not opened more than 800 yards from the target. In ground attack missions it proved wise, first to shoot a little below the target, if strikes could be seen on the terrain in question. After successful lateral correction, the aircraft was just nearer enough to the target that the shot then lay on the target.

(c) *Low Level Attacks*: Low level attacks were carried on in bad weather or where surprise was required. Success with bombs was small against most ground targets on such attacks, since the bombs had to be dropped with some delayed action in order not to endanger the dropping aircraft with fragments or blast. If possible, they pulled up to 900 to 1200 feet just short of the target in order to recognize the target better and more effectively attack it.

A special type of bombing at low level was the so-called turnip bomb run (a type of mast-high bombing). It was used against shipping and by some experts even against tanks.

Since the effect of bombs in low level attacks was usually minor, the main effort in such attacks lay in strafing. Low level attacks made from a low level approach needed especially good preparation, since the locating of targets and proper attacking units was difficult and absolutely had to click.

(d) *Leading Formations*: As a matter of principle, as far as the ground defenses permitted it, as many attacks as possible were carried through one after another. For this purpose strict control by the formation leader was necessary. He had to get his Staffeln onto the various targets according to their importance and still hold the formation together. It was the rule that the small units, like the Staffeln and Schwärme had to insure their own cohesion.

Since during such missions of long duration the formation was subject to fighter attacks, the formation leader had to use parts of his forces at altitude for fighter cover, in case no additional fighter cover had been provided.

If A.A. defense was anticipated, usually parts of the units were from the beginning entrusted with combatting the A.A. In other cases, the formation leader committed during the attack itself some elements for A.A. attacks. The minimum strength for attacking an A.A. position was a Schwarm, which could attack the position simultaneously from different directions with strafing and small bombs.

For every repeated attack, the correct attack position was resumed. For this purpose a relatively undefended area near the front was sought out, utilizing the great speed gained in the dive for evasive maneuvers. In this area the necessary altitude was regained and the next attack begun.

(e) *Radio Traffic*: Radio traffic was supposed to be limited to that absolutely necessary. During surprise attacks, radio silence had to prevail until the attack was carried through. R/T conversation took place usually only between the formation leader and the Staffel C.O.s, and, where Staffeln operated alone, between the Staffel C.O. and the Schwarm leaders. Other pilots were only supposed to use R/T in emergencies or to make special observations. The R/T between the formation and the ground attack control stations on the ground was conducted by the formation leader only. Call names were used, except in rare cases, not for security purposes but for purposes of better contact.

(f) *Anti-Tank Raids*: Anti-tank missions were conducted in the same manner as other ground attack missions, as shallow dive and low level attacks. For the special anti-tank units, cooperation with bomb carrying ground attack units to keep down A.A. defenses was especially important.

The most important type of anti-tank operations were those with large caliber weapons and rockets. With cannon of 3 cm. and 37 mm. the direction of attack was determined by the necessity of scoring hits of 90° angle of impact on the vulnerable parts of the tank, usually the stern. Shooting at heavily armored parts was useless. For RP attacks, these limitations did not apply.

The attack took place in Rotte or Schwarm formation, in battle column, and the interval between aircraft was large enough that the first aircraft attacking was not endangered by the ones behind it and so that mutual interference in aiming did not occur. Until reaching the effective range, 200 to 50 meters, they had to fly evasively in order to minimize the ground defense, which always got stronger and stronger. For attacks with RP the same principles pertained.

A few ground attack pilots have destroyed tanks with the turnip tactics, by approaching the target almost on the ground and released the bomb right next to the tank, so that it flew into the suspension and completely destroyed the tank.

(g) *Shipping Targets*: Against shipping targets the dive attack was most used. This was because of the defense fire, especially with warships and convoys. A freighter was attacked with at least a Schwarm, warships and destroyers with at least a Staffel. Attacks were made from various directions, to divide up the defensive fire. Large ships sailing alone could well be attacked with the turnip procedure. Light craft like motor torpedo boats could be attacked in shallow dives and strafed. Light landing craft were repeatedly attacked and destroyed on the Eastern Front by anti-tank aircraft using 3 cm. cannon and HE ammunition.

(6) **Reassembly and the Flight Back**. At the end of the ground attack operation it was important to reassemble the formation as quickly as possible. By radio or by signal (like waggling the wings) the formation leader gave the order for reassembly. In so doing he flew with the first elements, all throttled back, and continually curving to make a quick reassembly easier for the rest of the formation. This type of assembly always took place in areas where defense was weak.

The flight back took place in the same formation as the flight in. As often as possible, the altitude was not less than 3,000 feet and the route avoided defended spots just as on the approach. Over friendly territory, the formation flew back along roads used by our troops. They kept a little away from the roads themselves, so that friendly troops could see them but would not become too disturbed.

(7) **Landing**. The landing took place by Staffeln. The Staffeln landed in a column as quickly as possible. The Staffeln remained in flight formation over the field until their turn came to land.

(8) **Success Report**. For operations of ground attack units in support of the army, a detailed success report for the mission was very important. The sooner this report got to headquarters the quicker it could be utilized. Therefore after landing the various pilots assembled around their Staffel CO. The CO's took down the reports about the victories, observation reports, and serviceability of the aircraft. Immediately afterward, each went to the Gruppe CO. The latter had already reported to headquarters by telephone any special events which had occurred. On the basis of the reports of the Staffel CO's the detailed success report was now relayed on to the headquarters. It contained: victories scored, losses, conclusions about the enemy situation, front lines, ground defense, fighter defense, and other special remarks. Finally the new probable time of next readiness was reported, together with the number of serviceable aircraft.

CHAPTER 20

Mistakes and Omissions in the GAF Ground Attack Arm

By Generalmajor Hitschhold
At Latimer House, England, 24 October 1945

1.   The prerequisite for successful and lasting operations of ground attack units is air superiority. Wherever the Germans did not have air superiority, their ground attack operations were almost always ineffective. This lesson was confirmed in Africa, in Italy, and on the Western Front. There, suffering from high losses of aircraft, planned and effective support of ground operations was *not* achieved. Raising the number of ground attack units would only have been useful if air superiority could have been won back.

2.   The tactical support of armies from the air requires, in addition to attacks on small individual targets, action against large area targets. In the GAF there were no special TE bomber units set up for this purpose. Instead, as an improvised solution, bomber units originally organized and equipped for strategic operations were used. With the later attempt to use these bombers for their original purpose (converting of Fliegerkorps IV to long range bombing in the east) the effective use of these aircraft in the tactical area was stopped completely. Its absence was appreciably felt.

3.   The technical planning was not far-seeing enough. Despite the continuous increase in the effectiveness of enemy defense, up to 1943, the equipment of dive bomber units with the outmoded Ju.87 was continued. Only after the post of General der Schlachtflieger was created could the equipping of them with aircraft like the FW 190, which suited the combat conditions, be effected.

4.   The reconnaissance Staffeln which were very effectively attached to every ground attack Geschwader were not retained (even though they still existed with Stuka units) but were given up in 1942. The necessary reconnaissance for ground operations now had to be flown by the ground attack units themselves. Inadequate training of crews did not bring about all the success possible. The hitting power of concentrated formations was thus reduced.

Equipment and personnel shortages prevented the reestablishment of the reconnaissance units.

5. The short range of ground attack aircraft worked to the disadvantage of operations. Where there was a lack of forward airfields, operations in the depth of the tactical area might become impossible. In some cases all operations were impossible. Where the enemy had air superiority, take-offs and landings on airfields near to the front could be prevented as a result of action by enemy fighters. Moreover, the stay over the battle field, which should be as long as possible, was too limited if the airfields were far behind the front. The building of forward airfields with pierced steel planking, commonplace in the USAAF, did not happen in the German Air Force.

6. The delayed development of rocket projectile weapons was a great disadvantage. The combatting of certain targets like tanks and ships could have been considerably more effective. The goal of having every ground attack unit equipped, if necessary, for anti-tank work with rockets was not attained. This was due to the delay in beginning development and to the use in the interim of the inadequate 21 cm. army rockets which required a great amount of special training. No adequate amount of aircraft fuel for the required training could be made available.

   Furthermore, the specialization of anti-tank ground attack units resulted in tactical disadvantages. Because of their special training, they could only be used under certain circumstances, especially against tanks. Thereby long gaps between operations often came about for such units, in which they could not be used as ordinary ground attack units. In general, the development of rocket projectiles and the necessary sights was begun too late. The ground attack arm showed a way to combat targets effectively from low altitude and great ranges without coming into the anti-aircraft fire around the target.

7. The lack of rockets, bombs, or cluster bomb units (which gave good results in low level attacks) was felt especially in Russian offensives which were often conducted in bad weather. Ground attack aircraft at such times had mainly to be used for strafing attacks only because bombs dropped with delayed action fuses (to protect the aircraft against damage from their own bombs) had little effect.

8. In respect to tactics, no basic mistake or deficiency can be called to mind.

9. Because of lack of fuel, the training of new pilots was too short. A deep-

ening of flying experience could not be attained. In the ranks of new pilots, this led often to great losses in their first operations and to small successes, especially on operations in difficult situations where enemy defense was strong. The necessary training in instrument flying and blind flying had to be almost entirely left out.

10. The replacement and supply system of ground attack officers was far too small. After we suffered heavy losses of Staffel and Gruppe COs, it was often impossible to replace them with satisfactory officers with good experience. This led repeatedly to situations where NCO's led Staffeln in operations.

The training units could not entirely be Staffed with experienced and fully qualified officers.

A planned school for formation leaders and Staffel COs (formation leaders course) could not easily be carried out, because officers would have had to be called in from their training or operational units for the course. A reserve of officers which were temporarily not fully occupied was never available. The same thing came up when officers had to be sent to pilot schools, officer training schools, and staffs. The interests of the supply of new men and the success of operations prevented the units sending only bad officers to meet these needs. Replacements for those sent to these tasks were seldom supplied. The consequence was many vacancies in the operational units. A planned exchange of men between the front and the homeland to give crews timely and sufficient rest time was out of the question.

11. The operations of ground attack units was controlled by commands staffed by officers who partly had not experience in ground attack operations. Their decisions were often impractical and did not get the most out of the units. It was sought to have these positions occupied by experienced ground attack men, but in view of the lack of officers in the ground attack arm this was very difficult.

Courses for all the officers in command positions were planned from the autumn of 1944, but they never were carried through. In these courses the high commanders, their chiefs of staff, and operations officers, were to get a broad perspective over the operational principles and possibilities of air force units in cooperating with the army.

12. The lack of understanding throughout the army or about cooperation with the air force made [more difficult] the successful cooperation of the two forces. The army often made demands which were impossible to carry out. On the other hand, the army did not always utilize the effect of air raids

which were carried out. A planned training of all army officers in air operations was lacking. This was first recognized very late.

13. The establishment of the office of General der Schlachtflieger, combining oversight of the ground attack and dive bomber units under one *Waffengeneral*, did not take place until too late. The result was that the following main jobs were not carried out on time:

    a. Evaluation of flying units which operated in the tactical areas, combining of their experiences, the evaluation of these and incorporation into training.

    b. Unified technical planning for ground attack units (especially belated conversion from the Ju.87 to the FW 190).

    c. Expansion of cooperation with the army, especially in supporting the training of the army.

    d. Training of formation leaders.

14. The operation readiness of ground attack units often suffered by repeated transfers, because the units did not have enough transport space to take with them sufficient technical equipment and personnel. Not enough transport aircraft were available for this. Furthermore, the equipping of formations with trucks was not adequate, and the ones available were not equal to the terrain conditions which often confronted them, especially in the bad weather period in Russia. In addition the available number of trucks was continually being reduced so that the maintaining of operational readiness of units was difficult and the number of sorties went down.

Part 4
The Defensive War

This is the story of the evolution of organization, operations, weapons and tactics to meet the relentless Allied day bomber offensive that continually presented the Luftwaffe fighter force with an increasingly powerful and capable enemy and – in the form of the P-51 over Berlin – the instrument of its ultimate defeat. The vast majority of the fighter force was thrown into these losing battles, and they are the reason why it is estimated that the overall wartime mortality of Luftwaffe fighter pilots was over 90 per cent. (Postwar, Galland invited Douglas Bader, the legless RAF ace, to a German fighter pilot's reunion. Bader, upon entering, was obviously disappointed. 'I didn't think we left this many of you bastards alive.' Galland replied, 'Oh, you didn't. Most of these bastards were on the Eastern Front. Come, I'll introduce you.')

In this chapter, in addition to the postwar interrogations, are included three wartime documents, two written by Galland himself and one by the GAF Operational Staff from drafts by Galland and his staff. These show how Galland's responsibility to direct tactical and operational evolution was carried out and how the anti-bomber focus evolved from the initial battles (focusing on a few formations of fighters over France in 1942) to the massive climactic battles of 1944 (focusing on massed formations of fighters assembled from throughout Germany).

CHAPTER 21

The Evolution of
the Defense of the Reich

Interrogation of Generalleutnant Galland,
Oberstleutnant Bär and Oberstleutnant Dahl
At Kaufbeuren, Germany, 20–23 September 1945

In the build-up period of the Luftwaffe, the defensive and point-protection use of fighters was planned as a secondary mission. During the Polish Campaign only about 6 Gruppen were held back in the West for protective purposes. Even after the declaration of war by France and England, Germany did not reckon with any offensive aerial warfare from the West.

After the end of the Polish Campaign, the movement of all fighter units to fields behind the West Wall, in the Ruhr, and in northwest Germany took place.

The first successes of fighter units in defensive warfare were against large RAF Wellington formations attacking Wilhelmshafen in 1939.

Until the beginning of the campaign in the West in June 1940, German fighters were given only purely defensive missions. From the beginning of the French campaign until 1941, the fighter arm went over completely to the offensive.

In general, fighter units were under Fliegerkorps or Fliegerdivisionen. For temporary defensive operations, formation leaders were themselves responsible for operations. Already before the beginning of the campaign in the West in May 1940, while the fighter units were forming behind the front, two Jafus were set up, one for each Luftflotte in the West (2 and 3), but these Jafus did not actually appear until the Battle of Britain in August 1940.

Only after the movement of most fighter units to the Eastern Front in the Spring of 1941 did the fighter force in the West have to go over to the defensive again. The well-known operations of German fighters of J.G.2 and J.G.26 in the West in this period were not the predecessors of Defense of the Reich, but the actual beginning of it. The air war took place over the western coastal areas; behind these areas there was little activity, reflecting the limited range of enemy daylight operations.

Building Up of Signals Systems

This was begun at the end of 1940 along the Dutch, Belgian and French coasts. In the later course of events, night fighting with the XII Fliegerkorps won the unequivocal lead position in resource allocation.

The necessary signals facilities for defensive aerial fighter operations were neglected in 1939 and 1940 because of the offensive role of the fighter force in these years. The planning and the unexpected course of the Russian campaign now presented signals construction demands which were impossible to fulfill in time. This was especially true for night fighting and also for day operations. The period of need could have been bridged with sufficient fighter forces, but these were just what was lacking.

For Luftflotte 3 in France the following commands were set up: Jafu 2 and Jafu 3, Jafu Bretagne with the Subordinate Jafu Bordeaux (Unterabschnitt Bordeaux), and the Jafu Sudfrankreich (Jafu South France). From 1941 onward, Jafus 2 and 3 with their staffs became the first fighter control units of the daylight aerial defense system of the Luftwaffe.

Over the course of the daylight bomber offensive, 1942–45, the following evolution of American operations over Germany and occupied Europe were observed:

(a) Unescorted 4-engine bomber formations.

(b) Bomber formations with partial fighter escort on outward legs and reception on return flight. No escort over the target.

(c) Missions with escort in waves, from base to target and back. Fighter escorts throughout missions.

(d) Continuous fighter escort on way in and out without reliefs.

(e) Broad fighter escort sweeps ahead of and to the flanks of the bomber formations.

(f) Release of the fighters from the narrow escort concept, going over to fighter sweeps. Pursuit of German fighters down to their fields, which were also heavily strafed.

(g) Splitting up of the large bomber formations into smaller formations.

1942

The year 1942 was the decisive year in the struggle for air superiority in the West. Under the given conditions, it was necessarily lost, even though every German fighter pilot had done more than his share. The decision was clear as the USAAF in the Fall of 1942 appeared in the ETO. The air offensive against Germany began in the second half of this year with the clear division of missions: Americans by day and RAF by night.

The measures seized upon by the German High Command to counter-act this offensive cannot be regarded as planned. They included only the most pressing momentary stop-gaps. A clearly defined defensive plan never evolved. The grounds for this were not in a false underestimation of the enemy. Rather, the entire interest of the Luftwaffe was focussed towards Russia. The over-throw of the Russians was, in 1942, seen as the most important condition for a successful continuation of the war.

So the Luftwaffe ran along from 1942 onwards. It fell farther and farther behind in the eventualities of the strategic air war. Finally, in 1944, a clear recognition of the situation (and some results) came about.

At the beginning of the first attacks by four-engined bombers against the occupied countries in the West in August 1942, only three fighter Geschwader (with about 120 fighters each) were on the Channel coast and in Holland (J.G.2, J.G.26, and J.G.1.) These Geschwaders gained the first battle experience against unescorted and escorted heavy bomber formations.

In Germany itself at this time were no fighter units besides the two OTUs, Erganzungs Jagdgruppen West and Sud, which had little or no operational significance. These OTUs, together with factory-testing Staffeln and the Fighter Schools, could put up only a few Schwärme, which as a result of their organization and other missions could not later successfully be used against escorted heavy bomber formations.

1943

When, in January 1943, the daylight attacks began to traverse North-west Germany, including the North Sea Coast, a new Geschwader, J.G. 11, was set up in the area of Jagddivision 2, near Bremen. This Geschwader flew, along, with J.G.1, based in Holland, against the first missions over German territory since the daylight attacks of the RAF during the Polish campaign.

In 1943 Jafus 2 and 3 were placed under the Higher Jafu West (Hohere Jafu West), the predecessor of the II Jagdkorps, not yet approved by the High Command.

At the beginning of 1943 several fighter Gruppen were withdrawn from the East and the South, and transferred to Northwest Germany to build up the Defense of the Reich. In the summer of 1943, J.G.27 and J.G.3 were transferred into Germany with all their Gruppen for the protection of the Ruhr and the basins of the Rhein and Main Rivers. Besides these Gruppen, two high altitude formations were set up for combatting high-flying reconnaissance aircraft such as Mosquitos. They were J.G.25 in the Berlin area under Obstlt. Ihlefeld and J.G.50 in the Rhine-Main basin, both equipped with the

Me. 109G-5, with pressure cabins and ether methanol or GM 1 injection in their engines. They were set up by order of Goring.

In the fall of 1943 was created II Jagdkorps with Jagddivision 4 under it, containing the area of the former Jafu 2 (now Jafu 4), and Jagddivision 5, containing the area of the former Jafu 3 (now Jafu 5). Jagddivision 6 was planned for South France, but was not set up.

In Germany itself, under Luftwaffenbefehlshaber Mitte (GAF Command for central area, later Luftflotte Reich) developments were a little further along. Fighters under Luftwaffenbefehlshaber Mitte were commanded by the XII Fliegerkorps of Kammhuber. Influenced by the clear organization and fine signals network of Kammhuber's XII Fliegerkorps, Divisionen were formed early. Since Kammbuber's unit had night fighters almost exclusively at first, the Jagddivisionen first set up under it were really night fighter Divisionen. The day fighters which were set up to operate under XII Fliegerkorps as Allied aerial activity increased over Germany in 1942–43 were controlled not by the newly created Jagddivisionen of XII Fliegerkorps, but by the old Jafus which were already there, also under Kammhuber's XII Fliegerkorps. During 1943 the functions of the night fighter Jagddivisionen were changed into the I Jagdkorps, controlling through Jagddivisionen 1, 2, 3, and 7 all the day and night fighter units in Germany. (1945 Editor: the I Jagdkorps stayed under Luftwaffenbefelshaber Mitte, later Luftflotte Reich). Its CO was Kammhuber, until Beppo Schmid replaced him in Fall 1943. Schmid kept command until Winter 1944–45, when he turned command over to Hut for the Ardennes offensive and himself took over Luftwaffenkommando West, the unit which replaced Luftflotte 3 when the Germans were driven out of France. Under Schmid in late 1943 and in 1944, Jagdkorps I became the most powerful command in the control of the fighter defense of Germany. The next higher command, Luftflotte Reich, which controlled and commanded *all* Luftwaffe units in Germany, was not important for the actual running and planning of fighter operations.

Jagdkorps II, set up in France and controlling Jagddivisionen 4 and 5, was under Luftflotte III. The first CO of Jagdkorps II was Jung, who was succeeded by Bulowius at the time of the invasion in June 1944. Bulowius functioned well during the terrible retreat into Germany, and there Peltz, himself a bomber man, took over the Korps, to lead it disastrously through the Ardennes offensive and the 1st January attack on Allied airfields. Schmid was not even a pilot, but he was far better than Peltz. Jagdkorps II was dissolved in the first catastrophic months of 1945.

Meanwhile the enemy from the West flew, on the 15 August 1943, the

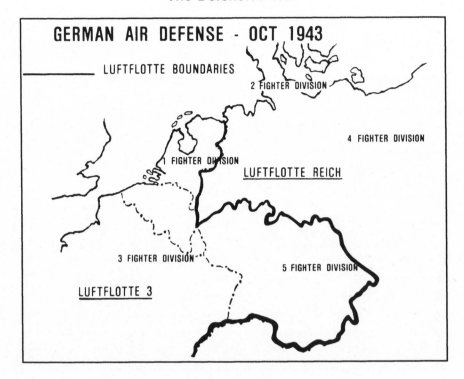

GERMAN AIR DEFENSE - OCT 1943

LUFTFLOTTE BOUNDARIES

2 FIGHTER DIVISION

4 FIGHTER DIVISION

1 FIGHTER DIVISION

LUFTFLOTTE REICH

3 FIGHTER DIVISION

5 FIGHTER DIVISION

LUFTFLOTTE 3

first really deep penetration raid into the Reich; the first attack on the Schweinfurt ball bearing industry. At the same time, the southern air front was opened with attacks on Southern Germany and Austria from the Foggia area.

It was planned to set up Jagdkorps II in the south East but this was cancelled. No fighter Units were available to warrant the setting up of another corps. With the coming of the second air front from the south, Jagdkorps I therefore had to combat also the attacks from Africa and Italy into Germany.

As a counter, in September 1943, J.G.27 was sent to the Vienna area and J.G.3 to the Munich area. Z.G.26 was used in northern Germany and Z.G.76 in Southern Germany in conjunction with the fighter units in these areas. Thus, by the time of the second attack on Schweinfurt on 14 October 1943, all the fighter and Zerstorer forces then stationed in Germany could effectively be brought to bear. In this action, the Zerstorer units with the 21 cm. RP proved to be especially effective.

The bomber mission of 14 October 1943 was the last attack by four-engine bombers without fighter escort to the target area. After that,

Thunderbolts and Lightnings (usually in small numbers), were with the bombers continually over the target area.

1944

At the beginning of 1944 the fighter escort was continually strengthened by the Allies, making the combatting of bomber formations more and more difficult. Especially for the twin engine fighters (Zerstoren), the missions became, as a result of their technical inferiority, more and more dangerous. Most German fighter formations at this time flew attacks from head on. This type of attack required very good flying and shooting ability. Because our units still exhibited high cohesion in formation flying, the attack from head on was still possible. Some successes resulted.

However, despite the later success with head-on attacks by the Sturmgruppen, the attack from the rear became standard in the fighter force. Closed-up flying of the entire Gruppe of fighters with the smallest possible interval between aircraft, opening of fire from very close range, and good discipline were prerequisites for the successful carrying out of attacks from the rear. On the whole, this type of attack brought more victories than the attack from head on, which was harder from a flying and gunnery standpoint. Especially for the young pilot and because of the progressive decline of formation flying skills, we considered that the attack from the rear was best.

Still another Jagddivision, the 8th, had to be set up in the Vienna area and in Hungary. In Hungary the German Jafu Hungary led the German and Hungarian fighters there. In Silesia and Jafu Schlesien and in East Prussia the Jafu Ostpreussen were set up under Jagddivision 1. For a while the idea of setting up a Jagdkorps against the East was toyed with. In this was to be included the Jafu Rumanien, Jafu Bulgarien, and Jafu Griechenland (Greece), all of which were temporarily under a higher Jafu Balkan. Day and night fighting were combined under these Jafus. Despite the participation of Rumanian and Bulgarian fighter units in fighter operations, the air defense of the Balkans was prevented, by lack of strength, from ever getting out of the token stage.

Terrific overloading of the organizational set up and the High Command would have resulted if either the Russians or the Americans had opened up a third air front from the East against Germany. Even the operating of American fighters from the East in cooperation with bomber attacks from the West would have brought a great deal of difficulty for the High Command in the Defense of the Reich.

In early 1944, the concentration of previously dispersed fighter forma-

tions into fighter geographical areas took place and the use of larger formations was accomplished. These were called Gefechtsverbände. The purpose
of this change was to bring larger fighter forces against the bombers in smaller
intervals of time and space. Up until then the fighter Gruppen had run one
after another – into the fighter escort. The Gefechtsverbände formed were
J.G.1 in Holland, J.G. 11 and 3 in the Westphalia and Rhine areas, J.G.z.b.V
(with three Gruppen under it) in the Rhein-Main basin, and J.G. 27 covering Linz, Passau, and Vienna.

In May 1944, the first planned enlargement of Gruppen in the Defense
of the Reich took place. This included raising the strength of each Staffel
from 12 to 16 aircraft. More significant was the adding of a 4th Staffel per
Gruppe, (drawing these Staffeln from Geschwader in the East). These changes
brought about the long awaited '1000 Fighter Missions'. The Luftwaffe would
now be capable of sending a thousand sorties against a massed USAAF
bomber mission. But this never took place.

A still closer concentration of the Gefechtsverbande was made for the
purpose of mass missions at the end of May 1944 with the transfer of six
fighter Gruppen into the Nürnberg-Ansback-Würzburg area. These were
placed under the Staff of Geschwader z.b.V. (A special staff set up to control miscellaneous units which were separated from their home units.) The
centralized position of those Gruppen under Geschwader z.b.V was favorable for them to engage attacks from the South as well as for attacks from
the West.

This strengthening of fighter units did not continue, however, because of
the invasion on 6 June 1944. This forced the transfer of almost all fighter
units to the West, except for Geschwader z.b.V, J.G.300 and J.G.301 (these
units had been set up for single engine night fighting and converted in
Summer 1944 to day fighting in bad weather). As a result, on 7 June 1944,
there were only 4 regular SE fighter aircraft ready to start in the Defense of
the Reich.

Now there followed the conversion of the SE night fighters to day fighting, and J.G. 300 and 301 were converted. In the middle of June the transfer of the single existing Sturmgruppe, J.G.3, from the invasion front back
into Germany took place. By the end of June, the conversion of J.G.300 was
so far along that IV/J.G.3 could be combined with J.G.300 into a
Gefechtsverband, under the Geschwader staff of J.G.300. Thus for the first
time since the beginning of the invasion a formation strong enough to give
battle was set up for the Defense of the Reich. Its average strength on a
mission was about 100–120 fighters. The first successful mission of this

formation was on 7 July 1944, when the ex-night fighters of J.G.300 gave a good account of themselves. It should be noted that the conversion of these SE night fighters to day operations took place with no break in operations.

In mid-July, II/J.G.300 was formed into the second Sturmgruppe of the Defense of the Reich. At the end of July a third Sturmgruppe, II/J.G.4, was organized, drawing its cadre from the two Sturmgruppen already in existence. The missions of July and August 1944 were flown only by those Sturmgruppen and their escort Gruppen, IV/J.G.3, II/J.G.300, and II/J.G.4. Meanwhile, in the Reich, the rebuilding of the Gruppen beaten down on the invasion front was taking place. A reserve of about 700 fighters was built up for the purpose of strengthening the Defense of the Reich. Hitler ordered instead that this reserve be thrown into the invasion front, where German forces were already in full retreat. Despite this, three large Gefechtsverbande could be formed in the north of Germany with fighter units withdrawn from the West. For the big missions of 11, 12 and 13 September 1944, 400–500 fighters were again put up against the enemy. On these missions it was possible to use the various Gefechtsverbande concentrated in time and space. Although these missions brought considerable victories against the bombers, a large number of German fighters were shot down by the American fighter escort, mostly Mustangs.

As a result of these losses, especially against fighters going after the bombers, in a series of conferences, among them one at the Hq. of Hitler on 15th September, 1944, the Geschwader Kommodore demanded a clear division between escort and attack fighters (Sturmjäger) with the ratio of 3:1 or at least 2:1. The highest order of the high command remained as before: the principle that the main function of German fighters was to shoot down bombers and that combat with fighters was to be avoided (Galland says: 'I was in sharp opposition to this order. It was, in my opinion, false to try to get to the bombers with the Sturmjagers escorted in this type of defensive fighter formation. I would have allotted a fighter escort to the Sturmgruppe in a ratio of 1:1. For the rest, I would have had the other 50 fighters attack the enemy fighter escort without giving them any escort missions for the Sturmgruppen. The Tactical Regulations which were given out at this time were given out against my will.')

In the meantime the Western Front had been thrown back to the Siegfried Line. Fighter operations during this retreat had been extremely ineffective. On the Rhein a new grouping of forces resulted:

JG 26 at the northern end of the line.

J.G. 27 in the Bonn area.

J.G. 2 in the Frankfurt area.

J.G.53 on the southern end.

All the rest of the Jagdgeschwader were in the area of Jagd-division 1 in Central Germany around Berlin, either flying against bombers or building up again. The southern front was stripped of fighters, the same as South Germany and Austria. The great effort which was still possible was termed 'The Big Blow', a massive proposed attack on a daylight raid on Berlin. This required a realigning of all Geschwader and concentration of forces in the Berlin area for a great action.

Temporarily J.Gs. 3, 4, 11 and other units had to be transferred into the Holland area for combat against English airborne operations at Arnhem. They returned later to the area of Jagd-division 1.

Now the 'Big Blow' was feverishly prepared for. By mid-November, the Geschwader were up to the increased strength. J.G. 27 was pulled back from the West to take part in the 'Big Blow' in the area of Jagd-division 1. There were now available J.G. 300, 301, 1, 3, 4, 6, 11, 27, and 77, all under Jagdkorps I, with a considerable proportion of inexperienced pilots. Jagdkorps II, with JG 2, 53, and 26, was to combat the bombers on the way out. The forces under Jagdkorps I could, for the most part, have flown a second mission against the bombers on the big day, so that at least 2,000 fighters of Jagdkorps I could have flown the first mission and 500 the second, while Jagdkorps II could have put up at least 150 fighters. 80–100 night fighters were ready to take part and attack stragglers.

The 'Big Blow' (planned by Galland) never took place. Up until the transfer of all these forces into the West to support the Ardennes offensive, bad weather prevented the carrying through of the mission. Then, in late November and early December, all the Geschwader but J.G.300 and J.G.301 were transferred into the West, to be used up in a type of combat for which they were not trained, experienced or equipped. With the Ardennes offensive, the history of the organized Defense of the Reich comes to an end. It went on through January in sporadic form and continued until the end of the war with the Me.262 missions.

Conclusions

(a) The building up of the Defense of the Reich was organic only as far as the command and control organizations were concerned. No special units were always assigned to defense against bombers.

(b) All decisions were made too late and then were not far-seeing enough.

(c) Decisive in the Defense of the Reich was not the command organizations, but the strength of the fighter units.

(d) The Russian campaign and the African and Italian campaigns prevented the preparation and building-up of adequate forces for the Defense of the Reich.

(e) In complete mis-recognition of the situation, the necessary materials, production, and personnel were not given to the fighter force.

(f) The final recognition of the situation came in summer 1944, when it was too late.

(g) The final recognition of the situation in 1944 was manifested by the preparation of the first two 1000 fighter missions and then the Big Blow. All these attempts were liquidated either by the High Command or by the situation.

(h) Despite all these errors, the decisive factor in the Defense of the Reich was the American fighter. Without the fighter escort and its depth of penetration, it would have been possible to stop the day attacks.

(i) The operational superiority won by the long range American fighter was only to be counteracted by a German fighter arm which was superior in strength, fighting ability, and technical achievement. The means for building up such a force were not made available to the fighter arm.

(j) The threat posed by escort fighters was not properly appreciated by the German High Command. They were not interested in them because they did no direct damage to Germany; nevertheless, a success against the bombers could only be achieved when the fighter escort was beaten down or knocked out altogether.

(k) The tactical employment of German fighters in the Defense of the Reich was often false, for reasons set out in point (j).

(l) The training of pilots and the production of aircraft were not well coordinated, but were constantly out of harmony, due to the Russian campaign, lack of fuel, and the keeping up of bomber production.

(m) The problem of large fighter missions in very bad weather against enemy formations over the clouds was never successfully solved by the Germans in regard to training, flying safety, flying control, radio navigation aids, and equipment.

(n) It was not appreciated what had to be done to break down Allied air superiority and what the consequences would be if this superiority was not broken down.

(o) The armament program neglected quality for numbers, not developing new types with more powerful engines. A force inferior in numbers can only hold its own through superior quality.

(p) Only the Me. 262 had the necessary superiority. The story of its development and belated use tell the reasons behind the final dramatic collapse of the Luftwaffe.

CHAPTER 22

Attacks on Heavy Bombers

Interrogation of Generalleutnant Galland
At Latimer House, England, 15 October 1945

The first experiences against heavy bombers by GAF fighters were the attacks on RAF Stirlings. Stirlings had weak defensive armament. The GAF shot some down despite large escorts, causing the British to withdraw them from daylight operations.

The next heavy bomber encountered by the German fighters was the American B-17. First attacked from the rear, this resulted in heavy losses for the German fighters. It was realized very quickly that the armor and armament of the fighters must be increased.

The head-on attack on bombers was developed by Hauptmann Egon Mayer in November 1942. The first victory using these tactics over a B-17 came on 23 November 1942 over St. Nazaire as the result of a head-on attack by a F.W.190. The GAF operated on the principle of breaking up the formations by a head-on attack and then concentrating on single bombers by attacks from the rear.

When the B-17's began making evasive maneuvers as a defensive measure against head-on attacks, the GAF realized that they must develop a safe and effective attack from the rear.

The GAF encountered no difficulties in shooting down Russian bombers.

Special Methods of Attacking Heavy Bombers. Dive bombing, towing bombs on cables, parachute bombs, steel nets, hand grenades, very heavy cannon and other unusual methods of attack were experimented with, but none of these were practical or effective and were not employed more than a few times. Air-to-air bombing and rearward-firing rockets were promising but developments came too late in the war.

Attacks on Medium Bombers. Medium bombers were not attacked from head-on because of the great closing speed. GAF fighter pilots did not fear the fire from the rear of medium bomber formations as much as they did that of heavy bombers.

CHAPTER 23

Weapons for Combating
Four-Engine Bombers by Day

Interrogation of Generalleutnant Galland, Oberstleutnant
Bär, Oberstleutnant Dahl, Oberst Petersen
At Kaufbeuren, Germany, 12–14 September 1945

General: The mass defensive fire-power of the close formations of American heavy bombers and the invulnerability of the bombers to hits showed, after the first aerial combats between German fighters and American bombers, that existing fighter armament was ineffective.

The Me.109 was at this time (1942–early 1943) armed with one MG 151 (2 cm.) and 2 × MG 17 (7.92 mm) and the F.W.190 with two or four MG 151 and 2 × MG 17. The ballistics of these weapons did not permit effective fire at ranges greater than 500–600 yards. The defensive fire of the bombers was, however, effective even at these ranges.

Since, in addition, German fighters could not satisfactorily master the mass attack from the rear, or from the front, the demand grew for new weapons. The tactical and technical requirements for the basic armament of fighters was decisively influenced by this situation. But the situation could not permit waiting until new models were in production. Emergency stop-gap measures and entirely new methods had to be found. The ultimate goal of the entire effort was the destruction of an entire close formation with special weapons and devices.

In SE fighter aircraft, TE fighter aircraft, and night fighter aircraft the following MG and cannon were used in various combinations according to model:

MG 17 7.9 mm.	200 meters effective range.
MG 81 7.9 mm.	200 meters effective range.
MG 131 13 mm.	400 meters.
MG 151 15 mm.	600 meters.
MG 151/20 20 mm.	400 meters.
MGFF 20 mm.	400 meters.

MK 103 3 cm.	800 meters.
MK 108 3 cm.	400 meters.
BK 5 5 cm.	800 meters.

The following solutions were arrived at, partly through systematically planned development by industry and the Technical Office, partly from proposals from operational units; from the various GAF Research stations; from the special testing unit, Erprobungskommando 25, set up for the purpose; from suggestions from industry, research, and from science:

1. **Me.109.** Building in 2 × MG 151 under wing armament with 60 rounds each. This addition proved good on the Eastern Front and in Defense of the Reich as long as the American fighter escort was not too strong.

Advantages: Doubling of fire power, maintenance of commonality of weapons, and good incendiary effect.

Disadvantages: Loss of 20 km/h speed, great loss of maximum altitude, and reduction of maneuverability. It was manufactured as a complete unit and could be fitted and dismounted by ground personnel. In 1944 production was stopped because enough were stocked up. Use declined as a result of American air superiority.

2. **F.W. 190.** Fitting of 4 × MG 151 under wing armanent, in two containers with about 50 rounds per gun.

Disadvantages: Loss of about 50 km/h in speed, and otherwise same as on the Me.109. Manufactured as complete units and not much used because of the great American air superiority. Was used in J.G. 1.

3. **F.W.190.** 2 × MK 108 *in* the wings with 50 rounds each as logical development of Number 2 above. Produced in series and proved good in Sturmgruppen.

4. **F.W. 190.** 2 × MK 103 under wing armament with about 40 rounds each, in addition to 2 × MK 151 and 2 × MG 17. Tested in a few models.

Advantages: High muzzle velocity, great range, and good fire effect.

Disadvantages: Speed loss of 60 km/h, aircraft not stable while firing, lowering of ceiling and reduction of maneuverability. The aircraft was overloaded with this armament.

5. **F. W. 190.** 2 × 21 cm. RP under wings. This RP was an adaptation of the ordinary German Army RP Nebelwerfer. The tubes were rifled and were jettisonable with explosive bolts. Time or impact fuses were used. Adopted upon proposals from operational units.

Advantages: Effective range of 800–1200 meters, outside of range of bombers' defensive fire. Good psychological effect on the bomber crews.

Disadvantages: Speed loss of 40–50 km/h plus loss of ceiling and maneuverability. Lack of range-measuring device and therefore inability to control the point of detonation. Also used at various times (the Normandy invasion, on the Eastern Front and in the Ardennes offensive) to shoot up ground targets.

6. **Me.109.** 2 × 21 cm. RP as above on the F.W.190. Me.109 was more underpowered with the armament than the F.W.190.

7. **Me.110.** 4 × 21 cm. RP, mounted in pairs under the wings. Could be discharged singly.

8. **Me.410.** 4 × 21 cm RP as in the Me.110.

9. **Me.410.** 5 × 21 cm. RP and 7 × 21 cm. RP in a battery under the fuselage. Only tested, not introduced, because of superiority of US fighter escort.

10. **Ju.88.** 8 × 21 cm. RP. built vertically into the fuselage of the aircraft to shoot upward into bomber formations from aircraft flying about 3000 feet below. Nullified by US fighter escort.

11. **He.177.** 24 × 21 cm. RP built into the fuselage, firing straight up. As Ju-88.

12. **F.W.190.** 1 × 21 cm. RP under the fuselage, firing backwards. One Staffel in defense of the Reich was so equipped, but combat testing was not finished, since inability to carry a drop tank hindered operations. Tactics: Fly low over the bomber formation from the front and shoot the rocket when the formation was directly underneath. The RP overtook the bomber formation in its 2-second flight and exploded in the middle of it.

13. **Me.109.** 2 and 4 × 15 cm. Army RP fired from cardboard rifled tubes under the wings, jettisonable. Further development was to be the same rocket fired from rail mounts and with collapsable fins to permit close mounting to the wings. Testing stopped because of US fighter superiority.

14. **Me.110 and 410.** 500 kg. demolition or shrapnel bomb with rocket propulsion and range of 1000 yards, with greatly curved trajectory. To be fired from the rear into bomber formations with a time fuse. Testing was stopped because of great difficulties with the rocket unit and range-finding.

15. **Do.217 and He.177.** Use of the Henschel 293 and 298 remote controlled

rocket propelled glider bombs, with wire control from mother aircraft. Ignition with proximity fuse. Technical experiments discontinued because fighter escort made operations impossible.

16. **F.W.190.** X4, a small flying bomb with rocket power and remote control by wire, a Rheinmetall-Borsig development. Testing not finished. Difficulties with the fuse and wire control. Not used on operations, but was to be used with the Me.262 if ever perfected. Tactics intended were to attack from rear from 1000 yards, steering of the flying bomb from the mother aircraft by the procedure of keeping the target in line with the bomb during flight. Shooting down of a whole bomber formation might have been possible.

17. **All Types.** 100 kg., 21 cm. incendiary RP, shot from rifled tubes and containing a great number of incendiary pellets which were propelled from the exploding rocket with a speed of about 650 feet a second. Could be used with all aircraft types which could mount the rocket tubes and was only an improvement of RP ammunition. Not used in operations because attacks on bombers with such large caliber rockets was at that time already outmoded.

18. **Me.110.** 37 mm. Flak 18 or Flak 42 A.A. cannon. Tested experimentally in combat by one Gruppe of Z.G. 26 with satisfactory results for a while. Difficulties with the functioning of the weapons at cold temperatures. Also low rate of fire and small ammunition supply, 28 rounds. Not in series production, aircraft especially equipped for testing. Testing stopped because of great losses inflicted on the TE fighters by US fighter escort.

19. **Me.410.** 2 × MK 103 and 2 × MG 151 built into the fuselage. Produced as the factory-built armament of some Me.410's. Not used in Defense of the Reich because by the time it was ready, the Me.410 had to be withdrawn from operations.

20. **Me.410.** The 5 cm. tank cannon (Kwk 5) was converted into the aircraft cannon Bordkanone 5 for use in this aircraft, and equipped with belt feed for 12 rounds, at 60 rounds a minute cyclic rate of fire, and muzzle velocity of about 300 feet per second. Planned for use in aircraft against tanks and tried out in Summer 1943. After its appearance it was deemed by Hitler to be the Luftwaffe weapon of the future, in opposition to the opinions of the technical and tactical experts and the operational units themselves. Goring also favored the BK 5. Hitler tried to carry over into the air the success of anti-tank units on the ground, completely misunderstanding the requirements. Again and again he ordered the BK 5 as the primary armament for

heavy fighters and TE fighters. Impossibly high weight, great space requirements, low rate of fire, limited likelihood of hitting the target as a result of the natural movement of the aircraft, low reliability, small number of rounds and the necessity of remaining so long in firing position to achieve hits with the slow rate of fire were the main disadvantages of the whole theory. Only laymen could conjure up the 'fact' that it was ballistically possible to shoot a bomber down at 1000 yards with one shot. Thus also arose the demand for:

21. **Me.262.** With the BK 5.

22. **Air-to-Air Bombing**. Tried from fighter bombers, TE fighters, and jet fighters. Fuses experimented with were time, barometric, and electric remote controlled. Bombs used were demolition and shrapnel cases of 250 and 500 kg. bombs filled with 1, 2, and 10 kg. fragmentation bombs. The whole project failed because of improper sights, measurement of altitude, and non-functioning of barometric and electric fuses. The effect was only to be achieved by fragmentation and incendiaries and not by blast. This project was continually pushed by laymen and empire builders.

23. **Cable Bombing**. Use of 10 kg. bombs slung on cables about 300 feet long and hung singly on F.W. 190's. Tactics were to attack from the front and exit flat over the bombers. Tested in combat with two unconfirmed victories. Experiments stopped because the bomb tended to trail behind the F.W.190 rather than hang down, because the bomb swung about too much, and because the aircraft had to come very close to the bombers to achieve victories.

24. **Detonating Cord**. Hung from small counterweighted parachute and dropped into bomber formations to mine the air space. Tests proved that amounts required were too great and success too small.

25. **Special Materials**. Liquid and powdered materials were experimented with for clouding up windshields or clogging engines, but it was found that they could not be carried and dropped in the necessary quantities.

26. **Weapons which were used with photo-electric cell firing**. In the F.W.190 three MK 103 rocket tubes with a single shot each pointing upward at 70–80° were fired by photo-electric cell when flying under the bomber formation.

27. **Harp**. 21 cm. rocket tubes mounted on both sides of the F.W. 190 fuselage firing obliquely upward.

28. **Rohrblock.** Several 3 cm. barrels either perpendicular or oblique with recoil arrangement. To minimize recoil, the whole weapon dropped out when fired. The weapon could also be built to fire downward.

29. **Automatic multi-barrelled weapon.** About sixty 2 cm. barrels in a bundle electrically fired in a fraction of a second could fire up or down and gave a good shot pattern. See 26.

30. **Jagerfaust (fighter fist).** Three 5 cm. barrels built into the wings of the F.W.190, Me.262 and Me.163 firing upward. No recoil, because the barrel dropped out when the shot was fired.

31. **R4M Rocket Projectile.** Of all special weapons, this 5.5 cm. RP with collapsible fins and about 400 grams of Hexogen explosive proved to be the best. It was introduced at the end of March 1945. It was shot from a rail which, on the Me.262, could be mounted outside of the turbines under the wings, 12 on each side, with little aerodynamic disturbance. The fitting of 24 more R4M RP was possible either under the fuselage on a frame or under the wings between turbines and fuselage. The RP's were shot off one after another in a fraction of a second so that in combination with the natural dispersion a shot-gun like pattern was made and one hit sufficed to destroy a bomber. The loss of speed from the Me.262 as a result of mounting the R4M was insignificant. The RP were mounted with an upward inclination of 8° and fired at 600 meters, at which range they had same ballistics as the MK 108 shots.

32. Important requirements for the success of special weapons against air targets were:

    a.   A practical range finding device, a problem which could not be solved optically. The electric devices, Oberon-Elfe, did not come until too late for use.

    b.   A sure and fool-proof method of discharge by photo-electric cells, which was not practical for use until March 1945.

34. As a gunsight, the gyro computing reflector EZ 42 (Adler) was tested and used in the F.W.190. Series production came very late because of bombing of the industry. In the Me.262 it was technically hard to mount the EZ 42.

CHAPTER 24

Typical Fighter Mission Briefing in Defense of the Reich

Interrogation of Oberstleutnant Bär
At Kaufbeuren, Germany, 21 September 1945

Briefing

The briefing always took place in the unit's briefing room with the Gruppe Kommandeur presiding. Present were the pilots, Staffel COs, the Technical Officer, the Weather Man and the operations officer. An example of a typical briefing follows:

Around 6:45 AM the assembly of pilots and the reporting of strength to the Gruppe CO takes place. At 7:10 physical training is given with torso bare, including body bends, twisting exercises, arm exercises, knee bends and a short run. At 7:15 the briefing begins.

1. The meteorologist draws a large weather map with bright crayons. Using this he predicts the possibilities of attack from the West and South. Further he describes the direction and condition of fronts, lifting of fog, dangerous areas (low clouds, heavy rain, and fog), areas where bad weather can be detoured, the prediction for the next day, winds at altitude, and icing altitudes. The CO gets various pilots to repeat the general weather situation.

2. The technical officer gives the CO a chart of serviceable aircraft by Staffeln and announces any special technical points to be watched for.

3. The signals officer turns over charts of the Y-Aircraft which are serviceable and mentions any special points to watch about signals traffic.

4. The actual briefing by the Gruppe CO now begins. In general he has already had a briefing from the Division. In it the Division explained to him the possibilities of missions from the west and south on the basis of weather and Listening Service reports.

'Assuming that a mission is expected from the north, the Gruppe will lead the Gefechtsverband in case the north mission materializes. Sequence:

Staff leading, 7th Staffel on the left, 8th on the right, and 9th behind. The Staffeln will be slightly below the one ahead. Attacks from head on are to be flown. Remember, approach from same altitude as the bombers, aim well, don't shoot from long range and remember to pull up and slip away after the attack. Assembly after the attack will take place according to the situation as to sun and enemy fighters. The second Gruppe will follow us and third Gruppe will provide cover, with its light (no external armament) fighters. The Geschwader will assemble at 3000 feet. The second assembly with two light Gruppen of J.G. 4 will take place over Dummer See, at 25,000 feet. I will lead the Gefechtsverband and my deputy will be the CO of 7th Staffel. The following airfields are to be used for intermediate landings after the mission, all well supplied with mechanics and facilities: Oldenburg, Delmehorst, and Rothenburg. The senior pilots on these fields are responsible to me for immediate servicing of aircraft and reporting to Division of the aircraft on the field for a second possible mission. Further, make sure all the aircraft are rendered serviceable as soon as possible so they can return to our base here. Take care on landing on these intermediate fields, watching for enemy fighters and bomb craters. Disperse your aircraft immediately after landing and camouflage them. All pilots but the senior ones will remain with their aircraft and the senior pilots will go to field operations to report to Division how many aircraft and who have landed, their successes, and how many are ready to start again.'

Then comes the check of the papers of the pilots, their emergency packets, with burn bandages and salve, and rubber tourniquets for arterial bleeding. Pilots who make emergency landings are to return at once by train, bringing their radio with them. The safety and guarding of the aircraft is to be taken into account. In case of hospitilization, notify the unit, if possible, through the doctor.

The special subjects – especially assembly places and airfields, intermediate landing fields, and emergency landing regulations – the formation leader has repeated by one of the pilots. It is also recommended that from time to time the Staffel COs hold these briefings under the supervision of the Gruppe CO, since the Staffel CO may some day have to replace the Gruppe CO.

At the conclusion of the briefing the pilots go to the unit dispersal areas, where their aircraft are standing ready for take-off. There, the Staffel COs assign the aircraft and appoint the Schwarm and Rotte leaders. Workshop flights are also carried on. By good weather, the Gruppe is usually in 30 minute readiness and cannot leave the field, as ordered by the Division. For this reason the Staffel usually fitted out their dispersal or parking areas very liveably, often with a small kitchen, sport facilities, and washing facilities improvised out of drop tanks. Until the take-off, everyone stays in the dispersal areas.

CHAPTER 25

A Typical Mission
in the Defense of the Reich

by Oberstleutnant Dahl
At Kaufbeuren, Germany, 20 September 1945

Force Assumed: A fighter Geschwader with one heavy Sturmgruppe and two light escort Gruppen. Geschwader is stationed in the Nurnberg-Ansbach area.

The weather over the entire German area indicates that a heavy bomber attack is to be expected. Weather permits flights in from the west as well as from the south. Weather over the entire Reich is suitable for defense.

The Geschwader CO is called by phone around 5:30 a.m. by the Division CO. In this conversation the Division CO makes known the plans of the High Command (including the Jagdkorps and Luftflotte), for example: 'Today on the basis of weather forecasts, missions from the south as well as from the west are to be expected. Weather for defense is ideal. Your Geschwader will be used to combat the mission from the west, but if the mission from the west only penetrates into the occupied zone (France, Belgium, and Holland) you will combat the mission from the south. Ready times as usual, i.e., when the Listening Service picks up the bomber assembly over Italy your Geschwader will go into 15 minute readiness.'

The Geschwader CO speaks, after this, with his Gruppe COs and relays to them the pre-briefing which he just got from the Division CO. The Gruppe CO's now hold the pre-briefing for their pilots.

The Geschwader HQ, which was fully occupied and in operation since dawn, especially if a mission seemed likely, gives out to the Gruppen the organization of the formation for the day, assigns the Y-Aircraft (those fighters which are equipped with one FuGE 16 ZY VHF set for fighter control purposes) call signs, as well as the chain of command in formation (deputy leaders). The Division commentary will be tuned in by the Geschwader and Gruppen as soon as the 15 minute readiness starts (this commentary comes by telephone, radio in Morse and voice, and OKW station).

Around 8:20, the Division commentary gives out the enemy situation after the bombers cross the English coast. All three bomb divisions are in the air. In a continuous commentary the position of the bomber formations point over the Scheldt estuary at 9:00 a.m. with course due east.

The Geschwader now goes into three minute readiness and a short time later into Sitzbereitschaft (with pilots in their aircraft). Pilots are in their aircraft in the dispersal areas around the edge of the field, ready to start. By loudspeaker over the Staffel hook-up the enemy situation is continually broadcast to the pilots in their aircraft. The bomber formation holds its due east course for a while but just west of the Rhine it turns to the southeast and heads for the Rhine-Main industrial area around Frankfurt.

In the meantime the Division CO has held repeated telephone conversations with the Geschwader CO's. The Jagdkorps has decided to use the Geschwader against the bombers approaching from the West. There are no signs of a mission from the South. Around 9:40 the Geschwader goes into sitting readiness, at 9:50 the point of the bomber formation is Southwest of Cologne over the Eifel area. The Geschwader now receives its order to start.

All three Gruppen now make a scramble start, assemble over their own airfields at 3000–6000 feet in 6–10 minutes and fly to the Geschwader assembly point. There, the Geschwader CO is already in the air and he forms up the battle formation (Gefechtsverband). Behind him lies the Sturmgruppen and the close and top escort hang on to them. The assembly altitude has been ordered beforehand and was fixed at 10,000 feet, under the ceiling. The assembly and the forming up of the Gefechtsverband can take no more than 20 minutes calculated from the time of take-off of the Gruppen. After this space of time, the Gefechtsverband must be ready to set course and start for its objective. The Geschwader CO announces by radio to the Division the completed assembly and the readiness of the formation to set course.

The Division now gives the order to set course:

'Set course at 320° and climb to combat altitude of 25,000 feet.' The Geschwader goes out of the left turn it used in the assembly and starts on the prescribed course, with the formation leader throttling back so that the Sturmgruppen can keep well closed up behind him. The close escort divides and goes half to the left of the Sturmgruppen and half to the right; the top escort sits 3000–6000 feet above the formation, stacked up from front to rear. In this formation the fighters climb at 220 m.p.h. IAS and climb at 600–900 feet per minute.

During the take-off, assembly and on course, strict radio discipline is observed. In the formation as little talking as possible is done, but the Division continually sends up its commentary to all pilots, describing the enemy situation. The location of the fighter formation is known to the Division at all times through Y-Procedure (or by Benito), and the Division can order the formation wherever necessary. In case the Division tells the Geschwader location information, code names and numbers are used to reduce the possibility of betrayal through the Allied listening service.

The formation continues to climb in the described formation toward the Rhine-Main area. Over Würzburg they reach an altitude of 23,000 feet. The formation leader already sees contrails ahead of him to the left and shortly thereafter sees Flak over Frankfurt. By the radio he announces this to the Division. Around 10:50 he can distinguish the first bomber formations. The Division gives him the green light to attack and releases him from ground control. Until then he has not contacted enemy fighters.

The formation leader orders external tanks to be dropped and attacks a bomber formation of about 60 Fortresses which has just dropped its bombs and is turning away to the right. The Sturmgruppen attack from level rear and go through with one pass. After the first attack the Sturm fighters (FW 190's) assemble to the right below the bombers. The German escort Gruppen are already engaged in light air combat with American fighters. The German fighters succeed in attacking still another bomber formation before it reaches its target and it jettisons its bombs. After this, there is air combat with the sizeable American fighter escort force until the vicinity of the Moselle River is reached. There at about 11:30 the air combat is broken off.

The few German Schwärme still holding together, as well as the aircraft flying alone, now receive the order to land in the vicinity of Mannheim. Around 1200 all have landed in the prescribed area, without further interference from enemy fighters. On these intermediate airfields each pilot is received by the field operations room and there he gives a short report of his mission. The formation leaders call the nearest responsible fighter command headquarters and give a short report by priority phone call. After all the aircraft have been serviced with fuel and ammunition the fighter command (Jafu, Division) gives the order to each field that all aircraft are to return to their bases from the intermediate fields, since no more enemy activity is in progress, or at least all the enemy formations are too far away to be caught by a second mission.

Usually these so-called 'Second Missions' did not lead to much success. Through the breaking up of the fighter forces in the first missions and the landings on many different fields, it was very difficult to form the pilots and aircraft into really effective fighting units.

After return to the home bases, the formation leader gives the operational report and the victory and loss statistics. The critique of the mission by the Gruppe CO with his pilots (and if possible with the Geschwader CO) takes place as soon as possible after the mission, to keep a clear picture of the conduct of the mission. The operational report is made by telephone and confirmed in writing. In addition the Geschwader CO and sometimes the Gruppen CO's call the Division CO and report by telephone about the mission, discussing the results and object lessons of the mission, making proposals for improving tactics. In case of special new enemy tactics or equipment the formation or unit leader may call and discuss the matter with the General der Jagdflieger or the Inspector of Day Fighters (East or West).

CHAPTER 26

Conduct of a Company Front Attack

Interrogation of Oberstleutnant Walther Dahl
At Kaufbeuren, Germany, 20 September 1945

Approach of the Sturmgruppe in Vic Formation

Upon sighting the enemy bomber formation, the formation leader gives the signal to attack by rocking his wings, or by radio. The wings of the Vics now pull up until the aircraft are in line abreast, with the formation leader throttling back a bit so the others can catch up. The approach is made from behind.

The 'company front' as seen by the tail gunner. This wartime USAAF tactical diagram shows a formation such as Dahl often led. Poised to attack, the FW190s of the Sturmgruppe have moved from 'vics' into line abreast. The three escorting Gruppen of Bf 109s are in elements of four, echeloned up-sun. The close escort will follow the 190s down to attack the bombers and cover the 190s' recovery.

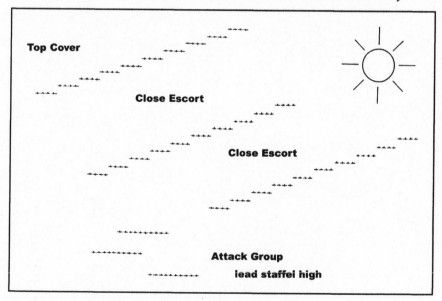

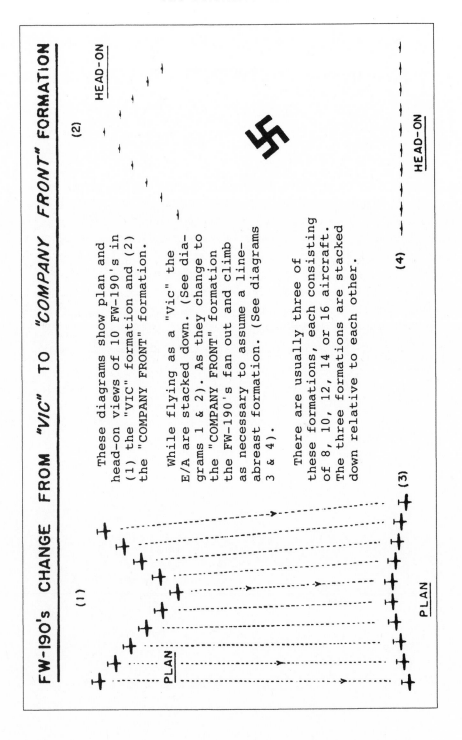

FW-190's CHANGE FROM "VIC" TO "COMPANY FRONT" FORMATION

(1)

(2)

HEAD-ON

These diagrams show plan and head-on views of 10 FW-190's in (1) the "VIC" formation and (2) the "COMPANY FRONT" formation.

While flying as a "vic" the E/A are stacked down. (See diagrams 1 & 2). As they change to the "COMPANY FRONT" formation the FW-190's fan out and climb as necessary to assume a line-abreast formation. (See diagrams 3 & 4).

There are usually three of these formations, each consisting of 8, 10, 12, 14 or 16 aircraft. The three formations are stacked down relative to each other.

(3)

PLAN

(4)

HEAD-ON

PLAN

The fighters attack in a line, the formation leader dividing up the target according to the formation of the bombers, for example: 'Bomber formation on a broad front with little depth (altitude from top to bottom of bomber formation). The CO will attack the center, and the forces to right and left will go to right and left respectively'.

Open fire from shortest possible range, about 400 yards, during the approach with all weapons simultaneously, firing bursts until close enough to ram. If no victory is yet scored, ramming should result by crashing against the bomber's tail with prop or wings.

Exit should be made from the formation to the side and down and reassemble at the same altitude with the bombers about 3000 yards to the side and 1000 yards below. The basic principle to be observed in reassembling, is that the assembly is to be made on the same side from which the entry into the bomber stream was made. The advantage thus gained is that the escort Gruppen are on the right side after the attack to protect the reassembly of the Sturmgruppen without having to change sides. If little or no fighter opposition is encountered, a second attack can be carried out by the Sturmgruppe as shown above.

CHAPTER 27

Experiences in Combat
Against Boeing Fortress II and
Consolidated Liberator

Letter from Generalleutnant Galland to Operational Units
From Papers of J.G.54, #9 of 1943

On 23 Nov. 1942 III/J.G.2 was in action [over St. Nazaire] against a force [49] of 4-engined bombers approaching in several waves. [Actually, one formation of nine B-17Es, suffered most of the losses.]

On the basis of experience with such formations up until now, the formation leader ordered an attack on the enemy formation from the front.

1.   The CO [Hauptmann Egon Mayer] himself led an element of three [F.W. 190s] and began his first attack from left front ahead. When in range, fire was opened with a lead that gave the impression that the cone of fire was going by the front of the enemy aircraft. In pulling up to the left he saw hits in the right wing of the Boeing Fortress. The wing broke off, the Fortress turned over and spun in amid heavy explosions.

In the get away after this attack No. 2 and 3 men of the CO's element of three were shot down or received heavy hits.

Close observation of the enemy defense during this attack and the next attacks brought the following facts to light:

On the approach there was no defensive fire. In the get away after a sharp pull up to left or right, no defensive fire at first, then suddenly there was heavy defensive fire which first passed behind the German fighters but which however heavily hit the German fighter as the bomber's range and altitude advantage increased.

2.   After this several attacks were flown on Fortresses from front low and on the last attack hits were seen in the fuselage and wing roots. In turning in under the Fortress a light ball of fire was observed under the fuselage and thereupon the Fortress spun in twisting and turning and exploded after receiving more hits from the rear.

3.   After several attacks with observed hits, the MG ammunition was expended. Nevertheless, the CO attacked a Consolidated Liberator [actually a B-17] from about 1030 (from ahead and to one side) with little speed. During the firing the German fighter was skidded in the direction of flight of the Liberator by simple rudder movement. Strong explosions were observed at the first shots. The aircraft pulled up slightly and dived straight down without spinning. No one bailed out.

4.   **Object Lessons:**

    a.   The attack from the rear against a four engined bomber formation promises little success and almost always brings losses. If an attack from the rear must be carried through, it should be done from above or below and the tanks and engines should be the aiming points.

    b.   The attack from the side can be effective, but it requires thorough training and good gunnery.

    c.   The attack from the front, front high, or front low all with low speed was the most effective of all. Flying ability, good aiming, and closing up to the shortest possible range are the requisites for success.

    d.   The exit can succeed only in a sharp diving turn in the direction of the bomber formation or single bomber. The most important factor is the angle of curve in which the fighter leaves the bomber formation.

    e.   Basically, the strongest weapon is the massed and repeated attack by an entire fighter formation. In such cases the defensive fire must be divided up and the bomber formation broken up.

signed:
GALLAND

CHAPTER 28

Tactical Regulations for SE and TE Fighter Formations in Air Defense

by Adolf Galland

Der Oberbefehlahaber der Luftwaffe   *Hq. 3 Sept. 1943*
General der Jagdflieger   *157th copy of 300*

The Tactical Regulations of GAF Planning Staff Ia Ops General der Jagdflieger Br. B. Nr. 416/43 is to be destroyed and replaced with the following new material. It is to be distributed down to Staffeln.

A. Control

(1) It is to be insured with all means that *one* enemy attack wave and if possible the one that penetrates deepest be combatted with the mass of all fighter formations continuously. For this the most important requirement is the early cooperation between the neighboring and rear Jagddivisionen.

(2) This first requirement for the joint operation of larger formations is to be achieved by the timely assembly of at least two Gruppen and their vectoring onto the enemy along one 'Y' Beam. These formations are to be led in the air by their Kommodore on *one* R/T frequency.

(3) For running orientation of the control commands and of the formations in the air about the strength, location, altitude, and course of the penetrating enemy formations, TE observation aircraft (Fuhlungshalter) will be used. For their operations special regulations are in preparation.

(4) The vectoring-on of all fighter and TE fighter formations without Y-Procedure (Benito) will be accomplished by the newly instituted Reichs Fighter Commentary (Reichsjagerwelle). It is to be continually tuned in by all SE and TE fighters in Defense of the Reich without Y-apparatus, by all night fighters operating by day, by all factory fighter units, and by all operational units of the training Geschwader. Aircraft with 'Y' apparatus will tune in on it (the Reichsjagerwelle) only after intermediate landings in the pursuit of enemy formations which have penetrated deep into the Reich.

(5) Upon landing on strange airfields, the senior fighter pilot (officer) must immediately combine all fighter pilots present into one fighter formation, regardless of what units they belong to, and then attend to the quickest possible serviceability of the aircraft.

The operational order is received from the fighter command of the area concerned who is to be kept continuously informed as to the strength of the units.

If communications with the fighter command are lacking, the leader of the formation operates on his own authority. (Taking off on sighting the enemy or on the basis of Reporting Service announcements.) After take off he will use as a call sign the name of the airfield. Reports of the location of the enemy formation will come over the Reichs Fighter Commentary in the clear.

The formation will be dissolved only on order of the fighter command. The released pilots are then turned over to their regular units.

(6) Airfields especially supplied for intermediate landings of fighters are to be marked in on the maps of pilots and are in addition to be so marked that they are recognizable as such from a great altitude.

(7) Kommodores and Kommandeure of the SE and TE fighter units must be constantly informed of the entire weather picture and its influence on enemy activity in the various battle areas.

B. Formation

(1) Every fighter formation (Gruppe to Staffel in size) is to combat mainly one and the same bomber formation. If it jettisons its bombs or is completely broken up it is to be left alone and the next formation flying within visible range is to be attacked.

(2) All leaders in the air, from Schwarm (4s) leaders up, are to be identified in the air by white rudders. Single fighters and separated Rotten (2s) are to form up on these aircraft immediately regardless of which formation they belong to. The leader of the Schwarm or larger unit thus formed must attack without delay the bomber formation again.

(3) The first attack has the purpose of breaking up the enemy formation. After exact division of the target and from a good position, the attack is to be so begun and carried through that the fighters go in close together by Schwärme (4s) with little interval between Schwarme, one after the other, against the same formation. The exit, the direction of which is ordered before

the attack, must make possible the quick reassembling of the entire fighter formation.

(4) In repeated attacks, simultaneous attacks by many fighters are always the optimal approach.

(5) The attack from the front is from now on to be the *exception*, to be flown only in exceptionally favorable circumstances and by fighter formations especially successful in it.

As the *standard attack*, the attack from the rear with small angle of approach is ordered.

Closing up to effective range is to be supervised by all formation leaders in the air for their formations.

Pilots who without adequate reason do not close in to the ordered minimum range are to be court-martialed for cowardice in the face of the enemy.

(6) From now on, only bombers in formation are to be attacked (without regard to whether they are on the way in to the target or on the way out).

Only when the entire bomber formation is broken up or when there is no more possibility of getting to the bomber formation, are separated or damaged bombers flying alone to be fought to final destruction.

Aircraft mounting the 21 cm. RP are permitted after successful discharge of their RP to destroy single bombers separated from the bomber formation.

Factory fighter Schwärme (4s) and Rotten (2s), night fighters, as well as small operational fighter formations from the training units, may, as long as there is no possibility for them to join up in the air or on the ground into larger formations, attack and destroy single bombers separated from their formations.

ADDITION TO THESE EXCEPTIONS IS FORBIDDEN.

Formation leaders and fighter pilots who disobey this order are to be court-martialed for military disobedience with serious consequences for the safety of the Reich.

For the claiming and allowing of victories the following regulations are in effect:

D.R.d. L.u. Ob.d.L/LP Nr. 14223/43 geh. v. 8 July 1943

D.Ob. d.L./Gen.d. Jagdfl. Nr.4016/43 geh. v. 9 August 1943

(7) Fire will be opened in attacks from the front at most at 800 yards, and in all other attacks at 400 yards. Every case of opening fire sooner means waste of ammunition as a result of lack of courage.

(8) The goal of every attack is one aircraft. Aiming at the middle of the bomber formation or spraying the whole formation with bullets never leads to success.

(9) The aiming point and the tip of the front sight, not shooting according to tracers or smoke trails, leads to victories.

(10) All attacks from an angle of approach of more than 30° are ineffective.

(11) The fighting will be continued even in the strongest flak fire, in flak zones, and in flak barrier barrage areas.

(12) The bomber formation is to be hindered with all available strength and means, even if it has broken through to the target, in the aimed dropping of its bombs.

Distribution:
All SE and TE fighter units down to Staffeln.
Training Fighter Units.
Fighter O.T.Us.
Factory Fighter Units and Fighter Commands

I.A. (signing for Göring)
GALLAND

Air Defense of the Reich (Volume 2) The Fighter Arm (The Jagdwaffe) *Pamphlet Series, September 1944*

Oberkommando der Luftwaffe
GAF Operations Staff
Training Sect. Nr. 1410/44 Confidential

A. General

1. The missions of the fighter arm in air defense are insuring of the domination of the air over friendly territory and the destruction of enemy aircraft by day and night. The emphasis is put on shooting down as great a number of enemy bombers as possible before they reach their target.

2. In supplementing the other branches of air defense forces (A.A. and ARP) the fighter arm is able, because of its mobility, to concentrate strength for short periods at great distances.

3. The fighter arm is organized into day and night fighting units. Day fighters include SE and TE (Zerstorer) units (later called long range units), and the night fighter arm includes SE and TE units. On the basis of equipment and special uses the following special types are used in combat:
Rocket fighters, storm fighters, air recce aircraft, shadowing aircraft, and illuminating aircraft.

4. SE and TE fighter units combat by day enemy bomber formations. High altitude units tie up and combat the enemy fighter escort and make the attacks of the rest of the fighter force much easier.
Rocket fighters provide local defense for the most important targets.
Storm fighters (Sturmjager) possess especially strong armor. They destroy enemy bombers by close-range attacks and occasionally by ramming.

5. Against especially fast and high flying enemy aircraft like recce and

pathfinder aircraft, specially equipped aircraft are used. (Me.262 is meant here).

6. By night air recce aircraft observe the air combat area during the battle. Shadowing aircraft observe the movements of enemy formations. In bad weather, air recce aircraft or shadowing aircraft help lead the fighters onto the enemy bomber formations.

B. Organization

7. The tactical unit of the fighter is the Gruppe with four Staffeln. Each Staffel has 16 aircraft.

8. The Gruppen are organized into day or night fighter Geschwader. A Geschwader has as a rule four Gruppen.

9. The Geschwader are under Jagdfliegerführer (Jafus) or Jagddivisionen (fighter divisions); their number depends on the situation at the time and the available forces.

10. Jafus and Jagddivisionen can be organized into Jagdkorps which in turn are under Luftflotten.

11. Rocket and storm fighters are organized as the other fighter units are.

12. The air recce and shadowing aircraft are organized into air recce Staffeln. Usually one such Staffel is in operation with each Jagddivision.

C. Command Functions

13. The control of all forces engaged in the air defense of the Reich lies with Luftflotte Reich, according to the instructions of the High Command of the Luftwaffe. For control of the night and day fighter units a Jagdkorps is placed under the Luftflotte.

The fighter forces of other command areas which are exclusively devoted to air defense are likewise organized according to their strength into Jafus, Jagddivisionen, or Jagdkorps.

In the operational areas of the army and in certain coastal areas, fighter formations, because of their functions' not being exclusively for air defense, are organized under Fliegerkorps or Fliegerdivisionen,

14. The Jagdkorps is responsible for the marshaling of fighter forces according to time and place and for determining the centers of resistance

according to the situation. The Jagdkorps appoints the Jagddivision which is to lead the mission, and insure the timely transfer of control to a neighboring command area (Division).

15. The Jagdkorps issues orders for the employment of the air raid warning service. It is also responsible for the production of the air situation picture in its area, and must insure the quick and unfailing informing of all commands in the air defense as to movements of enemy and friendly formations.

16. The jagddivisionen or jafus control the units under them directly in combat. They are concerned with all measures taken before and during battle to insure the tactically and technically correct conduct of the defensive combat and cooperation with the other arms of air defense.

They are responsible for the production of the unified air situation picture for their areas and for the quick and unfailing passing on of it to all headquarters of the air defense systems.

Through the A.A. combat controller (Flakeinsatzleiter) at each Jagddivision, the cooperation of the fighter arm with the A.A. and with ARP troops is insured.

17. The controlling Jagddivision controls, for the duration of the battle over its area, all the forces sent into its area from other division or Jafu areas.

18. The Geschwader is responsible for the operations, supply and replacements for the Gruppen under it.

The Geschwader CO is responsible for the tactically correct execution of the missions of his Geschwader in combat, especially in day fighting.

19. The Gruppe as a tactical command unit is so equipped with personnel, material and signals that it can operate independently in combat. The CO leads his Gruppe according to the missions given him in the air.

20. The day or night fighter Staffel is the smallest unit which is independent for administrative and maintenance purposes, Operations and supply of all kinds are controlled for it by the Gruppe.

D. Aircraft Types, Armament, and Equipment
I. SE FIGHTERS

21. BF.109 (Messerschmitt)
SE low wing fighter, single seater, flying endurance without drop tanks 1–1 1/2 hours. Used as fighter (with 1–3 cannon or 2 × 21 cm. RP and 2 MG)

or as high altitude fighter with 1 cannon and 2 MG.

A short increase of power for climbing and greater speed is possible by using the GM 1 boost device.

22. F.W.190 (Focke-Wulf)

SE low wing, 1 seater, flying time without drop tanks 1–1/4 – 1–3/4 hours; more maneuverable than the Bf.109.

Use as fighter (with 2–6 cannon and 2–4 MG). 'With special equipment as night fighter too.)

23. Me.163 (Messerschmitt)

Rocket fighter.

II. ZERSTORER AIRCRAFT (TE FIGHTERS)

24. Bf.110 (Messerschmitt)

TE low wing, 2–3 crew, endurance without drop tanks 2–2 1/2 hours. Used as long range fighter. Armament 2–4 cannon or 4.21 cm. RP and 4 fixed MGs.

25. Me.410 (Messerschmitt)

TE low wing, 2 seater, endurance with drop tanks 1–3/4 hours. Used same as Bf.110, cannon have greater caliber (3 and 5 cm.)

III. WEAPONS, AMMUNITION AND FUEL

26. In the fighter arm the following weapons are used: MG, heavy MG, cannon up to 5 cm., RP with the necessary firing tubes.

In fighter aircraft, only fixed weapons are used. They are built into fuselage, engine and wings. Aiming takes place by pointing the whole aircraft with the aid of reflector sights.

27. As ammunition; regular MG ammunition and special types, including incendiaries, armor-piercing, HE, and Hexogen armor destroying ammunition are used. Rocket 21 cm. projectiles are used, corresponding to the Army smoke projectiles. They are hung under the wings in tubes. Their use takes place by day with time fuses against closed up bomber formations.

28. For the engines of fighter aircraft fuel with tetra-ethyl lead, either 87 octane (B-4) or 100 octane (C-3), according to construction of the engine is used. Tetra-ethyl lead raises the anti-knock qualities of the fuel. Arbitrary interchanging of B-4 or C-3 is not possible.

To prevent loss of power at high altitudes the special GM 1 fluid can be used as additional fuel. Nitrous oxide is fed into the engine by the GM 1 apparatus. Use is possible in the Bf.109 and F.W.190 over 25,000 feet for about 17 minutes, up to 50 minutes with the ME.410. An increase in speed of about 40–70 km/hour is obtained at about 28,000 feet.

Another method of raising engine performance is by water-methanol injection. This helps to cool the engine and brings about an increased performance by greater manifold pressure. Methanol has a favourable influence on anti-knock properties. The increase in power is greatest at low altitudes. It has an increase of about 30 km/hour at all altitudes up to *full boost altitudes* (where the engine had its best performance). Used in periods of 2–20 minutes.

E. Control and Combat

I. CONTROL

29. The fighter arm makes it possible for the command of the Luftwaffe to form temporary centers of resistance. Transfer of these strong points can take place during the battle. This must be taken into account in a far-seeing deployment of forces. Choice, improvement, equipping and supplying of airfields for fighters as well as all measures for radio navigation and control must be arranged accordingly.

30. The goal of the fighter commands is to lead large combined formations of fighters onto the enemy so that it can be destroyed before it reaches its objective. Continuous combatting of all enemy formations is the goal, but it is nevertheless dependent upon the situation and strength of forces.

Reserves are, as a matter of principle, not held back. The holding back of parts of units for the protection of certain objectives (local fighter protection) is a special exception. (This applies mainly to rocket fighters – Me.163).

Enemy fighter sweeps are for the time being only combatted as a secondary matter (strength situation). Against enemy recce aircraft only the smallest units (Rotten) are used.

31. A requirement for the control of fighter formations is as perfect a picture as possible of the air situation. This is the job of fighter command, which uses the Air Reporting Service for this purpose.

The variable enemy strategy coupled with numerous continually changing deceptive maneuvers makes difficult the clear formation of the air picture.

By night as well as by day in bad weather, above clouds, shadowing aircraft and air recce aircraft have special significance. They must be so operated against the already located enemy formations that they can give timely running data about strength, formations, aircraft type, and altitudes.

By timely relief of these aircraft by the command posts of fighter commands, continuous observation and identification of enemy formations is to be striven for.

32. Weather observance by aircraft and meteorological advice lead to weather predictions by the fighter commands. This decisively influences the preparatory measures for the battle (readying of forces, transfer of units, and instructions for the proper night fighter procedures to use).

The weather situation is to be continually observed during the combat, to arrange timely necessary changes in operations.

33. The Luftflotten, Jagdkorps, and Jagddivisionen determine the operational preparations and operational methods in advance in   Tactical Regulations (Kampfanweisungen). These include in detail:

Regulations for the conduct of combat.

Regulations for the use of different combat procedures.

Regulations for the cooperation of the various air defense forces.

Regulations for the control of ground organization.

Instructions for Radio Navigation and D/Fing devices.

Instructions for the supplying of ground facilities.

Instructions for the Weather Service.

34. In order to be able to have operational readiness on tap at all times and also be able to give the flying personnel the necessary rest and time for training and so on, the following degrees of readiness are used:

(a) for SE fighters (1) sitting (cockpit) readiness: take-off must follow at once, not more than one minute later. (2) take-off readiness: take-off must follow in 3 minutes, pilots near their aircraft.

(b) for TE fighters (1)   sitting (cockpit) readiness: take-off must follow immediately, in 3 minutes at the latest, for the greater number of the aircraft. Crews near their aircraft. (2) Take-off readiness: start must be guaranteed within 5 minutes of the aircraft.

(c) all other degrees of readiness are designated with the number of minutes or hours in which the start is to take place.

II. DAY FIGHTING

35. In view of the strong defensive fire of the close formations of enemy bombers and fighter escort, only the use of strong concentrated fighter formations promises success. Assembling of aircraft into strong formations, especially after intermediate landings following a mission, is always to be preferred to operations by small split-up forces. A later but concentrated attack usually results in more victories and less losses than too hasty operations by single aircraft or small formations. The assembly of fighters into large battle formations (Gefechtsverbande) takes place outside the approach routes of enemy fighter escort with their lateral covering of the area.

36. By day it is ideal to use units together in Division strength. Fighter combat should if possible take place outside of the Flak zones. If several enemy formations are approaching the employment of fighter forces against *one* formation and its destruction is to be preferred to the combatting of several enemy formations with weak fighter forces.

37. Contact is established by the vectoring of formations onto the enemy with the aid of various fighter control procedures. (Y-Procedure, Egon Procedure, and VHF D/Fing procedure). Aircraft not controlled from the ground listen to Reich fighter commentary (Reichsjagerwelle).

38. High altitude fighters are used primarily against enemy fighter escort. They are supposed to destroy them or lead them away from the bomber formation, before the other (German) fighters contact the fighter escort.

The use of TE fighter units (Zerstorer) is successful only against unescorted bomber formations or when the enemy fighter escort is fully tied up with the German fighter escort.

39. According to the manner in which the bombers fly, second missions against the bombers on the way out are a goal.

For this purpose a great number of airfields (fighter assembly defense of the Reich airfield) are so prepared that fighters from other areas of command which land there can orient themselves and find the same command and reporting facilities as well as comfort and supply facilities in order that they can quickly be put up for a second mission.

40. Fighters landing on strange airfields will, if a second mission is possible, be formed by the senior pilot present into a battle Gruppe for a new mission, regardless of their belonging to various units. The mission will be ordered by the Jagddivision of the area concerned. If signals connections are

lacking the battle Gruppe is to be ordered up independently by its CO on the basis of commentaries, sighting, and so on.

41. The first attack of the fighters has the goal of breaking up the enemy formation. In further attacks the simultaneous attack of several fighter or TE fighter units is always to be sought. If the enemy formation nevertheless breaks through to the target, at least the aimed dropping of bombs is to be hindered with all available strength and means.

42. The target of the attack of each fighter is one aircraft. Aiming at the middle or spraying of bullets over the bomber formation does not lead to success.

The attack easiest from the flying point of view is the attack from the rear with a slight stepping down of the attacking formation. Attacks from head on and from the side require a high measure of flying ability and exceptionally good gunnery.

F. Fighter Control Procedures

43. Fighter formations and individual fighter aircraft are vectored onto enemy aircraft from the ground with the help of various Fighter Control Procedures. By day, according to the weather conditions, vectoring until sight contact is established usually suffices. By night the controlling up to the range of the night fighter radar AI (about 3–4 km.) must take place.

44. In Day Fighter Operations, the following procedures are used:
    Y-Control and
    Egon Procedure (Erstling Weitführung – literally First Born Long Range Control VHF D/Fing Procedure)

45. By Y-Control, fighter formations are vectored onto enemy formations, or Rotten (2s) are vectored onto individual fast recce aircraft. The control takes place over two predetermined frequencies, which also must be maintained by the fighter formation during the turning over of control from one fighter control area to another.

The aircraft equipped with Y-apparatus are plotted by the Fighter Control station on the ground (hearing and range) and are vectored by course and distance onto an enemy formation, which is plotted with Radar (Wurzburg-1 Freya). In a closed formation, only one aircraft can fly as the plotted aircraft, or the exactness of plotting will suffer. If this aircraft is lost, another aircraft, designated in advance, takes over. All other aircraft with Y-apparatus may not turn on their apparatus.

The range of the fighter control stations is about 200 km. Range depends upon the altitude of the formation.

Average ranges with Y-Control.

At 3000 feet Altitude – 100 km. range.

"   6000   "   "   – 140   "   "

"   9500   "   "   – 180   "   "

"   13000   "   "   – 200   "   "

"   16000   "   "   – 220   "   "

"   19500   "   "   – 250   "   "

46. In the Egon Control Procedure, the position of the aircraft controlled is determined by hearing and range.

On the ground a Freya Radar Apparatus is used in a Fighter Control Station and in the aircraft the IFF apparatus FuG.25a ('erstling' – First Born) is used. Range at medium altitudes is about 200 km. Only the aircraft of the formation leader is controlled, all other aircraft switch off their FuG.25a. Locations, flight orders etc., are broadcast to the formation by the headquarters which gets these figures from the fighter control station. Genlt. Galland made the following statement after reviewing the above document.

This VHF procedure was only widely used in the fighter force in 1941 before the Y Procedure was introduced. Luftflotte III in France had developed the VHF procedure for the Geschwader under it. With the introduction of Y and later Egon, the VHF D/Fing procedure was no longer used for Fighter Control except where the other two systems failed because of jamming or mechanical trouble. VHF D/Fing was still used, however, for simple radio navigation in cases where aircraft had to be vectored back to their bases for emergency landings.

Part 5
Summing Up

This section contains a number of brief (and unsurprising) summaries of different Allied aircraft and their tactics. Galland's views of the end-of-war programs, including the obstacles placed in the way of his desire to deploy numbers of the Me 262 despite its technical immaturity, show his understanding of technology and operations. As Johannes Steinhoff, Galland's comrade in the Me 262-equipped JV 44 (and who was unable to contribute to this volume because he was recuperating from severe burns at the time the interrogations were undertaken) put it, 'The war in the air is a technological war which cannot be won by a technologically inferior fighting force, however high its morale or dauntless it resolution.'

The last chapter shows Galland's awareness that it was more than the failures in technology and operations he identifies which defeated the *Jagdwaffe*.

CHAPTER 30

GAF Opinions of Allied Aircraft

Interrogation of Generalleutnant Galland, Generalfeldmarschall Milch, Oberstleutnant Bär, Generalmajor Hitschhold, and Leutnant Neumann
At Kaufbeuren, Germany, 2 September 1945

1. **The Hurricane.** This was considered to be a rugged aircraft but was too slow for a modern fighter. It was very maneuverable and effective against bombers in 1940. After the Battle of Britain, armament consisted of 12 × 303 cal. machine guns. It was made better when the armament was changed to 4 × 20 mm. cannons. German information was that it destroyed as many aircraft (mostly bombers) as the Spitfire. It was used mainly against bombers, being covered and supported by the Spitfire.

After 1942, it was considered obsolete as a first line fighter.

2. **The Typhoon.** This was an exceptionally fast aircraft. It could outrun a Me.109 and F.W.190 in level flight. It had excellent armament and armor for ground strafing, but was not maneuverable enough to combat the Me.109 and F.W.190.

3. **The Lightning (P.38)** This aircraft was very fast and had a good rate of climb below 20,000 feet. Visibility backwards, downwards and over the engines was very poor. It was considered a good strafer due to armament, visibility, speed and silent motors. Its main drawbacks were its vulnerability and lack of maneuverability. On the deck, it could out-run the Me.109 and F.W.190. German fighters would always attack the P-38s in preference to other Allied escort fighters.

4. **The Airacobra (P.39)** This was a very inferior fighter aircraft at all times during the war. Its maneuverability, speed, dive and climbing qualities were were poor. It was one of the easiest of the Allied fighters to shoot down.

5. **The Warhawk (P.40)** This aircraft was inferior as a modern fighter. The models with only 4 × .50 cal. machine guns were considered to be too lightly armed. It was slow and could not dive or climb. Its best quality was that it could out-turn the Me.109 and F.W.190 below 12,000 feet.

6. **The Mustang (P.51)** This was the best American fighter because of its long range, climb and dive characteristics, fire power and maneuverability. It was very vulnerable to cannon fire. It would break up during very violent dives and maneuvers.

7. **The Thunderbolt (P.47)** This aircraft was exceptionally fast in a dive, but could be out-distanced at the start of a dive by the Me.109. It would absorb many cannon hits and still fly.

CHAPTER 31

Allied Fighters and Equipment

Interrogation of Oberstleutnant Bär
At Kaufbeuren, Germany, 28 August 1945

1. **American Fighters.** The Mustang is the best escort fighter up to six thousand metres. Thunderbolt is, as a fighter bomber, very efficient as it has a radial engine and long endurance. The Lightning is an old type aircraft but is efficient as an escort fighter over water because of its ability to fly on one engine.

2. **British Fighters.** The Tempest is a very good fighter but was not well known by Bär. The Spitfire is fast and maneuverable, has a good climb and excellent armament but does not have long range. The Typhoon is good as a ground attack aircraft because of its speed in horizontal flight. The Allied tendency towards heavy fighter aircraft is not good. R/T was considered as very good on all types of aircraft.

The US.50 calibre would have much trouble against the Russian Il-2. It would have been better for the Allies to have airfield defense units equipped with 20 mm. guns and other units equipped with 12.7 mm. guns. The best solution would be found in interchangeable guns in the same type of aircraft. The 12.7 mm. guns were sufficient for defense of large bomber formations.

3. **Allied Fighter Pilots.** Bar states that in all countries the fighting spirit is high as long as that Air Force is superior. As fighters, the Americans were better than the British because they fought to the end and were very brave sometimes to the point of foolishness. The English fighters were only good when they had air superiority. The French fighters were good acrobatic pilots but they had no fighting spirit. They lacked discipline and Bar thinks they lived too good a life and that they were not rugged like the Russians.

As P/W's, the English pilot never talked. He was always cold and had the feeling of his native superiority. The American pilot was very strong as a P/W, as long as the situation was favorable for the American forces. If unfavorable, as in Africa, he used to be quite talkative.

4. **Formations Employed by Allied Fighters for Escort Missions and Others**. The formations were good as the Allies always had the superiority of numbers.

5. **Tactics**. The concentrated attack of U.S. fighters against enemy formations in order to disperse them was always very efficient. However, the American fighters always waited too long to attack. These tactics would have been disastrous if the Germans had air superiority.

CHAPTER 32

Allied Aircraft

Interrogation of Leutnant Neumann
At Kaufbeuren, Germany, 28 August 1945

1. Aircraft

a. **Russian**

Yak-3, -5 and -7 were the fighter types most commonly used. With the exception of the Yak-3 they were all too slow but good in turning ability. The Yak 3 was named the 'Spitfire of the East'. All types of R/T's were non-existent. Methods of communications were old and primitive.

b. **American**

Mustang. This was a good long range fighter. Guns were efficient against fighters but not against bombers.

Thunderbolt. This was the best fighter-bomber.

Lightning. A good escort fighter for long range over water missions as it could be flown with only one engine. It had a most efficient armament set-up as all the guns were grouped in the nose.

c. **British**

Tempest. This was considered to be the fastest aircraft.

Typhoon. This was a very fast aircraft, but weak in a curving fight. Neumann knows very little about Allied R/T and knew nothing of the tail radar used by Allied night bombers.

2. Allied Fighter Pilots

a. **Russian.** The Russians were weak as fighter pilots. Neumann noticed great progress in Russian tactics and equipment since the spring of 1944.

b. **American.** The American fighter pilot had great self-confidence and possessed a high fighting spirit. Neumann states that Americans had no discipline and spoke of some shooting of German pilots in their parachutes.

c. **British.** No opinions.

3. Tactics

a. **Russian** – Neumann doubted that the Russian ever had any suitable or good tactics. They continually had to be forced to the attack. Russian dive-bombing was always bad and very rarely used.

c. **American and British** – He makes no statements on tactics. Neumann claims they were beaten by a great superiority of material.

CHAPTER 33

Plans of the German Fighter Force for the Continuation of World War II

Interrogation of Generalleutnant Galland
At Kaufbeuren, Germany, 16–18 September 1945

a. The following statements are not plans for a future war, but concern the projected developments for the fighter Force if the last war had not ended when it did. Most of the plans are discussed with reference to the air and ground situation as it existed at the beginning of 1945 before the Russians and Allies broke the Oder and Rhine lines respectively and it is presumed that Germany might have continued that war with the fronts on the ground much as they were at that time. As it actually did happen, the pushes from West and East made air war impossible for the Germans and resulted in the effective dissolution of the Luftwaffe by the end of April. This is how the Fighter Arm planned, at the outset of 1945, to continue defensive warfare in the air.

A. Technical Developments

(1) **Conventional Fighters**: Trends were towards high altitude fighters with long endurance. The Tank Ta-152C and 152H were in production and one Gruppe already had the Tank Ta-152 at the end of the war. These aircraft were to be powered with new high performance engines, the Jumo 213 and the Jumo 222. The Me.109H, a large Me.109 with a center section added to the wings for higher altitude performance and powered with the DB 603 or June 213, was cancelled late in 1944. Production of the F.W. 190 and Me.109 was to stop in 1945.

(2) **Weapons for Conventional Fighters and Jets**: The 30 mm MK 103, with good ballistics up to 800 meters range, was to be introduced for use against bombers. It would replace the MK 108. The MG 213, either 2 or 3 cm. was to be the standard fighter armament, replacing the MG 151 2 cm. The MG 213 had a cylic rate of fire of about 1000 rounds per minute and better ballistics than the MG 151 or MK 108. The R4M RP was eventually to replace

cannon for use against bombers, possibly with a (proximity fuse) photo electric cell device, which was almost perfected. The EZ 42 computing gyroscopic sight was to become standard equipment and a radar range measuring device for use with it was being developed.

(3) **Accessories**: For high altitude aircraft, special pressure cabins such as in the Tank Ta-152, cabin heating and de-icing, and high altitude parachutes (equipped with oxygen supply and with barometric pressure release) were planned and perfected. New types of external fuel tanks were not carried under the fuselage, but over the wing roots (flared in) or directly on top of the wings (flared in). It was found that the increased load of gasoline was most efficiently carried in these places.

(4) **Radio**: Navigation aids such as the Hermine were ready for use. By using simple click-stop tuning in various radio navigation stations, the map grid coordinates of the aircraft were shown on sliding scales in the aircraft, reducing navigational work to a minumum.

(5) **Zerstorer (Heavy Fighters)**. The Do. 335 with three 30 mm MK 103 cannon was planned as a fighter with ability to get away from the Allied fighter escort and at the same time to knock down bombers from a long range. It was also to be used at night against Mosquitos. The Do. 335 was in production when the war ended.

(6) **Jet Aircraft**. The Me. 262 was to be further developed to increase range, with drop tanks, better fuel, and a built-in Walther Rocket unit in the fuselage to increase climbing speed. More armament was to be built in and more armor was to be fitted for protection in attacking bomber formations. The He. 162 Volksjager was not capable of much further development, except that it was to be improved until it came up to the first promises of Heinkel. Further developments would probably have resulted in the building of aircraft powered by both piston engine and jet units.

(7) **Rocket Aircraft**. The Me.163 with its short endurance and weak armament of 2 × MG 151 2cm., was to be replaced by the Me.263 with its doubled flying time and heavier armament of 4 × MG 151 or 2 × MK 108 (3 cm.). A further armament for the Me. 263 was the use of two 5 cm. rockets firing upward (or downward) from the forward wing roots, triggered by a photo-electric cell. The whole field of Flak rockets (like the Natter) was under the fighter arm. The pilots of these projectiles would be fighter trained, but the whole organizational set-up was still indefinite.

B. Planned Organizational Developments

(1) **Conventional Fighters.** With the fighter force fully on the defensive, Gruppen would have been held at a strength of about 70 aircraft, of which about 50 would be serviceable at any one time. This was the maximum number which could start and assemble in a reasonable length of time. Big groups were also necessary so that the large fighter force could be fitted onto the small number of German operational air fields.

Operations would have been flown in Gruppe strength getting away from the big Gefechtsverbands of Geschwader size. Later, the Gruppen would fly in sight of each other. Eventually it was hoped to use R/T in the air for mutual support work between Gruppen. For once and for all, the old type of strict Division fighter control was to be done away with. Each Gruppe C.O. was to have tactical freedom about how and when he attacked the bombers. Mobility of fighter units would have been no longer necessary if the fronts had remained stable.

Fighters were to be specialized further into light and heavy Gruppen with appropriate armament for their respective duties of attacking the fighters and bombers. Since it was expected to use all units from time to time over the front in support of the Army, the heavy Gruppen were also to be trained to shoot rockets and drop bombs while the light Gruppen could strafe and fight off enemy fighters over the battle area.

The fear was that the Allied high altitude heavy bombers might begin to come in at a bombing altitude about 5000 feet higher than usual, which would have made all the German fighters very ineffective. This forced the introduction of the Tank Ta-152. It was planned to convert almost the whole conventional fighter force to this aircraft or the Me.109H for high altitude work. A small force of single engine night-fighters would have been kept in case German AI radar was completely jammed, in which case the SE fighters could have kept up some kind of a defense. Almost all twin-engine day fighter units had been dissolved and converted to SE fighters in early 1944, and it was planned to re-equip them with the Do.335s. Twin-engine fighters would still be used. They would be needed to satisfy the Navy's demand for cover for their U-Boats when approaching the continent.

C. Jet Aircraft Organization and Employment

(1) The use of the Me.262 and He.162 would have called for certain innovations in fighter organization and control. Gruppen were to have three Staffeln of 12 aircraft each, with four for the Gruppe Stab, a total of 40 air-

craft. The 25 aircraft that would usually be serviceable would completely use up the average facilities of the German airfields available. Units were based on the Kette of three aircraft rather than on the Schwarm, consisting of four aircraft. Each Geschwader was to have three Gruppen because the Geschwader or the Gruppen were to provide their own fighter control and larger Geschwader would have been unwieldy. The employment of jets put great demands on fighter control. The great speed of jet aircraft made the time lag in reporting on the air situation of vital importance for fighter direction. Distance and direction estimations by formation leaders in the air were, for the same reason, often inaccurate. Jet fighters demanded very exact vectoring and information from the ground.

(2) The whole question of employment of the Me.262 was complicated by Hitler's order that it be used only as a bomber and by Goring's giving most of the aircraft to bomber units converted to fighter operations, assuming that the units could be ready for combat in time. Galland hoped to use the vastly superior Me.262 units against the Allied fighter escorts, which they could easily tie up by repeatedly diving and climbing to regain favorable position. Meantime the conventional German fighters could attack the bombers relatively unmolested, a job for which they were adequate from all standpoints, including armament, training, and aircraft performance. They had, by that time, little fear of the bombers' defensive fire.

(3) Actually the plan of using the Me.262's to attack the fighter escort never was put into effect, because by the time that the Me.262 fighter units (J.G.7 in early 1945 and J.V.44 in April) were ready for operations, the conventional fighter force as such had ceased to exist. The Me.262s then had to attack the bombers because nothing else could. The Me.262's of J.G.7 and J.V.44 had considerable success even though they disregarded the Allied fighters. Whereas the former ratio of victories to losses had, with conventional fighters, been 1 to 5, with Me.262s it was reversed, one loss being suffered for every five victories.

(4) The use of the He.162 Volksjager presented very special problems. The aircraft was never satisfactory, though performance and safety equal to that of the Me.262 were promised and probably would have been realized with further development. As it was, the aircraft went directly from the blueprint stage into final series production, without the usual testing and experimental stages. This was a marvelous feat of production, but the He.162 was not ready for combat at the end of the war. Its extremely short endurance, about

20 minutes, would have demanded it be directed in flight by a very skilled fighter control system. Combat missions would have to be timed so as to allow landings and takeoffs safe from the Allied fighter escort, which could easily destroy jets during landing and takeoff, when the jets could not accelerate or maneuver.

(5) The He.162 units were to be employed as regional fighters to protect certain areas. The fighter control organizations concerned with them would probably have been their own Geschwader headquarters. They were set up similar to Me.262 Geschwader. One wild dream supported by Saur, the production wizard of the Jagerstab, was to use Me.262s and He.162s in the same formations, with the Me.262's leading. The Me.262s would have had the only R/T for command communications. The two dissimilar aircraft operating together would have been worth nothing.

D. Rocket Aircraft

(1) The Me.163 was technically finished. It had been in combat, but the fuel shortage kept down sorties to a very low figure. Production was about 50 a month, but this sufficed, because the low number in action kept losses low.

(2) The three Gruppen of J.G.400, which had the Me.163s, were organized like Me.262 units, with three Staffeln each, 12 aircraft per Staffel. Since every landing with the Me.163 was an emergency landing it was wise to locate no more than one Gruppe at one field.

(3) The Me.163's had a radius of action from their base of only about 50km. In combat they flew singly instead of in formation. They tried, however, to attack the bombers in concentration whenever possible.

Fighter control with the Me.163 was very difficult. Seconds were important and each aircraft needed to be directed by ground control individually. The Me.163 could climb at an angle of 50° to an altitude about 3000 feet above the bombers, then shut off its power and estimate the situation, making its attack from the rear of the bombers at gliding speed. The dive away could usually be made with power on. The Me.163 otherwise depended on close turning to escape Allied fighters. The Me.163 would also have launched from rails in rocket assisted take-offs. It could have operated from the Autobahn.

(4) The Me.163 was to have been a 'pure' addition to the fighter program because it was not taking any fuel from other fighter types. It was also not relieving any other fighter units. The Me.263 had about three times the range.

E. Changes in Ground Organization

(1) *General* – S.E. fighter units in Germany could and did use poorly equipped grass airfields without hangars or runways. The need for camouflage was great. Eventually Allied attacks forced dispersal as much as 10 km. away from the field. Attempts to construct new and bigger fields always met with much opposition from the lumber and farming interests in the Government. A program begun in early 1944 called for the expansion or construction of about 150 runways in Germany itself. Some were to be built on old airfields, some just lengthened, some were to be simple runways without fields, and some were to be on the Autobahn. The runways were to be mainly for jet aircraft. Pilots of conventional German types did not favor the use of runways anyway. Shortage of materials prevented much progress on this program.

(2) Hitler wanted the construction of large circular bunkers for keeping fighter aircraft near their fields, but Galland objected that a bomb carpet laid over the bunker would prevent the aircraft taxiing out, even though they were undamaged. He consented, however, to the construction of some bunkers, because they actually could be well used for repair shops. Most units depended on dispersal and camouflage for protection.

(3) Jet aircraft like the Me.262 needed special concrete aprons at the end of the runways where they could be lined up for a scramble, since they had great difficulty in taxiing. Another problem for all units was the great shortage of tugs for towing aircraft. It was best to have one tug per aircraft, but units had to scrape to have even two per three aircraft. The strength of conventional fighter units went up sharply in Fall 1944, and made this shortage more serious.

(4) Despite all efforts to build new fields and improve old ones, the shortage became worse and worse. Those fields which were built or improved, usually near the fronts, were continually over-run. In 1945 there was a great shortage of jet airfields even though jet strength was very low.

F. Protection of Airfields

(1) Little was done in the way of construction of bunkers or underground hangers. Light Flak was depended on for protection against low level attacks. Galland believes it to have been very effective. Each airfield of any importance had its own Flak Kompanie under the Luftgau. Small caliber weapons of all kinds were used, including numbers of 50 cal. guns from American

bombers. Most fields had over 200 guns and at Munchen/Reim there were 270. Jets like the Me.262 required much Flak protection, well spread out at distances from the airfield, because the aircraft were very slow in landing and takeoff and required good protection.

(2) The Me.163 required special fueling equipment and great quantities of clean running water, which was not available at many fields.

G. Training Trends

(1) *Conventional Fighters* – Fighter training, much curtailed during the war and very inadequate, could not have been much improved because of the fuel shortage. If all other branches of the Luftwaffe, except day and night fighters, had been cancelled, some increase in training time might have been effected, but this was not foreseeable.

(2) *Me.262 Training* – Following his usual policy, Galland wanted to allot the first Me.262's to the operational units and convert them to the new fighter during ongoing operations to save time. Then, he would have supplied the OTUs and, last, the fighter schools. But he was only able to do this in the case of J.G.7. The bomber units got most of the rest of the Me.262s. III/Erg. Jagd Geschwader 2 was the OTU for the Me.262. It was next equipped, but the program never got much farther. No drastic changes in training were contemplated.

(3) *He. 162 Volksjager* – It was at first proposed that the entire training of He.162 pilots be conducted by the NSFK in gliders, but Galland and von Massow were able to kill this idea. They did however, approve of the plan to have the NSFK give He.162 pilots glider training in gliders built like the Me.262. The crazy idea that the Gauleiters (Political Governors) were to control operations of the He.162 was barely stopped. The Luftwaffe planned to continue He.162 training where the NSFK left off, in special Jagdschulen and OTUs, dispensing with the Me.109 and F.W.190 as transitional fighters as an experiment. This was never tried.

(4) *Me.163* – Training on this aircraft was to be continued as before. The NSFK gave preliminary training, and the fliers got regular fighter training in fighter schools minus formation flying. They first met the Me.163 in the OTU, IV/Erg. J.G.2 where they made unloaded towed flights, loaded towed flights, half loaded power starts, and five full load powered starts before going to the operational unit, J.G.400. The shortage of C-Stoff fuel made the entire Me.163 program very limited when the war was almost over.

CHAPTER 34

The Most Important Mistakes of the Luftwaffe as seen from the Standpoint of the German Fighter Force

By Generalleutnant Galland and Generalleutnant Schmid
At Latimer House, England, 23 October 1945

A. Mistakes in Organization and Planning

1. The job and the significance of the fighter force in a strategic air war was not recognized by the German High Command even in the years when the force was being set up. This resulted, among other things, in the wrong size relationships of the fighter arm to the bomber arm, in Autumn 1939:

about 30 bomber Gruppen

9 Stuka Gruppen

13 fighter Gruppen

Thus the fighter force was from the beginning too small to provide a basis of development to meet wartime requirements.

2. The fighter force was not considered a part of the strategic air force. From then on it took a second-rate position. This situation later bitterly avenged itself in the fields of organization, personnel, and materiel as well as in combat.

3. The fighter force had, in the High Command, no representation which could be taken seriously. The personalities of the Inspectors of the Fighter Force and the quick turn over in this position did not permit the office to become important. From this position especially in the building up and preparation period these should have become decisively important stimuli.

4. Neither in the building up, in attack nor in defense were German fighters ever combined under an overall fighter command. This was an organizational disadvantage.

5. The tempo of setting up and training the fighter force just before the war

was far too fast. Thus a wearing down of the quality of formation leaders, pilots and of the standard of combat training began too soon.

6.   After the beginning of the war, no new units of the Fighter Force were set up until 1942. At the beginning we had at our disposal nine Geschwader (J G 2, 3, 26, 27, 51, 52, 54, 77) and from 1942 to 1944, eight Geschwader were set up (J G 1, 4, 5, 6, 7, 11, 300, and 301) and enlargement by still a third more was attained by increasing the TO strength of the units. This setting-up of new units had to be carried on despite rising losses of men and materiel in order to even try to keep up with the enemy numerically. Naturally, the level of achievement and battle potency of the units sank. The build-up was therefore not organic and evolutionary, but forced, since in the two good years of the war, 1940 and 1941, nothing at all was done for an enlargement of the fighter force.

7.   For the build-up and training of the fighter force, the necessary training organization was lacking. (In 1941 there were only two fighter pilot schools.)

8.   In the High Command, the people always let themselves be surprised by developments, instead of planning in advance. I have indicated at another point the detailed story of the delayed beginning of the organizational building up of the Defense of the Reich. At least one and a half years were thus lost. This had great effect on the delayed development of radar equipment and other branches of technical matters.

9.   The concept of 'control of the air' had not been grasped by the High Command in its true meaning. It was never clearly admitted that air superiority in modern war was the first requirement for *all* operations of *all* branches of the armed forces and especially of the branches of the air force. If this had been recognized, the GAF would have had to begin to wrest air superiority back from the moment it was first torn away from it at El Alamein. This was only recognized and acted upon by insulting the morale and bravery of the fighter arm instead of taking concrete measures. In the grand strategy of the air war, no alterations took place.

B. Mistakes in Development and Technical Equipment

1.   A great number of the mistakes in this field are grounded in the lack of planning and organization. They will not be further discussed here. Decisive at all times was the lack of a Tactical-Technical Section in the General Staff.

2.   Our technical development program was not planned far enough into the future. In 1940, all developments which would not be ready for introduction into use within about two years were put aside, in order to accelerate the shorter term developments. This was a mistake of tremendous scope. For example, the Me.262, the further development of the F.W.-190, the gyro computing sight, engines of more than 2000 HP and many other developments were thus all delayed.

3.   In the effort to raise the production figures of items in series production, new developments were not forced into series models with the necessary pressure. Even the preparation for series production was somewhat neglected in the pressure to get new designs into series production quickly. In addition, there was a certain dangerous (and partly unwarranted) self-satisfaction at every new technical advance.

4.   For this reason the Me.109 was not taken out of series production for years, although this was absolutely necessary on the basis of performance figures from 1943 on. Similarly the beginning of the new series of FW 190 and of the Tank 152 was so delayed as to be almost ineffective.

5.   Only after the end of 1943 was the lack of fighters recognized and a program for greater series production set up. Until then, the monthly production figures were actually comical. The highest production point was reached nevertheless after the heavy damaging of aircraft factories and synthetic oil plants. At this time our losses were so great that the increase of strength went far too sluggishly. Moreover, as a result of the loss of air superiority, ground attack units, reconnaissance units, and night fighter units needed to equip themselves with fighter aircraft.

6.   A clear concentration of productive effort on fighters did not take place until mid-1944. The reasons for this lay in the demands of the High Command for bombers.

7.   An especially crass case of a great mistake in technical development is that of the series production of the Me.262. This theme has so often been discussed that there is no use going into it anymore.

8.   The series production of the He.162 was indeed a sign of decay in logical thinking, planning, and equipping. Instead of this the entire capacity of industry should have been thrown into the speeding up and broadening of the Me.262 series.

9.   Especially the following technical improvements were *lacking* for the Fighter Force in the various theaters of operations:

1940   Belly tanks for operations over England

Engines with maximum performance at least 3,000 feet higher than ones on hand.

FW 190s, especially for escort missions, for greater maneuverability and relative invulnerability.

Possibility of temporary increase in performance – Methanol/Water under max. performance altitude and GM 1 above this altitude.

Greater supply of new a/c.

R/T communications with bombers in the air.

Fighter Control procedures.

1941   Greater altitudes of maximum performance

FW 190

Methanol/Water, GM 1.

Better supply of a/c.

Fighter Control Procedures.

1942   Faster conversion to FW 190 and less use of Me.109.

1943   Heavier armament

Increase in performance of Me.109 (As engines, use of Methanol/Water)

Replacement a/c for the Me.109 (Me.209, Me.309)

Increased performance for FW 190 (2000 HP engine with better altitude).

Series production of the FW 190 D (with in-line engine).

Gyro Computing sights.

More aircraft

Longer endurance of aircraft.

1944   No more Me.109's.

Running out of the FW 190 A series and replacement with the FW 190 D.

Series production of the Tank 152.

Series production of the Me.262 as a fighter.

Fuel for operations of Me.163.

Gyro Computing Sights.

Longer Endurance of Fighter a/c.

Automatic Pilots for Bad Weather Operations.

Series production of the Dornier 335 as a TE fighter (Zerstorer).

1945 Entire Messerschmitt production to be concentrated on Me.262 production.

No more Me.109.

Ending of FW 190D production.

Entire Focke Wulf productive capacity to be concentrated on Tank 152.

Jumo 213 and DB 603 as fighter engines both over 2000 HP.

Series production of Me.263 and fuel for it.

C. Mistakes in Choice of Personnel and Training

1.   For principles of selection of fighter pilots the principle of setting up an elite standard did not occur soon enough.

2.   For the selection of fighter pilot trainees in the flight schools a low scale of requirements for physical, mental, and character qualities was set up. The bomber arm was clearly given preference in the allotment of personnel.

3.   The supply of flying officers for the fighter arm was numerically neglected in the first half of the war, and neglected also as to quality and training. Hereby arose the acute lack of formation leader candidates.

4.   The flying and fighter training of the trainees was too low in flying hours. The training facilities (fighter schools) had increased sixfold during the war. While there was, until 1944, a continual lack of fighter aircraft for training purposes, there were enough of these aircraft from this time on, but far too little fuel was available.

5.   With the increase in the rate of loss of fighter pilots – at the latest after 1943 – the training of the supply of new pilots should have been continually bettered, because the possibility no longer existed as before for pilots perfecting their training and getting experience in the operational units themselves. This was, on the other hand, numerically impossible and later, in 1944, impossible also for lack of fuel. There was simply a lack of training emphasis on fighter pilots and nothing but fighter pilots.

6.   The gaps in the training which most often became evident were:
   a.   Insufficient experience with the operational fighter types under combat conditions (too few flying hours).
   b.   Too little formation training in operational fighter types.
   c.   Lack of gunnery training.

    d. Lack of combat training.

    e. Almost complete lack of instrument flying training.

D. Mistakes in the Training of Formation Leaders, Unit Commanders, and Staff Personnel

1. As a result of the lack of reserves of formation leaders, it became the general rule that units had to replace them from their own ranks. This method proved completely unfeasible after 1943, because the quality sank very low and the Geschwader were no longer in a position to close the gaps. Only now was a systematic training of formation leaders begun in a regular course. This innovation should have been in existence from the beginning of the war as the 'University of Fighter Operations.'

2. At the beginning of the war, pilots of World War I were used throughout as Geschwader CO's. These men were no longer able from a flying standpoint to lead their formations in the air. In the Battle of Britain the first 'rejuvenation' had to take place. Even though this step in my opinion proved good, still too many good young Gruppe COs became Geschwader COs, and the evolutionary development of the formation leader corps was thus shaken. It would have been better to carry out this process slower or to have begun it in peace time.

3. As already noted, there was no fighter command office before the war and in the first year of the war. Only during the French campaign were fighter commanders (Jagdfliegerführer) set up under the Fliegerkorps, with little influence on operations. During the Battle of Britain their influence grew. With the beginning of the Air Defense of the Continent the Jafus and, later, the Jagddivisionen were the operationally controlling staffs. There was, however, a lack of accomplished, battle experienced, and able commanders and staff men for these staffs. Both types of officers should have had operational experience in the war and have been trained either as pilots or as staff men. That would only have been possible if this training had been begun in peace time. But even during the war the training of General Staff Officers from the fighter force was neglected. Thus is explained the lack of unit leaders and staff officers for the fighter force.

4. For many sorts of personal reasons Jafus and Jagddivision CO's were, during the course of the war, relieved of their jobs by the C. in C. (Göring). Thus the commands never could collect the necessary experience and have the necessary peace of mind.

E. Mistakes in Strategy and in Operational Tactics

1. Continuous lack of forces led after 1942 to a permanent overloading of the Fighter Force with too many missions. This affected both the planning of operations and their conduct.

2. After 1942 the fighter force fought on all fronts against numerically superior forces. But on no front were the operations of the GAF and especially the fighter force primarily directed toward winning back air superiority. Instead of this, the operations of bombers, dive bombers, and ground attack units in the support of the army were supposed to be escorted by fighter forces using defensive measures.

3. The draining off of fighter forces from the Western Front in 1941 for the Russian offensive was bearable at most for a few months. For a longer duration, the air superiority passed first to the English and, from 1943, still more decisively to the Americans.

4. The building up of the Defense of the Reich against attacks by American four engine bomber missions failed from the beginning because of lack of forces. A timely withdrawal of forces from the east and from the south was never decided upon; instead individual Gruppen were transferred one by one. Thus we were always behind the strengthening of American forces, without once winning a lead position.

5. The High Command operated with fighter Gruppen and transferred them here and there according to the main effort of battle, instead of regarding the fighter *Geschwader* as the organic, undividable unit. In this way the Gruppen went into the different phases of operations always confused, the influence of Geschwader organization was lost and the largest amount of operational value was not extracted from the fighters.

6. The ground organization and signals net of all kinds, especially in rear areas behind the various fronts, were very much neglected. In retreats and in the building up of the Defense of the Reich, therefore, the units usually ran up against considerable shortages.

7. In operations during bad weather fighter units were completely overtaxed in view of their state of training and equipment. Great losses due to bad weather shook confidence in the High Command and caused great uncertainty in the units.

8. Especially in the Defense of the Reich, the High Command never let an